# DISCURSIVE ACTS

# COMMUNICATION AND SOCIAL ORDER

*An Aldine de Gruyter Series of Texts and Monographs*

**Series Editor**

David R. Maines, *Pennsylvania State University*

**Advisory Editors**

Bruce Gronbeck • Peter K. Manning • William K. Rawlins

# DISCURSIVE ACTS

R. S. Perinbanayagam

ALDINE DE GRUYTER
New York

# About the Author

**R. S. Perinbanayagam** had his early education in Ceylon (now, Sri Lanka), obtained his Ph.D. in sociology and anthropology from the University of Minnesota, and its presently on the faculty at Hunter College of the City University of New York. He is the author of *The Karmic Theater: Self, Society, and Astrology in Jaffna* and *Signifying Acts*. His journal articles have been published in *Sociological Quarterly, American Sociologist, Symbolic Interaction, Anthropological Quarterly*, and *Psychiatry*.

ALDINE DE GRUYTER
A division of Walter de Gruyter, Inc.
200 Saw Mill River Road
Hawthorne, New York 10532

The paper used in this publication meets the minimum requirements of American National Standard for Information Sciences—Permanence of Paper for Printed Library Materials, ANSI Z39.48-1984.

∞

**Library of Congress Cataloging-in-Publication Data**

Perinbanayagam, R. S., 1934–
      Discursive acts : R. S. Perinbanayagam.
          p.      cm.—(Communication and social order)
      Includes bibliographical references.
      Includes index.
      ISBN 0-202-30366-7 (alk. paper).—ISBN 0-202-30367-5 (pbk. :
alk. paper)
      1. Discourse analysis.   2. Dialogue.   3. Conversation.   I. Title.
II. Series.
      P302.P445 1991
      401'.41—dc20                                              90-47962
                                                                        CIP

Manufactured in the United States of America

10  9  8  7  6  5  4  3  2  1

*"Language enters life through concrete utterances (which manifest language) and life enters language through concrete utterances as well."*

Mikhail Bakhtin

# CONTENTS

# PREFACE

In the following pages I endeavor to relate various recent theories of language and discourse to earlier theories of signs and selves to produce a description of the structures and processes of conversations in everyday life and their consequences. These conversations constitute the procedures by which selves are given shape and substance. Conversations lead to the emergence of selves, and selves in turn create conversations. In and through reciprocal conversation, two selves reveal what each wants to be taken as: together they not only find each other, but themselves as well.

In analyzing conversations I have sought to use the strengths and insights of various classical and contemporary theorists rather than dwelling at length on their limitations and weaknesses. In Tamil poetry (*Naladiyar*, v. 135, for example), and in Sanskrit poetry too, I have read of a mythical bird that, if it is offered milk mixed with dross in a cup, will be able selectively to drink the milk and leave the rest behind. This approach can be very useful in dealing with social theory because there is no theory about humans, insofar as it is produced by other humans, that will not prove to be erroneous on some points and correct on others. Therefore, I have used a number of them in developing my own theory of signifying acts. through the management and control of language, and the various consequences thereof. This has led me to a notion of discourse as an interactional act capable of containing multiple significations, all of them delineating a self and an other in varying forms of dialogues and relationships.

The theories of language and meaning I used have been subject to vigorous critiques in recent years. The work of the structuralists Ferdinand de Saussure and Roman Jakobson has been subject to a particularly sustained attack as some of structuralism's early advocates have withdrawn their support, or produced their own *aufhebung* in deconstructionism. Nevertheless, it seems to me that the essential points of the structuralist movement are irrefutable, because the discursive strategies that even the most determined critics use in their own texts reveal the presence of all the structuralist categories! Like the famous character in Moliere, they will find that not only are they producing prose but a prose that is subject to structuralist formality. Of course, there is a great deal in structuralism that needs to be challenged and replaced. But for

ytic description of the human symbolic product it has
cularly when supplemented by the thought of those
nd who stood on its shoulders. In any case, theories
d as commodities demanding fetishistic loyalties or
complete programs forever demanding critique and

...he work presented here parallels in many ways that of work done
under other rubrics—sociolinguistics, conversation and discourse analysis, and ethnomethodology. This work, however, is not an attempt to
supersede that done under the influence of these perspectives, but
presents the same matter from a different standpoint. That is to say,
enthnomethodology and sociololinguistics focus on certain *formal* properties of conversations, and they have pursued the quest for these
properties with great methodological rigor, while eschewing questions
about intentions. In their work, as in that of many structuralists, discourse has become *depersonalized,* with the linguistic form itself becoming an autonomous entity hermetically sealed from the world of selves,
interaction, conflict, and suffering. My own interest is in displaying the
*dialogic* properties of such discourses, conceiving each element in them
as pragmatic and directed. The dialogue that results from the artful
management of discursive acts intertwines various selves and constitutes moments in the career of these selves. Nevertheless, I have benefited from the work of these scholars, and I recognize that it was they
who opened the field for inquiry.

In many ways these pages are an enlargement and exemplification of
themes discussed in my earlier forays into the analysis of language,
interactions and social relationships. Here I take dialogue to be the
central event of human being and doing; in fact, I take it to be the
defining principle of all actions and interactions. Drawing from a variety
of sources, I seek to construct a theory of interaction between humans
that is dialectical in all senses of the word; that is to say, a theory
concerned with dialects are double processes, as well as with speaking
and the logic of relational processes.

Some sections of the last two chapters, now revised and elaborated
upon, have appeared previously in *The Sociology of Emotions* edited by D.
Franks and D. McCarthy and *Studies in Symbolic Interaction,* (JAI Press). I
wish to thank the editors and publishers of these journals for permission
to adapt these sections here. I have, for the most part, used published
versions of conversations to illustrate my thesis. In addition, I have also
used various pieces of conversations that I had collected on my own and
recorded as soon as they occurred. These are cited as "field notes."

I would like to thank Professors Doyle McCarthy, Marvin Scott and
David Maines for reading earlier drafts of this work and making helpful
comments. Ms. Nalayini Fernando typed the manuscript from several
handwritten versions and I am truly grateful for this.

# Prologue

# — 1 —

In the series of stories known as "Tales from the Thousand and One Nights," Shahrazade finds herself in a peculiar predicament. The king of Persia, disillusioned by the disloyalty of his queen, has decided to love only virgins. Each will spend a night with him, only to be beheaded in the morning. Shahrazade is determined to avoid this fate: "When the king had taken the maiden Scheherazade to his chamber and had lain with her, she wept and said: I have a young sister to whom I wish to bid farewell" (Dawood, 1973:22–23).

The king sent for the sister, Dunyazad. When she arrived, she threw her arms round Shahrazade's neck and then seated herself by her side. Then Dunyazad said to Shahrazade: "Tell me sister, a tale of marvel, so that the night may pass pleasantly. 'Gladly,' she answered, 'if the king permits.' And the king, who was troubled by sleeplessness, eagerly listened to the tale of Shahrazade" (Dawood, 1973:23).

Listening to a tale that turned out to be endless, the king became so preoccupied with the stories Shahrazade spun, that she was saved from a beheading. Indeed, besides avoiding her fate, she got the king to have two children by her. Shahrazade's discourse begins with one story whose characters want to tell a story of their own, a story that contains characters who have their own stories to tell. This sets up a discursive braid that leads on and on with both the teller and the listener engrossed in the story, and the story within a story, and the story within it . . . But there is really only one story—the one a self tells another as they go through life. The story, or as it will be called here, the discourse, if not all, is what we convert all into. The human being is blessed, or cursed as the case may be, with language and uses it to occupy his or her mind as well as to occupy his or her relationships with others. The stories he or she tells others, he or she tells himself or herself and the stories he tells himself or herself only, constitute the sum and substance of a life. The stories that are told and retold, sad ones or happy ones, complete or incomplete, about how to do something, or about what happened to us today, about what we expect from the other, from life, and after life, let others enter and so know our minds.

Several hundred years after Shahrazade, the German playwright Peter Handke (1973) investigated the significance of sentences "with which you can tell yourself a story," spoken by a character, claiming that they defined as well as imprisoned him (1973:68). The play is *Kaspar*, and is the story of the emergence of language and selfhood in a child raised in isolation until he was seventeen. At the beginning of the play he is physically uncoordinated and frightened, and capable of uttering only a single sentence. Near the end of the play he is able to say:

Once plagued by sentences,
I now can't have enough of sentences.
Once haunted by words I now play with every single letter.
(Handke, 1973:111)

The play attempts to show how this is achieved—how a languageless entity is socialized into a human identity. But Handke also manages to convey the impression that this is a rather dubious achievement, viewing the acquisition of language and selfhood as both a trap and a gift.

In the opening scene, Kasper Hauser knows only one sentence that he keeps repeating. The sentence is, "I want to be a person like somebody else was once," (1973:72) and it is this sentence that is repeated in this form and in slightly altered forms throughout the rest of the play, becoming embedded in longer units, ending inside a climactical speech of several sentences. Each dramatic sequence in the play conveys a differing significance to the acquisition of more and more elaborate speech and in a dramaturgic tour de force manages to communicate by these same sentences the deep irony and ambiguity involved in the acquisition of language and hence meaning, culture, and humanity. These sequences, analogous to scenes in a play, are described by Handke as follows:

Phase I:     Can Kaspar, the owner of one sentence, begin, and begin to do something with this sentence?

Phase II:    Can Kaspar do something against other sentences with his sentence?

Phase III:   Can Kaspar at least hold his own against other sentences with his sentence?

Phase IV:    Can Kaspar defend himself from other sentences and keep quiet even though other sentences prod him to speak?

Phase V:     Can Kaspar only become aware of what he speaks through speaking?

Phase VI:    Can Kaspar, the owner of sentences, do something with these sentences, not only to other sentences, but also to the objects of other sentences?

Phase VII:   Can Kaspar bring himself into order with sentences about order, or rather with ordered sentences?

Phase VIII: Can Kaspar, from the order of a single sentence, derive a whole series of sentences, a series that represents a comprehensive order?

Phase IX: Can Kaspar learn what, in each instance, is the model upon which an infinite number of sentences about order can be based?

Phase X: Can Kaspar, with the sentence model he has learned, make the object accessible to himself or become himself accessible to the objects?

Phase XI: Can Kaspar by means of sentences, make his contribution to the great community of sentences?

Phase XII: Can Kaspar be brought to the point where, with rhyming sentences, he will find rhyme and reasons in the objects?

Phase XIII: Can Kaspar put questions to himself?

Phase XIV: Can Kaspar, with uninhibited sentences which he applies to his old inhibited sentences, reverse the inverted world of these sentences?

Phase XV: Can Kaspar defend himself at least with an inverted world of sentences against inverted sentences about the world? Or: Can Kaspar, by inverting sentences, at least avoid the false appearance of rightness?

Phase XVI: Who is Kaspar now? Kaspar, who is now Kaspar? What is now Kaspar? What is now Kaspar? Kaspar?

(Handke, 1973:55–56)

In the final speech, now that Kaspar has learned to speak and to speak in fact rather voluminously, the question that occurs to Handke then is about Kaspar's identity. Now that he has become fully human, he asks, "Who is Kaspar now? Kaspar, who is now Kaspar? What is now Kaspar? What is now Kaspar? Kaspar?" The acquisition of a language and a humanity does not indeed solve anything: the very fact of such acquisition creates problems that cannot be solved as readily as the problems created by a lack of language. The learning process itself is described by Handke as "speech torture," and the entire staging of the play emphasizes Handke's conviction that this is an achievement of dubious merit: a disarranged and forbidding-looking stage and a cyclopean eye of a light, which suggests various lights used in getting confessions out of unwilling captives, are the background in which Kaspar is taught to speak. Kaspar comes on stage awkwardly, barely able to coordinate his limbs, displaying an air of astonishment. His clothes are awry and their colors clash with the colors on stage. When he begins to move he is seen to be very mechanical and "artificial" in his gestures. When he speaks, he utters again and again the single sentence quoted earlier. When he sits down, he finds he is unable to get up again with any ease. When he does finally manage to get up and walk, he goes about muttering his sentence and touching the objects on the stage. But he is unable to react to the things he touches because they have no meaning for him. That is, he wanders around aimlessly in a world without significance because the objects in that world have not yet been named for him. He then stops his movements, going to sit on a sofa as voices begin to be heard all around him. Someone else has taken matters in hand, and he, she, or they are going to teach him to speak. The play then begins to take verbal shape, with offstage prompters addressing various passages— themselves big with significance—to Kaspar. Witness this passage, the prompters' opening gambit: "You have a sentence with which you can tell yourself everything that you can't tell others . . . you have a sentence with which you can already contradict the same sentence" (1973:67). Later on in the same phase of the play Kaspar is told by the prompters: "With the sentence, you can pretend to be dumbfounded. Assert yourself with the sentence against other sentences. Name everything that comes in your way and move it out of your way. Familiarize yourself with all objects" (1973:68). And on it goes. The power of language, its essential properties and functions—its "possibilities" as Handke might put it—are described in the very exercise by which Kaspar is being taught to speak, but with a consistent undertone of irony. The social-psychological functions of language are as evident to Handke as the structural and sociological ones. Witness the following: "You can hear yourself. You become aware. You become aware of yourself" (1973:70), and later on he has the prompters say to Kaspar, "and you learn with the sentence that there is an order and you learn with the sentence to learn order" (1973:71). In the hands of the playwright the story's implications for discourse, interaction, and consciousness are presented clearly and concisely, albeit in a poetic rhythm and diction. In sum, Handke's play forcefully poses the questions that most concern students of human linguistic interactions.

Stories and sentences as they are told and heard provide the matter that creates interpersonal presence and interactional resonance and engagement. They make the days of a life proceed apace with a minimum of anguish and ennui, proceed without thought of murder, as in Shahrazade's case, or even suicide—for a while at least. And like Shahrazade's stories, all discourses are embedded in other discourses, which are embedded in other discourses, through which we make ourselves and our worlds. Kaspar entered a dialogue and imprisoned himself, while Shahrazade created one and saved herself.

# The Dialogic Self

— 2 —

Everyone, after all, is born in solitary confinement, and like Kaspar and Shahrazade, manages to survive by conducting discourses with whomever else may be around. A life then becomes a discourse, and discourse itself has a life of its own, embedded though it may be in the lives of people. "The life of a human being does not consist merely in the sphere of goal-directed verbs. It does not consist merely of activities that have something for their object. I perceive something. I feel something. I imagine something. I want something. I sense something. I think something. The life of a human being does not consist merely of all this and its like. All this and its like is the basis of the realm of *It*. But the realm of *You* has another basis," wrote Buber (1970:54), and for him, "Whoever says You stands in relation, in a dialogue" and "All actual life is an encounter" (1970:62), and "In the beginning is the relation" (1970:69). It is out of such meetings and relationships that a self emerges and is sustained—indeed lives. It is in such ongoing interactions that one makes contact with a world and meshes with others. In the course of these interactions, the self of each participant *addresses* the other and such discourses become the signifying medium in which the self occurs. Such a self is not just there, nor is it a *being* that is there. Rather, the self is variable and reflective, nuanced and shaded, and, as an object to itself and to others scintillates and reverberates in varying waves and beats and is forever responsive to the signifying stimulation of the environs— people and things, the things people say, and the things that things say. The self needs this signifying culture in which to exist and thrive, and it is in it that it assumes its reality and exhibits its varying colors and shapes.

Buber himself says, "Signs happen to us without respite; living means being addressed, we would need only to present ourselves and to perceive" (1972:10). But the addresses "come in such alternating cascades that many build armors against them. Each of us is encased in an armor whose task is to ward off signs" (1972:10). These signs are also interpreted and used to sustain the self and present a self—and these cascades of addresses need to be differentiated into elements and examined for their signifying qualities. The interactional process is then an engagement between two mutually present social objects that seek not only self-understanding but an understanding through the sensuous discourse of the other as well.[1]

Mikhail Bakhtin too has argued that dialogue is the model that must be adopted for conceptualizing interhuman relationships. Criticizing the practice current in linguistics (and I may add in many new schools of study called sociolingusitics and conversational analysis) of using separate entities like *listener* and *speaker*, he notes that they make the listener's role too passive and nonparticipatory. "The fact is," he writes, "that when the listener perceives and understands the meaning (the language meaning) of speech, he simultaneously takes an active and responsive attitude towards it. He either agrees or disagrees with it (completely or partially) and augments it, applies it, prepares for its execution and so on . . . . Any understanding is imbued with response and necessarily elicits it in one form or another: the listener becomes the speaker" (1986:68). In an act of speech, if the listener is an active, participatory, and responsive one, the speaker too takes steps to ensure that this will happen. Bakhtin observed, "The expression of an utterance can never be fully understood or explained if its thematic content is all that is taken into account. The expression of an utterance always *responds* to a greater or lesser degree, that is, it expresses the speaker's attitude towards the other's utterances and not just his attitude towards the object of his utterance" (1986:92; italics in original). This complex attitudinal structure will be manifested in "the overtones of the style, in the finest nuances of the composition. The utterance will be filled with *dialogic overtones* and they must be taken into account in order to understand fully the style of the sentence" (1986:92; italics in original). In addition to the presence of dialogic overtones in the utterance, Bakhtin further notes that they possess *addressivity*: "As distinct from signifying units of a language—words and sentences—that are impersonal, belonging to nobody, the utterance has both an author and an addressee. Both the composition and particularly, the style of the utterance depends on those to whom the utterance is addressed, how the speaker (or writer) senses and imagines his addresses and force of the effect of the utterance" (1986:95). Another feature of this addressivity, he argues, is that "when I construct my utterance I try actively to determine his response. Moreover, I try to act in accordance with the response I anticipate, so this anticipated response, in turn exerts an active influence on my utterance" (1986:95).[2]

In many ways, G.H. Mead's theories of meaning, the social act, and symbolism anticipated Bakhtin's ideas here. Indeed, Bakhtin's argument needs a notion of the social act to buttress it. In the work of Mead, *the aim is not only to understand oneself, but to make oneself understood by the others*. Among the many ways in which Mead indicates this is by the notion of "taking the role of the other" and the related notion of "taking the attitude of the other" (1934:254, 363). How can one do such a thing? The moment one talks of taking the *role* of the other, it is clear that the other is making an effort to see that he or she is being, shall I say, properly taken. Notice here that the issue is being discussed not in terms of how do I know the *mind* of the other, his or her thoughts, feelings, etc., as "inner" private sensations; notice that it is not asked "How do I know that the other is in pain?" (Malcolm, 1966:371), but, what is his or her role? That is to say, an actor seeks to conform to a particular role and he or she does this by presenting "cues" (Turner, 1962)—words, bodily gestures, dress, facial expressions, changes in voice, that enable one to continue to present changing inflections of the role he or she is playing. This enables the other to attend to them as well and respond in informed ways to the one who is issuing them. One is then *making* a role, as he or she plays it just as the other is *taking* it. Ralph Turner noted, "It is this tendency to shape the phenomenal world into roles which is the key to role-taking as a core process in interaction" (1962:22). Such "shaping" is undertaken by means of various verbal and visual details, and the role comes dramaturgically alive in terms of the effects of these details.

The question then is, not how do I know the other is in pain, love, or derision, but is he or she *presenting* or *playing* the role of one being in pain, love, etc.? How, indeed, do I *act* toward the other, take the next step, or establish an interaction or relationship, insofar as he or she is playing this particular role? In other words, each human being is engaged in two processes: (1) He or she seeks to be understood by others and to bring some *control* to the ways in which he or she is to be understood. (2) He or she seeks to understand the other, as far as is necessary, in order to act toward him or her: "I interpret the other as he or she interprets me." In this *reflexive interpretation*, there is also a double uncertainty in that one is often being understood more than one wants to be understood and less than one seeks to be.

That is to say, meaningful interactions are not just an exchange of meaning with the help of symbols, and certainly are not mere mechanical reactions or for that matter mere physiological reactions (whatever that may mean) to stimuli in a simple-minded behavioristic way. Interactions should rather be viewed as selves participating in *encounters* not merely with someone else but with the other as the source of varied discourses. The assembled opus that reaches us from the work of others as words, sentences, and paragraphs is adorned with rhymes, assonances, and rhythms, composed with metaphors, metonyms, ironies, synechdochies, paradoxes, or oxymorons arrayed in simple, compound, and complex sentences. These sentences can in turn be elusive, seductive, virile, forceful, aggressive, domineering, and thus demand attention in these terms. Or else they can be challenging, mysterious, and puzzling, causing surprise and demanding reflection and analysis before a response is made. In responding to a sentence there is always the joy of decipherment, of unraveling the inherent mystery of its mass and shape, its light and shade, its allusions and graces, and in the capture of a recalcitrant signification, indeed in the enjoyment of the "pleasure of the text" as Barthes (1975) called it.

The relations between people, then, are between the *objectified* discursive acts of each participant. Truly, the relations between people can be best described as *interobjective* relations, in which the self encounters the other in and through the varied discourse that the other produces, discourses that are acts in every sense of the word. In discourse one therefore finds the self and its intentionalities objectified, so that the other may attend to them. In creating these discourses, a human constructs acts directed toward others that embody his or her own intentions—indeed his or her very self. In taking the other's role we take and interpret these discursive texts that do not merely provide pleasure but are the very matter by which we manage to live with others. In sum, the intentionality of the other is manifest in the details that constitute discursive texts, details manifested as signs.

Charles Sanders Peirce also produced a view of the interactive process in which the notion of dialogue was important. In his treatment, however, dialogue had logical referent rather than a social-psychological one. In such dialogic processes, signs are put into play. A sign, says Peirce, is a "*representamen* which stands to somebody for something in some respect or capacity. It addresses somebody, that is, creates in the mind of that person an equivalent sign or perhaps a more developed sign. That sign which it creates I call the *interpretant* of the first sign" (1955:99; italics in original). The second sign is "a more developed sign" at times, says Peirce, indicating not only that the recipient responds actively and creatively to the first one, but also maintains a *continuity* with it. This continuity is the dialogism in Peirce.

Roberta Kevelson, in a perceptive analysis of Peirce's dialogism wrote, "Dialogism is a process of reasoning which attempts to account for the method by which new information is discovered, processed and integrated into a continually evolving open-ended system of reasoning which parallels the actual method of creating human discourse" (1982:161). The relationship between an earlier part of the argument and a later one, or between an earlier moment and a later one in a discourse, is derived as a "continuous predicate" by Peirce. In Kevelson's words again, "In Peirce's sense every cohesive text is a *Continuous Predicate*. One infers from Peirce that the continuous predicate is a cumulative evolving network of relationships that parallels and resembles the continuity of consequential or clock-time; and it is only through analysis by defining its parts, that we break the continuity" (1982:164; italics in original). Knowledge of other minds, the apprehension of the other's intentions, and the understanding of the other's "subjectivity" are not achieved by clairvoyance or "assumptions" or idealistic reductions, but by interpreting the signs of which the other is the source and seeing them as parts of ongoing sequences. These signs are typically presented as discourses by a self-conscious agent. To ensure that they become available to the other and that the other becomes available to the self, humans conduct discourses that are dialogical. In such discourses an agent constructs acts that can elicit a response that continues the earlier one in a meaningful way. These acts allow the selves of the participants to enter into a dialogic relationship and mesh discursively with each other. The predicative continuity that one finds in the discursive acts becomes transformed into a predicative continuity of the selves involved in them. It allows the selves to sustain themselves as well as the dialogue itself and to anticipate further moments in it for their selves.

## The Self as a Sign

Through these dialogic processes, an individual is able simultaneously to bring a self as an object into its own conduct and being and to indicate thereby a self that others can take into account for their own purposes. If that is so, the questions that arise are: How is this possible? What are the instrumentations and methodologies by which the self is able to objectify itself, indicate things to itself, as well as do the same to others? The answer to both questions is to be found in the Peircian conception of a sign and the related process of what may be called signing.

Peirce (1958:41) argued that everything that humans know is derived from their understanding of the world and everything that they know is determined by what they have already mastered. He further argued that they can think only with signs and every conception they have is a cognizable, i.e., signable, phenomenon. Insofar as the self that philosophers and social-psychologists have discussed is an item of knowledge, it must perforce be subject to these Peircian rules of thought. Since the self is an item of knowledge that was not derived purely by introspection, what elements of the external world did in fact go into its constitution? Since we have no power of intuition, which of the previous cognitions, and whose, are used to constitute the self? Since all thinking is undertaken with signs, which of the universe of signs is used to constitute a particular self? Insofar as the incognizable is inconceivable, the self must be both cognizable and signable and conceived thereby.

In a very instructive paper, Milton Singer spoke of the "signs of the self," arguing that the self is a "system of symbols and meanings" (1984:53 See also, 1982). If the self is a system of symbols and meanings it is apprehensible by a mind and it is in the minding process that the self will find its presence. As such it is neither elusive nor mystical but is as concrete and tangible as the signs that a mind is able to assemble as the "intentional interpretant" to present for the "effectual interpretant" (Peirce, 1977:197). Peirce describes these as follows:

There is the *intentional* interpretant, which is a determination of the mind of the utterer; the *effectual* interpretant, which is a determination of the mind of the interpreter; and the *communicational* interpretant, or the *cointerpretant*, which is a determination of the mind into which the minds of utterers and interpreters have to be fused in order that any communication may take place (1977:197).

Signs then originate in one mind as intentional acts and create effects in another, together constituting what Peirce called a *commens* (1977:77) or a common identity of intepretants. Further, these signs, at an earlier moment in the history of the said mind, were produced by another mind and addressed to it now becomes the intentional interpretant in the new signing event. This process then is the vortex in which selves are generated and sustained. The sign thus is double-edged in a double sense: It connects the signifier to the signified, i.e., the vehicle to the concept in the mind of an agent, on the one hand, and the mind of one to that of another through the signifier, on the other hand. It is in such an ongoing dialectic of signs and their interpretants that the signs become the self. *Once the self gets constituted, as a commens it begins to exercise a legislative and executive function on the production of further acts of the mind and in responding to the acts of others.* Further, the assembly and presentation of what may be termed the *maxisign of the self* by the minding organism will seek to exercise control over the responsive interpretation that others make to itself. In this sense, the maxisign of the self has a double-edged character as do other signs: It signifies to the mind issuing it as well as to the others receiving it. *Once constituted, the maxisign of the self will achieve its own power and demand sovereignty over all its acts.* The acts that issue from it thereafter will add further dimensions to the already constituted self, thereby allowing it to grow, expand, and enrich itself or diminish and impoverish it. The signs of the self may have a certain stability at any given moment in its career, but in the long run the self is unstable insofar as it is capable of accepting new signs and abandoning old ones. The self develops by temporally and logically related moves from one moment to another, thus achieving a narrative status for itself until death.

However, this does not mean that the objects that become the signs of the self must necessarily have a prior empirical existence. No doubt many of them do: my attitude of hostility, contempt, and derision toward another can exist and become the elements of the maxisign that is the other's self. It is equally possible that these attitudes that the other conceives as being mine are imaginations and fictions constituted by the other. Nevertheless, to the extent that they become signs to the other, they achieve semiotic power and intentionalities of their own and can become elements of the maxisign that is the self of the other. In Joseph Ransdell's words, "Sign powers are in the signs themselves, and any changes in these powers, or the accruing of such powers to objects not previously having them, are due primarily to the signs themselves and *their* actions, not to people's actions (though the action of people is usually contingently instrumental in this respect)" (1980:151). Hence signs that are intended by another, as well as those whose intentionality is constituted exclusively by a respondent, both become elements of the maxisign of the self. In time this maxisign becomes stabilized and becomes a habit of a self and its continued production and reproduction in acts and relationships become difficult to dislodge or abandon and will function in all ongoing interactions.

Selves are maxisigns because they are simultaneously iconic, indexical, and symbolic. They are *iconic* insofar as they create images and decorations that represent the self for itself as well as for others. Such images are equal only to themselves and represent nothing but themselves. Selves are *indexical* to the extent that they have nouns and pronouns appropriate for them and referring to them, e.g., names of varying indications such as first names, Christian names, family names, clan names, caste names, tribal names, and pronouns indicating gender and sometimes status and honor. They are *symbolic* because selves typically incorporate a variety of terminologies, universes of discourse and social worlds that G.H. Mead (1934) called the "generalized other." When transformed into synecdochical units, these are used to symbolize the self; the world of Christianity and its specific universe of discourse, for example, are reduced to either the noun Christian or the adjective Christian, representing the person or some of his or her activities.

The emotions featured in social acts also can become signs of the self: emotions are neither mysterious emanations from the body or the soul nor insubstantial and fleeting phenomena, but social objects subject to historical and ontological analysis (McCarthy, 1988). Constructed just as any other object is, they too are subject to historical and sociological influences. That is, rules made by a historically antecedent social group establish how signs that signify emotions are to be used. Thus, emotional experiences, as all other experiences, are sooner or later signed into semiotic forms.

The self then is a semiotically constituted habit that the mind constitutes over the years in order to handle the actions and interactions that constitute a life. It does not exist in any sense other than as signs determined by earlier ways of cognition and conduct. There are many such ways of acting, with the one selected at any given moment having a double relationship: one to earlier ways, and one to the situation that is emerging in the nowness of the moment. These moments are points in an evolving mode that implicate and create opportunities for either the consolidation of old habits or the initiation of responses to the situation that become the seeding for cultivation of new habits. That is, the self has no ontology independent of the methods used to describe it or show it or think it; it is coterminous with the terminology and iconography of each culture, situation, and context in which it is presented, described, or conceived.

Such methods, however, and the terminologies that issue from them, are *reflexively potent*, becoming signs that project inward to the mind and outward into the thinking processes of others. The fundamental status of a self, then, is that of a sign that produces a double interpretant. If these interpretations are compatible, there is a coherent self; but if the two are totally at odds, a confused and unstable self emerges. Thus if the reflected social process is confused, the self too will be confused; if the social process is clear, the self also will be clear. In George Herbert Mead's words,

> It is by means of reflexiveness—the turning-back of the experience of the individual upon himself—that the whole social process is thus brought into the experience of the individuals involved in it. It is by such means, which enable the individual to take the attitude of the other towards himself that the individual is able to consciously adjust his self to that process, in any given social act in terms of his adjustment to it. Reflexiveness then is the essential condition within the social process, for the development of mind. (Mead, 1934:134)

The self therefore is an assemblage of signs, a more or less coherent text that a mind claims as its own and identifies as a presence in the world of others. Although an inescapably minding activity, it can be manifested in various tangible forms: A descriptive vocabulary of self, an arrangement of an image, and an appearance through clothing, jewelry, or bodily marks. This does not mean that the self is achieved once and for all, petrified forever after in the life of the body and mind. Rather, the mind and other minds conceive of and handle it as if it were fixed and stable, although it is continually being altered, enriched, impoverished, beclouded, and qualified in and through interactions and discourses. That is to say, the self is a process (Blumer, 1969:62), although it can be organized into a stable maxisign. It is a text, defined here as an organization of signs into a maxisign that is a feature of the minding process of the organism, an organization of the signs it has received from others as well as those it has produced on its own.

## Signing the Self

The very rationale for constructing a self separately is to identify and activate a presence in a world of others to prevent, no doubt in varying degrees, submersion into a general morass in which no initiative or decision, no individuated emotion or reason, can have play. The degree of such separation and differentiation may vary from culture to culture, but the sociological need to do so cannot be gainsaid.

In establishing a self one seeks to establish a separateness. However, a clear and precise separation can only be established by *identifying* with something and *disidentifying* with something else. "The self as an object," wrote Mead, "is dependent upon the presence of other objects with which the individual can identify himself" (1938:428). To identify with an object, the self must seek and discover elements of similarity with which it can identify. To do this well and with some conceptual and perceptual definition, it must also seek to disidentify itself with other objects, thereby establishing a separateness and a difference by means of an opposition. As Peirce wrote, "Existence is that mode of being which lies in opposition to another . . . A thing without opposition *ipso facto* does not exist" (1931, volume 1:435).

The self emerges and manifests itself at a point when a mind establishes a maxisign similar to others in some respects and different from others in other respects. In addition, within the group with which it shares similarities it will seek to create certain differences from others in that group. The process of posturing a maxisign that is different from one set of others in substantial ways, and another set of others in less substantial ways, goes on in ever decreasing circles until the self is left alone with its uniqueness. It is neither completely different from the other selves nor completely identical to them.

Consider Harry Wozzek: He is a man, and as such shares characteristics with other men with selves; he is a young man and shares a number of characteristics with other young men; he is a Christian, a Slovenian, a Slav, and so on. In addition, he is Harry Wozzek, with a unique trajectory of social relations that have shaped him over the years, thus conferring certain unique characteristics on him. In achieving these various signs that constitute his self, he has wittingly at times and unwittingly at others, differentiated himself from certain other signs. He is not a woman, not a child, not a Jew, not a Pole, not black, and so on. Further, he is not Mecir Wozzek, who is his younger brother.

These separations and differentiations are undertaken as a matter of course in the life of all human beings. Some of these differentiations are given and demanded by socializing agents, while others are chosen by the mind itself as it matures and is able to choose for itself. Further, the socializing circles may emphasize certain signs and underplay certain others that also change as the days and months and years pass. An individual can do the same: select certain signs and develop them systematically for use as the main feature of the maxisign.

How can this be done? Or rather, how can this be done parsimoniously and efficiently? To begin with, by visual differentiation, i.e., by visual signs that establish differences and similarities. The monk's clothing identifies him with other monks through similarity and at the same time differentiates him from non-monks. Second, by action. Worshiping at a church or at a temple is an action that defines the self of the worshiper and sets him or her apart from those whose religious identity lies merely in verbal claims, as well as grouping him or her with those who worship at church or temple in a public and ostentatious manner.[3]

Finally, separations and differentiations are made by using discourse—by asserting and responding interpretively to them. Such discourses too are constituted by creating and emphasizing differences and variations, by articulating such differences with intent and design, seeking effects and influences in the world. Insofar as discourses are capable of producing richer and more complex differentiations and similarities than visual signs, they become powerful methods of constituting and sustaining the maxisign that is the self. These discourses typically are artfully assembled as acts composed for the responsive attention of others. The self, in fact, is constituted in a signifying discursive medium, a discursive culture in which every word and sentence, every tonation and intonation, pause and emphasis, metaphor and metonymy, syntax and symbolism, defines it and qualifies it in small or not so small ways. These features of discourse become the vehicles through which attitudes and emotions are conveyed and reach the self for interpretation and collation into themes and patterns. The self, in fact hears and sees around it other selves that produce signs in and through discourse, every one of which is redolent with meaning for the conceptualization and estimation of the speaking and the listening self. In and through such discursive acts, the ontological representation of complex ideas is achieved by equally complex representational processes. Simple identification between idea and sign, between a prop like a championship trophy and the idea of sporting success is sometimes enough. But more often ideas demand more intricately arranged representations. Such representations of complex ideas is tantamount to composition, indeed to writing and, in many semiotics of the self this is evident. Such assemblies are undertaken according to a discipline that seeks to use intentionally the varied significances of single signs to construct a coherent total significance. In short, the assembly of individual signs, be they icons, indices or symbols, is a writing at its best and purest—the practice of thought—and the presentation of ideas being inseparable from its manifestations as matter and style. If, "Speech is to be understood as a form of writing, an instance of the basic linguistic mechanism manifested in writing" as Jonathan Culler (1982:102) puts Derrida's thesis about the connection between writing and speaking, then the deployment of signs to constitute objects of any kind, including the self, must be so understood as well. In assembling a self, then, one constructs a text, but one that is nevertheless incomplete at any given moment. The self too is subject to the same interpretational pathos that afflicts all textual constructions: indeterminacy. The self itself is constituted in a series of ongoing deferrals in which "the very principle of difference which holds that an element functions and signifies, takes on or conveys meaning, only by referring to another past or future element in an economy of traces" (Derrida, 1981:29).

Insofar as this is the case, in constituting a discursive act, the linguistic, literary and vocal structures have to be carefully selected and composed as the representation of one's intentions. That is to say, discursive acts are typically articulated with the anticipated effect contained within them. In Bahktin's words, "When constructing my utterance, I try actively to determine this response. Moreover, I try to act in accordance with the response I anticipate, so this anticipated response, in turn, exerts an active influence on my utterance" (1986:95). The answering discourse, based on the effects intended, can be one of many kinds. It can be one of acceptance and incorporation of the intention of the original into the self of the receiver, or of an active and discursive resistance to the message of the original.

This dialogue, however private and interpersonal it may be, is never conducted in a private language of individuated signs. Rather, as Bakhtin argued, the signs used in such discourses are socially and historically conditioned ones. In the words of Ken Hirshkop, a perceptive student of Bakhtin's work, "The dialogical work accepted that its production was a historical act: not the signification of a static reality by a lonely subject, but an active discursive intervention conditioned by precise social and historical circumstances" (1985:93). If the dialogue is conducted by signs that are arranged into efficient patterns and if in the course of the dialogue they begin to constitute selves, they yet come from sources external to the constituting process. A historically antecedent and socially structured process, in fact, makes available a variety of signs with which selves and relationships can be constituted. Once again a Peircian argument comes to the fore: if all knowledge of the internal world is derived from hypothetical reasoning from our knowledge of external facts, and all cognitions are determined by previous cognitions, it is not only the nature of the sign qua sign that is likely to influence the conception of a self, but the quality of the sign, its location and relation vis-à-vis other signs, as well as a social structure.

The work of making a self with the signs that are cognized from the external world, as the signs themselves, occurs within social and historical parameters. Bakhtin's "dialogism" seeks to integrate the essential features of language with the interactional moment in which an utterance is made, and the interaction itself to a historically created social structure. "Discourse lives outside of itself in its living directedness towards an object; if we abstract it completely from its directedness, then all that remains for us is a demented corpse of discourse from which we can learn nothing at all about either the social situation or the life or destiny or a given discourse" (1981:164). It is not "active discursive intervention" (Hirshkop, 1985:93) as opposed to language and coded or precoded structures, but how the latter and former *interact* with an intervening self to produce a discursive act that should be the focus of our inquiries. The discursive act is not merely an "instantiating of a code," as Gary Morson (1985:681) claims in a discussion of the work of Bakhtin, but the *use* of coded signs to manifest intentions to self and other. In such a process the self that is using a language to produce a parole, with its own ingenuity, is also a self that arrived on the scene already equipped with a system of signs (Mead, 1934). Any discourse he or she can produce, to be interpretable by him or her as well as by his or her audience, must be coded—the codes described not only by Saussure, but also by Jakobson, Cassierer, and, or course, Peirce. Dialogic processes, insofar as they cannot be conducted by private languages, are conducted with coded structures that the self as a member of an antecedently constituted *linguistic* and *speech* community not only knows but by which the self itself is constituted.

## The Styling of the Self

Addressivity, as defined by Mikhail Bakhtin, is an intrinsic feature of discursive acts (1986:95). In discursive exercises characterized by addressivity, styles of self-presentation are created just as such selves are given a force and a selective presence. Style and force of this sort are manifested in appearance and in the ascertainable features of the discourse as it is issued and received. In styling the self, an individual takes the elements (signs) available to him or her, and seeks to assemble and articulate them to indicate a selective variation of the self individuated from other selves. In such articulations the creative aspects of the mind come into play. These articulations are creative not in the sense that they are invented out of whole cloth but that already available threads are woven into a immediately realized pattern at the moment of constitution and presentation. Such constitution and presentations of self through discourse are the opposite of recitations and acting in plays because in such purposive presentations constant attention is paid to the evolving situation while each discursive act is uniquely individualized. These discursive acts are constituted in the moment, in response to situations and contexts, but nevertheless they use structures that are already part of a self's repertoire of linguistic habits. The creativity lies in the selection of the particular linguistic forms chosen to meet the situation in hand.

The importance of creativity and agency in the normal discourses of everyday life becomes evident when we examine cases where they are seriously impaired. There are several kinds of people who are unable either to do creative articulations or to do them well enough for them to be meaningful: (1) the brain-damaged, (2) the biologically retarded, (3) the socially and culturally deprived. In each case where the language faculty is impaired by head injury, the social faculty is injured as well. Thus, there will be an uncertain and diffuse concept of self, a want of creativity, originality, initiative, imaginative boldness, and endeavor, in selected areas. One consequence of certain forms of brain damage is a failure of the faculty of "judgment," as Oliver Sacks calls it.

> Neurology and psychology curiously though they talk of everything else, almost never talk of "judgment"—and yet it is precisely the downfall of judgment . . . which constitutes the essence of so many neuropsychological disorders. . . . And yet, whether in a philosophic sense (Kant's sense) or in an empirical and evolutionary sense, judgment is the most important faculty we have. An animal, or man, may get on very well without the "abstract attitude" but will speedily perish if deprived of judgment. Judgment must be the first faculty of the higher mind. (1987:20)

If such judgmental faculty is diminished or destroyed, an actor becomes incapable of *recognizing differences and making identifications* of objects in the world. With such an incapacity the most simple functioning in a symbolic and syntactic world becomes difficult, if not impossible. He or she may become "the man who mistook his wife for a hat" (Sacks, 1987). Sacks also describes another man who after an injury to his head found himself in a position where "Not a single face was 'familiar' to him, but there were three he could identify; these were workmates: one with a blinking-eye, one with a large mole on his cheek, and a third because he was so tall and thin that no one else was like him" (1987:21). He was able to make only these distinctions and identify them.

In exercising these faculties for judgments, identification, selection, and assembly, the actor displays his or her faculty of creativity as well. Without these faculties there will be an impoverished discursive act, at times even a confusing and misleading one, so that no really effective response can be given and certainly not one with addressivity. That is to say, a failure of technical mastery will eventuate in an incapacitation in discourse, interaction, self, and relationships.

Indeed, intentionality and the form in which it manifests itself are coterminous phenomena: intentionality speaks to the articulator in the process of articulation itself and to others, as it becomes available to them. The intention is the sign and the sign is the intention, just as are interrelated systems of signs. That is to say, intentions as signs become inseparable from the style of the discursive act and consequently the style of the self that is available to others. Intentionality is not to be conceived as an independent and a priori mental or psychic state that finds a presence in consciousness and then finds a language with which to express itself. The discursive matter that the self produces is the intention of the self and manifests its force through stylistic devices. The discursive acts and the matter, i.e., the signs they manifest, speak for the self as they speak to it and to others. Hence, where there is discursive incapacity, there is also minimal interaction, self, and social relationships.

In styling a self an actor has a varied verbal and gestural repertoire with which to construct a precise and variously controlled self for an audience. Constructing this self would involve the selection of a suitable diction, an appropriate grammar, intonation, and address, as well as the relevant gestures and moves. When constituting these elements into a more or less coherent discursive act, an individual is enacting a stylized presentation. The self thus presented may perform and display love, lust, anger, and irritation, for example, and will have two forms of styling. (1) The subtle differences between love and lust or between anger and irritation will be made visible in the form as well as the content of the discourse. (2) An individual's personal and idiosyncratic verbal mannerisms will be worked into the discourse, too. An expression of anger or love will take into account the situation and the context in which it is being articulated. The presence of others, the nature of the others, the role the participant is assuming for the moment, and what happened immediately before the expression in question will all be taken into account in the formulation of the discourse that becomes the act. A more specific example of style: In expressing anger, voices may be raised, and sentences may be short and staccato, replete with either obscene or blasphemous adjectives, nouns, or incantations in one actor's performance, while another may perform anger as quietly controlled rage displayed in sarcasm and irony. In either case, the articulator is consciously presenting a self that is very particularized in the discourse and is addressed to a particular audience. Style embodies the extremely variable and crennalated intentions of the self vis-à-vis an audience. Style then is achieved by the deployment of signs that bear the stamp of the articulator so as to become identified as the style of his or her self.[4]

## The Self as an Agent

Insofar as the self is a maxisign with powers of its own it is able to exercise these powers and thereby influence other aspects of its activities. That is, it becomes an agent in its own right capable of imitating acts and constituting responses. The self as an agent of the signing process implies primarily a capacity to take an initiative in constituting an act. Although this is a more or less voluntary act, the possible anticipatory responses inherent in the signs control their selection. This capacity to select is analogous to the creative aspects of the self that G.H. Mead called the "I" (1934:173–78). Describing the "social creativity of the emergent self," Mead compared the "I" element of the self "to those values which are found in the immediate attitude of the artist, the inventor, the scientist in his discovery." He further noted, "these values are not peculiar to the artist, the inventor and the scientific discoverer, but belong to the experience of all selves where there is an I that answers to the me" (1934:214). That is to say, we are all artists, inventors, and discoverers of varying talents whose artistry and inventiveness are deployed in constituting the self and the discourse. And it is through discursive acts, their styling, and presentational delicacy that the I manifests itself.

The "me," Mead argued, was the organization of the attitudes of the community: "The 'I' is the response of the organism to the attitudes of the others; the 'me' is the organized set of attitudes of others which one himself assumes. The attitudes of the others constitute the organized me . . . [that] one reacts towards . . . as an 'I' " (Mead, 1934:175). If that is the case, who or what is doing the organizing and providing the response that becomes the me? If it is the I, then how did it come into being? Was it there at birth? No, Mead pointed out, the self is not present at birth but emerges later as a result of social experiences. It is here then, according to Giddens (1984) that we are faced with impossible and irreconcilable positions: something or someone is doing the organizing of the attitudes of the others, and creating a me, but if the entity doing the organizing is a social emergent too, it is not possible to explain how it came into being.

These difficulties are entirely artificial created by a commitment to the principle that there is always a beginning to phenomena. This primiti- vist conception has led to a number of theories about origins—myths of origin, for example. Human beings, unable to explain how they emerged or how the many emerged from one, fashion various myths so as to have a sense of a coherent beginning to their communities. Unable to explain the origin of many from one, many cultures have sought theories of autochtony to account for the origin of humans (Levi-Strauss, 1967). The imperative to explain origins is really a form of retrospective closure on the thinking process; we all have a definitive starting point and proceed onward from there, even if it is an improbable one. Those who seek a simple and definitive answer to the question about the origin of the I are also animated, it appears, by the same logical need that led the Greeks to claim that the first man was autochthonous. "Half serpent; he grew from the earth as plants grow from the earth," as Leach summarily puts it (1979:70). Discussions of the I have also fallen victim to this search for origins and a quest for finite explanations of its source (Giddens 1979:121). Many critics have argued that it must be either biological or social. The former, it is claimed makes the self too biolog- ical, thereby undermining all the other claims that Mead makes; the latter makes the theory self-contradictory.

One can, however, propose a Peircian solution to this problem. The I has no origin except in the social and minding processes and has no exact location in the physiology of the brain or in any other anatomical unit. Rather, the I and the me emerge as features of the learning of symbolism: minding, self-consciousness, and symbolic consciousness emerge simultaneously with varying degrees of intensity and complete- ness. The I and the me are therefore different forms of the minding process, different moments in the emergence of self, both of them manifest as signs. The Peircian rule applies to the I and the me, as to all signs: All signs are constituted by earlier signs. An infinite regress is involved here; all the signs that are being used now are begot by earlier signs, which were begot by still earlier signs. In such a regress it is fruitless to search for origins. Hence when Mead says, "The 'I' of this moment is present in the 'me' of the next moment" (1934:174), there is the problem of discovering where this "I of this moment" came from— or rather what begot this earlier sign. The answer indubitably is that it was begot by a still earlier sign. It is not then so much the *origin* of the I that one must seek but the nature of the sign that begot the new sign. Such a search yields the conclusion that the I has no origin as such in the body or brain or gene of the individual, but is part of a semiotic chain in which there is a constant emergence. Further, in the case of the self, sometime after birth during the *social* growth of the individual, the semiotic chain appears. Since, however, socialization is undertaken by a set of others using a universe of signs to achieve it, this signsystem exists as an infinite regress in the history of the community that is using the signs. The self that gradually emerges in the process of socialization emerges more or less coterminously into a fullness with the capacity for using language. This is not to deny that certain simple forms of self-consciousness may not be available to an organism independent of linguisticity. The fine shadings and qualifications, the constant emergence of variations and crennalated intentionalities, however, demand language to come to a fullness. The community participates in such an emergence and it is in this give and take of linguistic communication that the I becomes separated from the me so that the child begins to get a sense of his or her self as a complexly faceted process. It is this complexity that the self begins to sign, to itself and to others, by means of the two first-person pronouns. It is a complexity that incorporates the controller and the controlled in a social act as well as the *temporal* changes that occur in the relation between the two, as acts, and life, proceed.

If the signs depicting I and me are in infinite regress, each having been begotten by an earlier one, Mead's depiction of the relationship between the two needs some elucidation. He said, "If you ask, then, where directly in your own experience the 'I' comes in the answer is that it comes in as a historical figure. It is what you were a second ago that is the 'I' of the 'me'. It is another 'me' that has to take that role" (1934:174). As a historical figure then, the I is recollected as having been there at an earlier moment, while at the moment of its presence and occurrence it was not recognized. "It is in memory that the 'I' is constantly present in experience" (1934:174). However, once it is recognized as having been present at an earlier moment and having now become part of the me, what is the next step in the ongoing process of reflection and action? The I of these characteristics, it is clear, has been incorporated into the me in terms of the responses they elicited from the "organized community." The organism, however, now has a self with at least one new dimension—the I of the earlier moment—and still has to produce action in which the I too plays a part. The I also gives the "sense of freedom, of initiative" (1934:177).

To the extent that the foregoing is persuasive, then we can conclude that though the I may surprise and be source of a sense of freedom and initiative, yet it is at its moment of expression connected to earlier processes and forms. Its presence and actions are emanations from earlier actions and presences. It is not conceived, as it were, immaculately; rather it is begotten, however hurriedly and spontaneously, by the messy processes through which the organism and its mind have passed. In short, the I is responsive to the me of the organism and is begotten by it. If the I of this moment is present in the me of the next moment, it is the me of the present moment, in varying and, yes, unpredictable permutations and combinations, that issues the I of the next moment. The relationship between the I and me is not a linear relationship, where one is constrained to seek a point of origin, but a circular one.

In acting through discourses, the I and the me are simultaneously operating, though in varying proportionalities. Some acts can be said to be dominated by the me: a bureaucrat rigidly following the rules of his or her office may be one example of such acts; others may be dominated by the I: A madman who articulates his or her intentions without regard to immediate consequences can be taken to be one dominated by the I. In the typical acts of everyday life one presents discourses in which the I and me are operational in proportion to the structural position that the self is occupying vis-à-vis others; selves in positions of authority will be able to give expression to their selves in more forceful fashion and more frequently than those who are in subordinate or dominated positions. In both cases it can be said that the discursive acts bear the force of the self articulating it.

Typically, then, an actor expressing and objectifying intentions in shared forms obviates the mystery of his or her being, about his or her consciousness, through discourse. Such discourses are taken to have "authority" and "testimony" (Austin, [1961] 1970:115). In fact, the discourse articulated by a person is, in every sense of the word, full of himself or herself, full of his or her force. And this force of statements, the *signifying force*, refers to the differentiated purposes, attitudes, and "otheracions" (Ortega Y. Gassett 1956:169) that they manifest, achieved by managing the various constituent elements of the utterance, i.e., by styling them. Signifying force defines and delineates the intentions of the self in the very structures wherein the "stating," the "asserting," and the "uttering" are done. Such signifying forces have to be produced as routine parts of discursive acts, in their very assembly and constitutions.[5]

In sum, the force of an utterance signifies the force of the self being presented discursively in the interaction and the dialogue. Signifying force is presented in an organized and creative act embodying the intentions of the articulator. Further, the signifying force is immediately responsive to the context and situation at hand. Creative acts carry the force of the self, and it is through them that the self becomes an active agent of its creation, perforce takes responsibility for these acts and faces their consequences. And these consequences will reflexively affect the self in one way or another. At a simple dichotomous level, they can either enhance or devalue the self, thereby having a commensurate effect on further productions that may issue from the self. In any case, the self is dialogic in a double sense: at the moment of executing a social act it has both a sense of its existence as a self from past dialogic experiences and in executing a social act it anticipates its future existence as a self. Thus, the utterances and the force they manifest are limned with addressivity and intimations of the anticipated response.[6]

## Notes

1.   For a comparative examination of dialogic processes in the work of Martin Buber and G.H. Mead, see Pfeutze (1954).

2.   M.M. Bakhtin's work has been known for a long time in the West but has only recently been translated into English. Besides the work on speech genres (1986) the one of interest to students of interaction and discourse is his *Dialogic Imagination* (1981). For a discussion of Bakhtin's work see the special issue of *Critical Inquiry* 10 (Dec. 1983), 225–319, and the responses it elicited in *Critical Inquiry* (June 1983).

3.   The classic studies of the visual representation of self are, of course, Goffman (1959) and Stone [1962] (1970). It has been suggested that Goffman presents a Machiavellian approach to human relationships by proposing that a self must manipulate the other in order to achieve maximum payoffs for itself. This is as naive and parochial a reading of Goffman as one is likely to get. In all human interactions a self seeks to present itself by whatever means are available. Such a presentation is achieved by *managing* the signs, be they signs of stigma or honor, cynicism or sincerity, and by assessing or evaluating the context in which the presentation is occurring. To call this Machiavellian is to misunderstand both Machiavelli and Goffman. In fact, between the two of them, it is Goffman's work that is the more general and encompassing. It is not that Goffman's work is Machiavellian, but that Machiavelli's work—at least *The Prince*—is a truly Goffmanian description of the *political* uses of self-presentation and self-disclosure, of strategic revelation and concealment.

4.   For a discussion of the concept of stylization used here see Herbert Read, *Art and Alienation* (1967:56–76). Without actually using the concept itself, Dick Hebdige in *Subculture: The Meaning of Style* (1979) seems to be describing the way in which various members of countercultures stylized their selves. See also Fowler (1975) and Morris (1979).

5.   This is not to be confused with the various acts and their respective forces in Austin's work (1975). Speech acts, according to Austin, can be divided into (1) "locutionary acts" in which a person *says* something—these are propositional sentences, (2) illocutionary acts, through which a person performs an action, (3) perlocutinary acts, through which a person produces effects upon the hearer. From these acts we get locutionary force, illocutionary force, and perlocutionary force. From a pragmatic standpoint, these are distinctions without essential differences. Whatever one says is addressed to somebody else, be it another present self, an imaginary other, or a fantasized other. Similarly, when one is merely "doing something", it too is a form of address or, in other words, it too says something and locutionary and illocutionary acts are both undertaken in order to have an effect on someone or other. Thus, the category of illocutionary acts seems redundant. Locutionary force is said to be contained in sentences that begin "He said that . . . ," perlocutionary force in sentences beginning "He

convinced me that . . . ," and illocutionary force in sentences that begin "He urged me . . ." (1975:101–103). Perhaps these distinctions have some use in philosophy, but as for accounting for human conduct, they seem to be merely creating given effects in the world by means of the signifying force they are able to exert, the rhetorical vigor they are able to mobilize by the structuring of signs. Austin himself noted that his interest was in contrasting the illocutionary act with the other two and that "there is a constant tendency in philosophy to elide this in favor of one or other of the other two" (1975:103). In the study of interhuman communication in any case, they can all be elided into one.

6.  In many recent discussions of the self, person, and individual, it has been argued that the concept of an individuated and separated personhood is a peculiar aberration of Western thought (e.g., Shotter and Gergen, 1989). Clifford Geertz is often cited as the authority for this stance. "The Western conception of the person as a bounded, unique, more or less integrated motivational and cognitive universe, a dynamic center of awareness, emotion, judgment and action, organized into a distinctive whole and set contrastively against other such wholes and against a social and natural background is, however incorrigible as it may seem to us, a rather peculiar idea within the context of the world's cultures" (1979:229). Levi-Strauss too has inveighed against the illusion of a self (1979). Against this view one may cite an earlier work by Marcel Mauss. After investigating the "A category of the human mind: the notion of person, the notion of self" in a variety of cultures, he concluded, "From a simple masquerade to the mask, from a 'olre' (*personage*) to be person (*personne*), to a name, to an individual; from the latter to a being possessing metaphysical and moral consciousness to a sacred being; from the latter to a fundamental form of thought and action—the course is accomplished" (Carrithers, Collins and Luke, (Eds.) 1985:22). For Mauss, then, while there is no *one* way of conceiving the self or person there is nevertheless some individuating principle by which it is accomplished. It is not then that the self is merely a "final trace and survival of bourgeois individualism" as Frederic Jameson thinks, nor is it an aspect of "collective structures and ways of mapping out our decentered place with respect to them" (Jameson, 1982:86). In this view, urged here, it is not that there are some societies that cultivate the concept of an individuated self, while there are others that acknowledge the irreducibly decentered and collectivized nature of the product. Rather, it is that in different cultures the illusion of a self is created with *varying metaphors* of separation and differentiation. And furthermore, the notion that an individuated self is an invention of Western bourgeois individualism can come only from a profound ignorance or confusion regarding certain terms in Buddhism and Hinduism and equally profound confusion regarding the meaning of the word *self*. For example, there is no doubt that Buddhism, in its doctrine of *anatta*, denies the existence of a permanent entity that transcends time and place, called the "soul" in Christianity and *atman* in Hinduism. The word *anatta*, however, is composed of *atta*, meaning person or self, with a negative prefix *ana*. Clearly in order to deny the existence of a self in the sense of soul or *atman*, Buddhism has first to postulate a self! The Buddhist texts, themselves containing the extreme example of a doctrine that seeks to deny an entity that transcended life and death and rebirth, nevertheless find themselves compelled to talk of an entity/phenomenon that is able to take an initiative and consummate an act—indeed *objectify* itself. The *Dhammapada* says for instance, "Only a man himself can be the master of himself. Who else from outside could be his master? When the master and servant are one, then there is no true help and self-possession" (Mascaro, 1973:58). Here we have the notion

of a *social self* that sociologists and philosophers use and this is inescapably a *this-worldly* phenomenon describing a minimum of continuity of conception by an actor from moment to moment in the mundane world. Nevertheless, the self as used in social and philosophical conceptualizations is not either the *atman*, the *atta*, or the soul, but a socially and interactionally derived concept given shape and form discursively and dramaturgically to represent an entity that is separated from the group, no doubt in varying degrees. There is no doubt in my mind that the social self, represented most basically in the capacity to use a first-person pronoun as the subject of an utterance, is an essential feature of all linguistically minded species. In the end the uses of the concept of an individuated, but socially constituted self, can be defended on the grounds that it is a category "with which to think" or a category with which it is "good to think" as Tambiah (1985) wrote about totemic animals in a Levi-Straussian mode. This concept of self may be an illusion, but an illusion nevertheless with practical consequences that make a difference. It is then not so much a non-Westerner's incapacity to conceive of a self that seems to be the issue, but a Westerner's incapacity to conceive simultaneity: how a self can be both individuated *and* be a member of a collectivity at the same time. See also Hywell Lewis (1982) for a discussion of the need for a conception of a subject for an understanding of human being and doing.

# Acts of Discourse

In engaging in communication with another, a person is obliged to articulate his or her signifying gestures in ways that make his or her intentions *interpretable* with a minimum of doubt and confusion. Or, in the words of Peirce, the articulator must work at "how to make his ideas clear" and at presenting acts that speak for oneself. Dismissing arguments given in what he calls modern treatises on "logic of the common sort" about *clear* and *obscure* conceptions, and between *distinct* and *confused* conceptions, Peirce suggested that clarity of thought is achieved "when thought is excited by the irritation of doubt and ceases when belief is attained, so that production of belief is the sole function of thought" (1958:118–119). The doubts that are entertained stimulate a mind to activity in which "Images pass rapidly through consciousness, one incessantly melting into another, until at last, when all is over—it may be a fraction of a second, in an hour, or after long years—we find ourselves decided as to how we should act under such circumstances as those which occasioned our hesitation. In other words, we have attained belief" (1958:119). Belief is described by Peirce with the help of a musical analogy: "It is the demi-cadence which closes a musical phrase in the symphony of our intellectual life. . . . [I]t has just three properties: first it is something we are aware of; second, it appeases the irritation of doubt; and, third, it involves the establishment in our nature of a rule of action or, say for short, a *habit*" (1958:121; italics in original). These procedures provide the initial basis for achieving a "clearness of apprehension" (Peirce 1958:114) of our ideas.

Clarity of ideas is won by calculating their effects, and they are put into action as signed intentions. The responses that the articulation of the ideas elicit allow the establishment of their commensurability with the effects sought. That is, conceptions, however clearly they are apprehended, do not remain merely conceptions for long since they are transformed into public actions whose consequences are experienced. Various ideas in the form of delicately assembled signs are apprehended and transformed into acts, which in turn will mobilize effects in others.

In order to achieve these effects, signs must be apprehended more or less clearly and then transformed into intentional acts that achieve a resonance for the author. The selection and use of signs and their publication demand minute and subtle apprehension not only of the effects of the different signs but of the *combined effects* of the various signs. This is what humans do in everyday life: they conceive, assemble, and articulate, using the full relational powers of signs so that certain complex effects are mobilized. The acts that humans articulate are never mere "behaviors" eliciting other behaviors in return; rather they are complex and artful constructions for eliciting similar responses.

This is achieved, with varying degrees of efficiency and effectiveness, by signing grammatical, tonal, and symbolic categorizations. Such discursive acts enable an articulator to bring a measure of control and discipline into what others will take to be his or her intention without losing control of the situational significance sought. The structures of language in speech forms are intelligible, Bakhtin (1981:259) argued, only in social situations. It is, however, equally true that speech produced in social situations is intelligible only to the extent that certain language structures are used. Further, insofar as discourses have to convey complex and multiple significations, the multiple structures of language and the various transformations to which they can be subjected become indispensable instruments for such acts. These structures become pragmatically necessary as well as socially, culturally, and interpersonally useful. They enable the various activities of the social world to occur efficiently, effectively, and parsimoniously. Bakhtin's dialogism seeks to integrate the essential features of language with the interactional moment in which an utterance is made and the interaction itself with a historically created social structure: "Discourse lives outside of itself in its living directedness towards an object; if we abstract it completely from its directedness, then all that remains for us is a demented corpse from which we can learn nothing at all" (1981:164).

To deny the reciprocal influence of the social situations of speech and the various structures of languages is to be trapped in an either/or linear logic, when in reality human discourse and the discursive structures by which they are formulated are inseparable.[1] In fact, if one examines actual instances of discourse, it is impossible to avoid the conclusion that these processes equally influence the constitution of discursive acts. First, situating signs that stand for objects makes them better able to elicit the interpretational activity that Charles Peirce called *semiosis*. Second, the signs are arranged in a certain order so as to indicate given values, an activity that has been called *transformation*. It is by using these twin processes that distinct and clear conceptions and propositions are achieved, rising out of a system already constituted in a pragmatic fulcrum by earlier acts of discourse.

## Semiosis and Transformation

In acts of discourse the initiator and the respondent practice mutual semiosis. Peirce described the process in these terms: "A *sign* is anything which is related to a Second thing, its *object*, in respect to a quality in such a way as to bring a Third thing, its Interpretant, into a relation to the same object, and in the same form, *ad infinitum*" (1932: volume 2, 92; italics in original).

The sign is defined by Peirce as a process in which there is systematic relational activity among different phenomena. In this process the signs are said to possess their own power and intentionality, and minding itself becomes an act of semiosis. What are the details and intricacies of this process by which signs are systematically produced, in which objects and new signs are generated around the same object?

Let us see how this works in practice, with practice here being viewed merely as the production of words that others interpret to some end. Peirce maintained that when an object is designated by a sign and elicits an interpretant, a triadic relation is obtained. In such a relation, the sign *B* represents the object *A* and is produced in order to elicit the interpretant at least where interactions between people are concerned. Semiosis therefore seems to involve the production of a sign representing an object that elicits a response from another.

One may ask what is the nature of the process by which a minding organism, or a semiotic process itself, can convert, develop, and actualize the sign from the object? Does the sign, as it being produced, and thereafter, have a shape and a substance, and is there a relationship between the object and its sign other than the representative one? Obviously, there is an activity by which the signing is actualized, a process by which an object (be it a thought or a thing) is made into a logical, gestural, or graphic sign. It is this shape or sound that becomes the sign or the representation and is able to elicit an interpretation. The object itself becomes apprehensible to the initiator as well as to the respondent only by means of this shape or sound. Further, the object becomes something else in the sign that it has generated: in the sign, it is now simultaneously *more than* the original insofar as it now has influenced the attitudes of the sign maker and *less than* the original insofar as various elements of the original have been found to be irrelevant to the sign's purposes at hand.

Undeniably, the fate of signs is to be altered for flexible use. Of course, all such changes are undertaken in order to elicit not only an interpretant, but a more or less precisely anticipated interpretant, though such anticipations may not be fully realized in the event. Fitzgerald puts it nicely, at least as far as discursive processes are concerned: "In saying that the interpretant is triadically produced, Peirce is claiming that the sign, through which the interpretant is determined must be produced in view of the interpretant. The sign is useful because of its intended effect either on another or on the future self" (1966:74).

The intended effect on another is achieved not only by the powers of the articulated sign, but by how it is defined and accepted by the other. In the articulation of signs, then, there are two fundamental acts: (1) First, an articulator signs an object for his or her own purposes. In such moments, he or she selects and assigns a vehicle with which the object can be represented well for his or her own purposes and then announces it to others so that it can have an effect on them. (2) For the other person, the articulated sign has become an object to which he or she will now assign a *representation*, which also becomes an *interpretant*. There is always an element of uncertainty between these processes. That is to say, there is no reason to conclude that the transference of a sign from a self to another is either automatic or secure in its ability to elicit the interpretant it seeks or that the other will be able and willing to respond in the way sought by the sign. In sum, there is an initial signing by which an object, be it a thing or a thought, is apprehended, defined, and experienced, and a later signing by which it is articulated. In the production of discourse by which a self is defined and presented to others for interpretation, an agent has to use this moment to arrange his or her signs in such a way that they achieve not only a successful interpretation but an effective presentation of a self that is situationally and contextually appropriate as well. Semiosis, then, involves the processes of taking signs and using them deliberately to achieve successful effects, i.e., communication with self and other.

The notion of transformation, a central element in the theories of language, grammar, and mythology produced by Roman Jakobson, Noam Chomsky, and Levi-Strauss, is not usually associated with Peirce's work. However, there is a fundamental congruity between Peirce's view of cognition and semiosis and transformational processes. Discussing the processes of cognition Peirce argued:

1. We have no power of Introspection, but all knowledge of the internal world is derived from our knowledge of the external world.
2. We have no power of intuition, but every cognition is determined logically by previous cognitions.
3. We have no power of thinking without signs.
4. We have no conception of the absolutely incognizable. (1958:41).

These four "incapacities," as Peirce called them, direct our attention to the capacities by which cognitions are achieved. Tracing the consequences of these processes, Peirce concluded that "thought is what it is only by virtue of its addressing a future thought which is in its value as thought identical with it, though more developed. In this way, the existence of the thought now depends on what is to be hereafter; so that it has only a potential existence, dependent on the future thought of the community" (1958:72).

From this it follows that there is a space and a moment between an internal world and the external world in the first capacity, between the current cognition and the previous cognition in the second, between the signs of thinking in the third, and the various cognitions of the fourth. In these spaces and moments an activity occurs that alters or changes the sign into a different form and casts a different relationship onto other signs. It is this change, maturation, enrichment, or impoverishment that is a transformation: it changes from an external world to an internal world, changes a previous cognition into a current cognition, one sign into another sign and into the multitude of signs that constitute a discourse. In these exercises, knowledge is acquired by transformation, and insofar as all thinking is undertaken through signs, all transformations are also a process of semiosis. It is not that one is prior to the other, or a past of the other, but that semiotic processes are always acts of transformation. In such acts of transformational semiosis, a sign is produced to represent an object, an interpretant is defined in response to the sign, and the sign is related to other signs, which of course have *their* respective interpretants and objects constituting a precise signifying act. Such a view is a slight variation on Peirce's idea of semiosis: "By 'semiosis' I mean . . . an action, or influence, which is, or involves, a cooperation of *three* subjects, such a sign, its object, and its interpretant, this tri-relative influence not being resolvable into action between pairs" (1955:282; italics in original). The process by which these effects are realized is described by Peirce as follows: "A sign is not a sign unless it *translates* into another sign in which it is more fully developed" (1955:594); italics added). This is more fully explained as follows: "If after any thought, the current of ideas flows on freely, it follows the law of mental association. In that case, each thought suggests something to the thought which follows, i.e., is the sign of something to this latter. There is no exception therefore to the law that every thought-sign is translated or intercepted in a subsequent one, unless it be that all thought comes to an abrupt and final end in death" (1934: volume 5, 284).

If the semiotic process can be called a translation it behooves us to examine this a little more closely. Translation signifies a change of something into something else that is in all essential aspects equal to it. In such processes, both the translated and the translation are of the same value and significance and nothing but a superficial change has occurred. A translator from one language into another, for example, or from one currency into another, indicates no radical change in either side of the transactions thus conversion back into the original format can be made without any loss. In the semiotic process involving a change from one sign into another sign, the object—which has an effect on a person—is certainly therefore not a mere translation, because it has become something more than what it was before. To Peirce one sign changed into another is more fully developed or elaborated. (1955:99) If this is the case, then there is a radical change in the significance and form of the sign and hence the process is better called one of transformation rather than of translation. The process of semiosis, which "follows the law of mental association," is indubitably a process of transformation.

In spite of the differences among the various theorists about the usage of the idea of transformation, there is an underlying similarity as well. In all cases, transformation describes a process in which X, as a result of one operation or another, becomes $X + 1$ or $X + 2$, or $X - 1$ or $X - 2$ and so on. Further transformation and formation are not separate activities; rather, transformation is the central mental act. Insofar as there is no possibility of "the absolutely incognizable" and since every conception is derived from a previous conception, there can be no pristine formation. [Thus everything that passes for a formation is really a transformation of one already existing sign into another. Producing a "sign" is really assembling selectively other more complex sign-systems.] To read a sign is not to react to it mechanically, but to understand the sign in terms of other signs, to see relationships and connections, to apprehend it as similar to and/or different from other forms. Semiosis turns out to be a transformational process by which an object is converted into a sign, which elicits another sign called an interpretant. It appears then that interpretability is given to discursive signs by *processes of multiple and simultaneous transformations*. In order to achieve interpretability for one's signs, an agent must transform intentions into signs that are phonologically, grammatically, symbolically, linguistically, and socially acceptable. These are isomorphically achieved acts of transformation. The intentional apprehension, itself a sign, is given form in sound, order, grammar, and significance in symbols and structures of social and interpersonal situations. It is through these acts of transformation that both the logic of human living and its "psychology" are achieved. As Peirce noted, "Signs require at least two *quasi-minds*; a quasi-utterer and a quasi-interpreter; and although these two are at one (i.e., *are* one mind) in the sign itself, they must nevertheless be distinct. In the sign they are, so to say, *welded*. Accordingly, it is not merely a fact of human psychology, but a necessity of logic, that every logical evolution of thought should be dialogic" (1933:551, Volume 4; italics in original).

Mind, or rather minding, is both a logical and a psychological operation, and one and both of these operations are subsumed under that of transformational semiosis. These operations can also be called (1) grammatical semiosis, (2) phonological semiosis, (3) categorical semiosis, and (4) symbolic semiosis, referring, respectively, to Chomskyan, Jakobsonian, Saussurian, and Cassiririan/Langerian transformations. In this process a phenomenon, whether an object in Peirce's sense, a code in the Saussure's sense, a distinctive feature in Jakobson's sense, or a logical structure in Chomsky's sense, is changed into something noticeably different from the previous form.

## The Phonological Semiosis

The presence of discourse in one's immediate environment becomes known primarily by auditory means. One hears the words and sentences as articulated by a sentient being and it is to these that a responsive interpretation and a completing act must be directed so as to constitute an interaction. Discourses are apprehended as they are heard and comprehended as tangible and plangent forms and forces given by the prosodic features of the text. To begin with, these words, as they are assembled into the utterances that become the discursive act, must be enunciated in such a way that their separateness from each other and identity unto themselves are clear and unambiguous. Second, various changes in the course of enunciation must be made so that the nuances of the articulator's intentions are indicated. The first quality is given by managing the phonological features of a language and can be called, following Jakobson, *the phonotary act*. The second feature is achieved by controlling the pitch, length, loudness, rhythm, and stress on words and phrases, i.e., tone and intonation, and can be called *the tonatory act*. Jakobson notes that

> Since the sound matter of language is a matter organized and formed to serve as a semiotic instrument, not only the significative function of the distinctive features, but even their phonic essence is a cultural artifact. Phonic entities draw on the gross sound matter, but readjust this extrinsic stuff, dissecting and classifying it along their own line. The gross matter knows no oppositions. It is human thought, conscious or unconscious which draws from this sound matter the binary oppositions for their phonemic use. (1962:423)

Another way of describing these operations is to say that differentiated patterns are derived from gross sounds and used as semiotic instruments. In these exercises, the phoneme is an object, Jakobson is at pains to point out that has no significance by itself. As he states, "The phoneme's sole linguistic context, or more generally its sole semiotic context, is its dissimilarity from all other phonemes and signifies something different from another phoneme in the same position; this its sole value" (1978:60). Nevertheless it still stands as a sign by itself, and when it is combined with other such signs a word is created, and when words are combined with other words, sentences are created. Here, too, the phoneme functions as a sign that represents an object, a sound, and when it is combined with other sounds it achieves an interpretant and has an effect upon a person. The semiotic effect, then, is achieved by an act of transformation.

The phonetic equipment of the human is such that it can make a certain number and quality of sounds. These sounds have to be organized in such a way that both gross and subtle differences can be asserted by an articulator and read by a recipient. From a basic pattern of sounds an articulator produces varied phonemes that are organized so as to constitute words. This is the first step in the construction of a discursive act: the transformation of sounds into a discourse that embodies one's intentions. Slight variations in these sounds will alter the significance being conveyed and change the force of the utterance. The selection procedures consist of assembling phonemes designated to perform various tasks in a discursive act. To quote Jakobson, "What we recognize in spoken language is not sound differences in themselves but the different uses to which they are put by the language, i.e. differences which, though without meaning in themselves, are used in discriminating one from another entities of a higher level (morphemes, words)" (1978:74): different uses to which not only the language puts the phoneme, but to which the users—articulators and respondents—also put them, i.e., to define, assert, and announce intentions.

The construction of a discursive act thus consists of assembling intentionally phonemically clear and purposeful utterances organized on the basis of selection procedures that have become habitual. These procedures lead to the presentation of various speech sounds designed to perform selected tasks in a discursive act. In creating a discursive act an articulator has to engage in two operations:

(1) Combinations: Discursive acts, made of constituent signs, or occurring only in combination with other signs. "This means," says Jakobson, "that any linguistic unit at one and the same time serves as a context in a more or less complex linguistic unit" (1971:243).

(2) Selections: Discursive acts consisting of linguistic units that are the result of a selection between alternatives. "A selection between alternatives," says Jakobson, "implies the possibility of substituting one for

another, equivalent to the former in one respect and different from it in another. Actually selection and substitution are two faces of the same operation" (1971:243).

In ordinary discursive acts, the articulator manages both the metaphoric and metonymic, that is, the similar and contiguous poles of speech investing them with significance that is part of the discourse, as well as mixing them in such a way that an enriched text is heard. These are acts of phonological transformation in which the intentions of the self are deliberately manifested as organized sounds that are understood by the other and by the self, and eliciting a commensurate response. It also appears in normal discourse that an articulator can deliberately use the sounds of discourse to stylize his or her texts to indicate intentions and define the parameters of a self.

The various elements of discourse are never used without significant internal variations. These prosodic features of discursive acts consist primarily of three interrelated variables: *pitch, length, and loudness.* "Pitch," notes Alan Cruttenden, "concerns the varying height of the pitch of the voice over one syllable or over a number of successive syllables; length concerns the relative durations of a number of successive syllables or the duration of a given syllable in one environment relative to the duration of the same syllable in another environment; loudness concerns changes of loudness within one syllable or the relative loudness of a number of successive syllables" (1986:2). These are variables recognized by both the articulator and the listener. Articulators are expected to be as in control of their vocal equipment as they are of their auditory equipment, and when such control is used to indicate significations and their qualifications by means of pitch, length, and loudness, such voicings or articulations become a tonatory act.

D.C. Brazil argues that there are four variables that constitute the prosodic elements of a discursive presentation: *prominence, tone, key,* and *termination.* In producing discursive acts one often has to underline, emphasize, and give importance to one word or one segment of the discourse as the context in which the utterance occurs so indicates. This act of verbal underlining can be called prominence. In the course of a game of bridge, an inattentive player can ask his partner "Which card did you play?" The card that one plays is determined by the logic of the game as a whole, as well as a particular moment in the developing sequences of the game. In one context, the respondent must wonder whether the question implies that he or she has played the wrong card. If so, his or her response may have to give prominence to the "hearts" component of the utterance, which conveys the idea that he or she surely would not have played spades, clubs, or diamonds. Thus he or she would say, "The *queen of hearts*." Further, since the opponent has played the jack of hearts and his or her partner has the king of hearts and the dummy has no high card in hearts, he or she would give prominence to the "queen" segment. In any case, it is clear that tonal prominence has been used to convey the intention of the self in the context. The opposition between soft and hard articulation is what is being transformed here in terms of contextually determined intention. In this case, the articulator selects the hard form, gives it prominence in articulation, and thereby achieves the effects of his or her intention.

Brazil has called another tonal input a discursive act *rising* and *falling* tones. Citing Brazil's work, Coulthard offers the following, in which the downward line indicates falling tones, the upward line rising tones, and the arrowhead the ending.

1.   When I have finished Middlemarch I shall read Adam Bède.

2.   When I have finished Middlemarch I shall read Adam Bede.

Coulthard observes of the two forms, "Whatever additional implications these intonation choices may have, the first utterance is certainly addressed to someone who is expected to know already that the speaker is reading Middlemarch, but to whom the speaker's other intentions are an item of news. In the second example the question of the speaker's reading of Adam Bede had already arisen in some way and he is offering information about when he will read it" (1985:104–5). In each case, certain oral operations are performed in order to convey signifying intentions to an auditor, which are creative transformations of basic material into signifying instrumentations.

Further, in articulating utterances so as to constitute discursive acts, a speaker must select the relative pitch, or as Brazil calls it, the key "from a three-term system, high, mid and low" (Coulthard, 1985:11). The key that is high is high in terms of the previous tone unit and is used to indicate a *contrast* with it:

He GAMBled and $\frac{\text{LOST}}{}$.

In this utterance, basic information is given, but it is implied that both the speaker and the auditor expected him to win, notes Coulthard (1985:111). The high-pitched *lost* can also mean that in the context of the preceding discussion there was a statement made by the auditor that the subject had gambled and won, which the speaker is now decisively contradicting.

In discursive acts there is often a need to make lists and to engage in the addition of phenomena that share certain properties. This is tonally accomplished by:

He GAMBled and LOST.

In this articulation, no contrast between gambling and losing is implied. There is merely a confirmation of necessary relationship: he both gambled and lost. This is an *additive* indication.

In the pitch that is low-keyed, as in

$$\text{He } \underline{\text{GAMbled}} \text{ and } \underline{\text{LOST}}$$

notes Coulthard, there is an *equative* relationship. There is no flouting of expectations here or no unanticipated consequences, and both speaker and auditor know that this is what usually happens. Keying options are systematically used to indicate significations that are particularly appropriate in the situation and context in which the utterance is being made. These add finer shades to significance as well as assert the presence of the self in the discursive act. This, in keying the pitch in the first utterance at a high level for *lost*, the articulator is able to assert himself or herself by contradicting the other and announcing that he or she knows enough about the person in question to understand that he usually wins and that the auditor in this particular case is mistaken. Each of these assertions of the self is also an affirmation of the self.

The final element of information that Coulthard discusses is tonal *termination*. He notes that, in addition to choosing a pitch movement for each tonic syllable, "the speaker chooses to begin, in the case of falling tones, or end in the case of rising tones, with high, mid or low pitch." With the help of this manuver, he or she is able to predict, or ask for, "a particular key choice and therefore by implication, a particular meaning from the next speaker" (1985:116). When a speaker says, "You'll come won't you?" he can put it tonally as follows:

$$\text{You'll } \underline{\text{COME}} \text{ } \underline{\text{WON'T}} \text{ you}$$

where *come* is in high key and *won't* is in a medium key, with both words given prominence. In this case, there is a special determination of the expected answer, making it vain for someone to say anything but yes. The following gives the auditor a choice:

$$\text{Will you } \underline{\text{COME}}$$

because the termination is high-keyed and prominent. The answer can be either yes or no, either high- or low-keyed. We see here the choices a speaker can exercise: offering the question as a plea, a threat, a simple request, or an importunement. To do this, he or she takes the basic grammatical form and transforms its intonational structure, making the terminating sound not only a question but a question with special properties. Without any change in the surface structure of the sentence, the speaker has been able to reduce the choices the auditor can exercise, almost entrapping him or her into an answer by merely transforming the sounds, indicating not just a question, but an entreaty.[2]

Emotions are articulated in similar ways. Emotions, of course, are not merely occasional intrusions into discourse. Rather, every act, gesture, and speech is redolent with emotions, although the ratio of their presence is undoubtedly variable. Every statement made has an emotional element conveyed by tone: tones that record love, tenderness, affection, anger, contempt, hatred, indifference, ennui, etc. All discursive acts, then, are emotionally tinged, emotions that are defined and articulated tonally. Those who cannot do emotions tonally are typically considered interactionally incompetent, and indeed this is often regarded as lack of affect, and an impairment of self.

Further, discourses are articulated with socially correct tonal qualities, or what may be called, tonatory decorum. For example, official occasions, such as the swearing in of the president of the United States, demand a particular tone, in contrast to television commentator's announcement of a home run in a baseball game. Similarly, status and honor are reproduced tonally and intonationally in the articulation of discourses: inferiors are addressed differently from superiors, just as addressing children and pets calls for prosodic variations.

Irony and sarcasm are also conveyed by prosodic variations. In ironic discourses, statements made are meant to convey a signification opposite from that contained in the semantic unit. In perhaps the most famous ironic speech of all dramatic literature, Mark Antony refers to Brutus as an "Honorable Man" and then by means of systematic repetitions, conveys to his audience that Brutus was anything but an honorable man. In ordinary life, such indications become imperative; recognizing ironic and sarcastic tones in everyday discourses is a common occurrence. Typically, an articulator calls attention to the sarcastic or ironic intention by altering the tone, or intonation, of the utterance. Coulthard indicates an example of the former. If someone does something stupid and an observer remarks "clever," the context makes it ironic, no doubt aided by the observer's articulation of the word in such a way as to make its ironic suggestion unmistakable. Of course, if it is missed and the initiator of the stupid act does not recognize its stupidity, the intelligence and perspicacity of the observer becomes questionable. Coulthard, however, notes that the sarcasm becomes more pointed by the use of a tone indicating the observer was truly impressed by the cleverness of the act (Coulthard, 1985:102). In either case, the observer's discursive act is achieved by managing the tone of the utterance, and I venture to suggest further that whether a tone indicates that he or she is really impressed or is not being serious depends on the nature of the relationship that exists between the two.

While the context contributes the major component for ironic interpretation in longer utterances, intonation too is an important element in it. A cab driver who has not been tipped may feel hostile toward a passenger, and may say "Thanks for the tip" in a soft modulated intonation. All the tones are even. There are no rises or falls, and a sense of control and calm is thereby achieved. In other circumstances, acts of irony call for more forceful prosodic techniques, which call the attention of the auditor to certain words and phrases by stressing them in one of many ways. This can be done by altering their pitch, length, or volume, thereby signaling that certain qualifications are being introduced into the words' overt significance.

To sum up, the impairment of the language function that leads to two basic forms of disorder—similarity disorder and contiguity disorder—makes it impossible, or at least very difficult, for a self to announce its intentions and experience the effects of such announcements. The discursive act necessarily becomes truncated and fruitless, which renders physical impairment of the brain a cause of major social failure as well. The impaired person will find it difficult to enter into interactions and cultivate relationships, and will indeed be driven into isolation and emptiness. Others with similar impairments, the deaf and the mute, have certain problems unless they are properly trained and unless those who interact with them are trained in the same skills. The impairment of function is only an illustration of the overwhelming importance of discursive processes and transformations for everyone. Of course, this particular kind of impairment is only one among many. Indeed, even those who are not aphasic, deaf, or mute may be impaired. In fact, everyone's capability for constructing or interpreting discursive acts is a variable, and each one of us is always in danger of using the apparatus of language incorrectly. Anyone can distort similarity relations and contiguity relations, be deaf to tone, blind to color, insensitive to irony, sarcasm, nuance, and shade without being physically deficient.

Tonal variations are used to encapsulate and convey significance, the intentional significance of a self that is participating in a situation and developing a context, and a continuation of the processes for the production of the phonatory act that Jakobson discussed. These variable features of discourse, represented by tonality, are produced by managing distinctive features of the act of phonation (Jakobson and Halle, 1956).

Creativity in the course of the discursive act is not a mere luxury in the dramaturgy of a linguistically minded species, but an imperative without which conviction in one's own productions cannot be demonstrated. Further, the conviction demonstrated by the discursive presentation also indicates the articulator's responsibility for the words issued and the commitment of his or her self to them. These productions must bear the stamp of authenticity and originality, of being freshly minted, of immediacy of apprehension and construction. They must appear to be spontaneous and wrought in felt emotions and attitudes, and above all must be distinguished from mere mimicry. Prosodic mastery then becomes imperative whether one is speaking from one's own conviction or merely pretending to be doing so.

Indeed, it is when we consider how they are created for purposes of persuading audiences to accept authenticity when they have evidence to the contrary, that the importance of these tonatory qualities in everyday discourses becomes clear. In producing a play—where neither the discourse nor the agents that issue it have any authentic relationship to each other—dedicated labor is needed in order to give the discourse and the gestures that accompany it a nature that appears fresh and authentic. The production of a play is nothing more than getting the actors to enunciate and gesture in such a way that a congruent relationship can be created between them as well as between the character and situation in which the discourse is presented. While in the theater we expect the actors to articulate with conviction and commitment words written by somebody else, in everyday life we expect the speakers to be their own authors. Indeed, in some arenas the veracity of a statement is judged on the basis of its authorial authenticity alone, while in others, such as courts of law, a rotelike enunciation will mark a witness as a liar, or as one who has no authorial relationship to his or her words.

In discursive acts, then, the sound of the discourse ensures the verisimilitude of the self in the situation in which it finds itself. Further, the articulation of utterances that are parts of discourses contains words arranged into sentences. In uttering them, certain words or phrases are selected and emphasized intonationally in order to qualify the intention of the self contained in the sentence. Such changes give to utterances a distinct tone that carries the complex signifying intentions of the articulator and manifests the force of the self as it becomes relevant.

## Grammatical Semiosis

Chomsky's revolution in linguistics has given us a number of substantive conclusions that need to be incorporated into any theory of the act and its articulation. To summarize a few of the relevant ones:

1. Language is based on a logic and a reason that is specific to the human population.
2. This logic is manifest in the existence of deep syntactical structures in the brain of the human species, which are manifest in the language of the species.

3. As they are put into use by humans, these deep structures produce surface structures, which are manifest in the varieties of human discourse.
4. These surface structures can take many forms.

Chomsky argued that the deep structures of a sentence are syntactical ones; that is, they *connect* one element of a sentence to another, and one can find these structures in all human languages. Deep structures can give rise to a great variety of surface forms by a process or operation called transformation. That is, transformational rules allow a deep structure to be converted into a variety of surface forms, each carrying varied significations. To use Chomsky's more recent terminology, the language faculty consists of an "internalized language" that has a universal grammar, that is, a biologically derived capacity of the mind generates an "externalized language." As he puts it, "What is given to every child is some finite array of data, on the basis of which the child's mind constructs an internalized language that assigns a status to every expression, and that we may think of as generating some externalized language under one or another stipulated convention" (1986:31).

It seems however that it is *not* the "stipulated convention" alone that leads to the generation of the externalized language, but also the structure of intentions of a conscious and deliberate agent. It is he or she who seeks to assert, announce, and declare his or her intentions, thereby exercising his or her celebrated capacity for the "creative use of language in the process" (Chomsky, 1972:75), that generates an "externalized language." It is because an agent has an infinite number of intentions, with which he or she will seek to create effects in the world, that he or she succeeds in generating an infinite number of sentences or a close approximation thereof. *The grammatical transformational process is then nothing but the parsimonious embodiment of intentionality in a surface form that is based on a deeper one that is fecund with generational possibilities.* In other words, surface structures, as they are produced by an agent, inevitably become creatively constructed pragmatic instruments. The process refers to "output," to the conversion of one phrase structure into other phrase structures, and to the coming into being of many forms from one basic form. The basic form yields to an agent a parsimonious way of generating semantic structures, that is, a way of collapsing his or her intentions into socially and interactionally acceptable forms.

In grammatical transformations, says Chomsky, "one can distinguish the *surface structure* of the sentence, the organization into categories and phrases that is directly associated with the physical signal, from the underlying *deep structure* also a system of categories and phrases but with a more abstract character" (1972:28–29, italics in original). Instead of naming these structures in terms of an archaeological metaphor, they

could be called concrete and abstract or expressive and logical structures, respectively. The process of articulating sentences, then, involves
transformationally generating a number of concrete sentences from an
abstract formula and an expressive sentence from a logical structure.

Chomsky's transformational system is compatible with Peirce's for-
mulations in many ways. The logical or abstract structure is the object
that is, to use Peirce's expression, translated into a more concrete sentence, which thereby "determines an effect upon a person, which effect
I call its Interpretant" (quoted in Liszka, 1981:55). *While in Chomsky's
formulation the transformational exercises are mere grammatical ones, viewed
through the Peircian semiotic, they become grammatical ones in which the act of
transformation seeks to have a semiotic effect upon a person.* Thus transformations are inescapably semiotic exercises, just as semiosis is a systematic
and many-faceted process of formation and transformation. Consider
the work of Bever, Lackner, and Kirk (1974), who after reviewing previous work and doing some experiments of their own concluded "As we
hear a sentence we organize it in terms of underlying structures: sentences with subjects, verbs, objects and modifiers. Rather than recapitu-
lating the *full* grammatical derivation brought out in the linguistic analysis of a particular sentence, the underlying structure segmentation of
sentences and organization within sentences is projected immediately
and directly from the structural potentialities of the words in sequence"
(1969:142; italics in original).

In earlier work, Fodor and Garrett (1967), as well as Fodor, Garrett,
and Bever (1968), found that "listeners *actively* use their knowledge of
the underlying structure potentialities of particular lexical items in sentence comprehension" (Bever, Lackner, and Fodor, 1974, italics added).
If listeners actively process underlying structures in order to compre-
hend the other's articulation, it is because underlying structures are put
into play when articulating a sentence. *That is to say, transformational
exercises occur both within a speaker's activities and between speakers and their
listeners.* The object receiving this attention is the underlying logical
structure, which becomes available as a syntactic structure readily capable of being transformed into surface phrase structures as the situation
demands. The basic logical structure, then, is analogous to "thought" in
the Peircian problematic, or to a "cognition." What exactly is the ontological nature of the deep structure? Is it a consciously held belief, an
item of knowledge, a diagram, a tree? Or is it merely an unconscious
element, whatever form it may take, or is it a mere a neurological
arrangement? Insofar as it has to be *something* for it to be knowable and
usable, I opt for the conclusion, prodded by Chomsky's repeated usage
of the term "innate ideas" (Chomsky, 1986), that it is in the nature of a
thought or cognition, *at least in the moments before it is transformed into*

*expressive surfaces*. Such a cognition is an object that is converted into an *intentional interpretant* that, in the form of an expressive structure, is articulated in order to elicit an *effective interpretant*. Such activities are inherently teleological, though the emergence of an actual interpretant may be deferred. If the sentence is terminated, the sign will fall short of the perfect significant character; however, "It is not necessary that the Interpretant should actually exist. A being *in futuro* would suffice" (Peirce, 1932 volume 2, 92). The following sentence, then, exists as an underlying logical structure and as an intentional interpretant, a cognition and a sign. It is also a sign with complex features, which signify complex intentions. These features are manifest as "surface structures" and will be interpreted effectively in the same way as they were constituted. Consider an example:

"Caesar crossed the Rubicon" becomes a surface structure of phrases: S is sentence, NP is noun phrase, and VP is verb phrase.

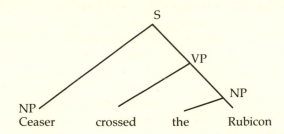

where S is sentence, NP is noun phrase, and VP is verb phrase.

This can also be expressed as

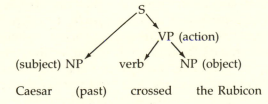

The underlying logical structure of the sentence is written to describe the functions of each phrase: the noun phrase that constitutes the subject and the one that constitutes the object, and the verb and the suffix that indicate the tense of the verb. The more significant of the results from these studies—Bever, Lackner, and Kirk (1974) note—is that it shows that the form in which sentences are understood and memorized corresponds closely to their underlying logical structure. Thus, any model for speech perception proposed in this tradition includes a device that isolates the logical structure corresponding to each lexical sequence (1974:121)

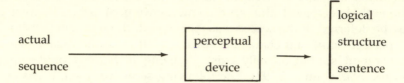

If this is the listener's view of the matter, then, the articulator's views would be

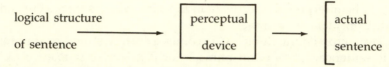

If we abandon the notion of the device used here and substitute certain Peircian notions, the argument would not only look more human but would also be enriched. Indeed the thesis that Bever et al. are proposing seems to be congruent with Peirce's concepts of semiosis. In this process of active listening to the other's sentences, use is made of the knowledge of underlying structures that the articulator is using to constitute his or her sentences. Chomsky himself summarizes his theory as follows: "Knowledge of a language involves the ability to assign deep and surface structures to an infinite range of sentences, to relate these structures appropriately, and to assign a semantic interpretation and a phonetic interpretation to the paired deep and surface structures" (1972:30). Insofar as the articulation of a discursive act is simultaneously grammatical, phonological and semantic, how does the intention of the self become manifested by an agent's capacity to select the semantic, phonological, and grammatical form in the same moment his or her intentions are generated? The answer is, of course, that the intentions of the self are generated simultaneously with the other operations, though once the process of articulating is set into motion, various modifications and qualifications can be introduced. Chomsky points out that some transformations are obligatory, while others are optional (1969:45), and that an articulator has greater freedom in the selection of syntactic component than the phonological component. Whether they are obligatory or optional, all utterances, and therefore all discursive acts, are the result of transformational exercises at the grammatical level. Each such transformation seeks to encode and embody the precise intentions of the articulator in the syntax of the utterance.

Transformational exercises, it seems, are the same as the semiosis of signs from intentional interpretants into effective ones. Transformational exercises, however, are discursive practices, even though they may have different surface forms of varying degrees of significance. There is no essential semantic difference, for example, between "Caesar crossed the Rubicon," and "The Rubicon was crossed by Caesar," but in an ongoing discursive series, articulators may change the order around. The value of grammatical transformations of this sort in discursive acts cannot be overestimated. They avoid monotony and introduce variety and alternation into a discourse. Even in this very elementary example there is a metrical and rhythmic difference between the two utterances; the first sounds short, clipped, and to the point, whereas the second one has a slightly longer duration and an altered rhythm.

The moment that *context* is introduced, however, there can be a noticeable difference in significance when the second form is used. In this case, if the sentence "the Rubicon was crossed" were uttered at a certain moment in an ongoing series in which sentences pertaining to the crossing of the river, by whom, when, and why were also presented, it would have an altered significance. Earlier utterances leave their marks on the meaning of a later sentence. The later sentence will have a slightly varied force even though the semantic content has not been altered by the transformation. The articulator can find himself or herself at a moment in the discourse where the fact that the Rubicon, let us say, a sacred river in a culture in which crossing it is taken as a major ritual offense, was crossed, and the speaker, wanting to forestall any attempt to pardon the crossing, can very well say, "The Rubicon *was* crossed." The transformational exercise here gives a new force to the utterance and asserts the presence of a self and its very definitive intentions. In such moments, articulators can exercise their *option* to transform sentences so as to maximize their signifying force. Discourses, insofar as they are continuing contextual processes, need these transformational options to be exercised. The need to elaborate and enhance one's significations in the course of producing discursive acts, to define precisely and clearly signifying intent and force, are perennial problems often dealt with by grammatical transformations. This is evident in the following instance:

A patient, responding to questions from a therapist observes: You know, I feel like I'm going to be released from this room and that I am going to be raging, in a raging fury, and nobody will know why (laugh). I just walk along, you know, nice and straight. If I get angry enough all at once, then would I get over it? Primal scream. I can't imagine, you know, feeling really, feeling like there isn't anything wrong with me. I was thinking about that the other day. What would it be like, you know, to feel that you really just, you know, you were where you ought to be, and everything is just really full? (Gill and Hoffman, 1982:61)

This paragraph contains a number of grammatical transformations that is used to signify discursively the intentionality of the self as well as to indicate the force of intentionality. Consider the opening sentence, which contains three simple sentences:

1.  I feel like I am going to be released from this room.
2.  I am going to be raging, in a raging fury.
3.  Nobody will know why (I am in a raging fury).

These are run into a compound sentence introduced with a vocative fragment, "You know." The running compound structure displays the interconnected nature of the sense of the three sentences as well as her emotion. The opening vocative fragment invites the auditor to agree beforehand with what is to follow; indeed it suggests that he or she already knows what it is she is about to reveal. The first sentence is again prefaced with a fragment that underlines the words that follow: "I feel" rather than "I know," a softer, rather apologetic claim. The sentence that follows this is a claim about her feelings and, in a striking construction, reveals a number of complex intentions. It contains a predicate, "raging," which is altered by the introduction of the preposition "in" in the next phrase, which now becomes a predicate, as "raging" becomes an adjective qualifying the object "fury." The patient is able to convey that she is going to be angry but suddenly changes to the more extreme condition of "raging fury." These intentions are nicely paralleled by the grammatical constructions employed. One can also notice the systematic usage of the fragment "you know" to qualify her sentences. This is surely a usage that intends to acknowledge doubts and anxieties and to invite the prior approval of the auditor.

These usages, then, are intrinsic parts of this discourse, and carry the signifying force of the articulator, the presence of the intentions of the self, and its immediate location in a particular context and situation. These transformations of the articulator are optional ones that she uses to convey her intentions, thus investing them with signifying force. These articulations are made not by self-conscious choices and deliberations as to syntactical form, but by the exercise of syntactical options that become habits by which an agent conceives intentions and sentences coterminously.

Consider another example, a malediction used by monks against their enemies during the post-Carolingian period: "Almighty God above, look upon the affliction of all who call upon you, who mercifully allows the tears of orphans and widows to reach your ears, look down upon us, your servants on behalf of your most holy and pious conferrers . . . and protect us from our enemies" (Little, 1970:394). Through this stage it is a very conventional prayer that soon becomes a long litany of *suggested* punishments for the enemies:

> Let their portion and inheritance be the fire of eternal punishment with Pathon, Abiron, Judas, Pilate . . . with whom they may be tortured with eternal punishment without end, so that neither with Christ and his saints in heavenly peace may they have a share with the Devil and his companions dispatched to the hell of torment, and may they perish for all eternity; may they be cursed in the cities, may they be cursed in the countryside, may they be cursed in the castles, may they be cursed in the islands, may they be cursed in the fruit of their wombs, may they be cursed in their homes, cursed when they enter, cursed when they leave, may they be cursed in all their places (Little, 1970:395; translated from the Latin by John McLaughlin)

The use of the word *may*, an optional construction, succeeds in articulating a request from God without making it an imperative and a demand at the beginning. However, as it rolls along, the frequent use of *may* indicates a more forceful request. The opening invocation is a properly supplicatory one: We are like children and orphans, your servants, and please take care of us. However, this intention of a supplicatory request in which God had the determining function is undermined by the systematic and repetitive structure of the sentences. The piling up of the details of the punishment that is requested and the rhythmic organizations of the discourse suggests a reversal of the dialectic of request and demand, an opposite of the representation of God and his relationship to his priesthood. The priests, accordingly, become the dominant characters and God the servant.

The use of these operations results not only in the creation of sentences but the construction of a discursive act that embodies the intentions of the self that is made available to an other whose responses will define the effects of the discourse. These effects have to be anticipated, and the very structure of the sentences codes these anticipations.

Needless to say, it is possible to supply numerous other examples. But it is evident from the few discussed here that discourses actively use the structures of grammar to invest them with signifying force and to display the self of the articulator. Indeed, they become acts that seek not only effects in the world, but very specific and deliberate ones.[3]

## Categorical Semiosis

In categorical transformation, the signs that represent objects are given significance by being compared and contrasted with other signs (Saussure, 1959). In this case the signs are subject to semiosis in such a way that they elicit two objects simultaneously: the one they represent and another either diametrically opposed to it or only in varying degrees. Each sign is put into one category or another, thereby establishing a systematic conceptual differentiation of one from another. Indeed, words are defined by the differentiations they embody, and in Saussure's system such differentiation is made in terms of "paradigmatic" and "syntagmatic" transformations. In making signifying utterances, every articulator must implicitly and habitually perform two interrelated operations: the selection of words that precisely represent intentions and the assemblage of the words so that they clearly indicate those intentions. That is to say, the words that constitute an utterance need to be known to the articulator in terms of what they constitute, what they do not constitute, and how closely they constitute what the articulator seeks to convey. There is no doubt that these finely graded degrees of signification and intention can be known and used only in *a field of signs*. From this field, some signs are selected and measured against other signs, and then against still other signs, so that a precise estimation is achieved. That is, a phenomenon not only occurs in a field of other objects, but is given shape and coherence, precise features, indeed a tangible reality, by contrast and comparison with other objects in the field.

This can be seen in fields other than language and meaning. In recent studies of visual perception David Marr (1982) provided an excellent summary of an approach that uses an information processing theory of vision. He described the findings as follows:

> By analyzing the spatial aspects of the problem of vision, we arrived at an overall framework for visual information processing that hinges on three principal representations: (1) the primal sketch, which is concerned with making explicit properties of the two-dimensional image, ranging from the amount and disposition of the intensity changes there to primitive representation of the local image geometry, and including at the more sophisticated end, a hierarchical description of any higher order structure present in the underlying reflectance distributions; (2) the 2½ sketch which is a viewer–centered representation of the depth and orientation of the visible surfaces and includes contours of discontinuities in these quantities. (3) The 3–D model representation, whose important features are that its coordinate system is object centered, that it includes volumetric primitives and that primitives of various size are included, arranged in a modular, hierarchical organization. (1982:330)

Vision, it turns out, is a complex process of analysis and assemblage occurring simultaneously. Each successful view is accomplished by continuing acts of *differentiation* between amount and disposition, the representation of the shape of the image, and the hierarchical description of higher-order structures present in the sketch. This is true for more sophisticated images as well; contours of discontinuities are visible in depth, orientation, and volume and are organized usually in modular and hierarchical terms. All of these operations, it is evident, are based on using contrasts and comparisons, or indeed engaging in measurements of differences and similarities. *The are, in other words, acts of semiosis in which objects are transformed into organized relationships with other objects whereby an order is created.* "This framework," says Marr, "is based on the idea that the critical issues in vision revolve around the nature of the representation used—that is, the particular characteristics of the world that are made explicit during vision—and the nature of the processes that recover these characteristics, create and maintain the representations and eventually read them" (1982:330).

If that is true of visual objects, it is also true of other signs. Placing them in a system of relations with other objects allows their value to be determined. Thus, a fundamental process seems to operate in the articulation of utterances. The transformational semiosis that is conducted in articulating utterances means, as Phillip Pettit succinctly puts it, "sorting out parts in a whole, elements in a string under syntagmatic constraints and paradigmatic contrasts" (1975:37). These categories have been most clearly shown in the work of Claude Levi-Strauss, who noted that symbols are subject to transformational rules whereby they are converted into new manifestations. While he applied these principles, derived from the theories of Jakobson and Saussure, to the analysis of myths and kinship systems, they can be applied to everyday discourses as well. In fact, Edmund Leach noted that the basic principles of structural analysis can be applied to "all verbal expression and ritual activity" (1976:26). He also gives a neat summary of structural analytical methodology:

1. We start with a mythical story that is linear, one thing happening after another, that is, the events occur in sequence, forming a syntagmatic chain linked by metonymy.
2. We then note that the story as a whole can be broken up into episodes: mythical story as recorded: episode A episode B episode C.
3. Each is then assumed to be a partial transformation of each of the others and on that assumption we rearrange the diagram to suggest that each of the subjects refers to simultaneous events and then "add up" the result. In the jargon, the first of these steps has transformed the original "syntagmatic chain" into "paradigmatic associations" (metonymy is converted into metaphor). Thus,

episode A
episode B
episode C
_____
summary: result by "addition"

(Leach, 1976:26–27)

Unlike the detailed elements found in the original episodes, the elements in the summary "additive" story are abstract. In the jargon, the summation process converts "paradigmatic association" into a "syntagmatic chain," metaphor transformed into metonymy. (Leach, 1976:25–

26). When arranged in this manner an articulator and a respondent are able to arrive at a more or less common interpretation of a story—even if the story has no particular articulator.

The same conditions obtain in the production and interpretation of the discourses of everyday life. Consider a patient's communication to his therapist:

> There are a few little minor things that I have noticed, eh, that don't shed any new light on that we've been talking about, but just show the consistent pattern of, eh, the way my mind works. The nurse we've had, eh, leaves Wednesday morning. She was going to leave this weekend, but we had her stay a few more days. Leaves Wednesday morning. And my wife and I view the, her leaving entirely differently. And at least in my viewing it, I can see, is my usual, eh, rose-colored approach; I don't see it—I mean having the full responsibility of the baby, when the nurse is there, I suppose and when she had the final responsibility—as too, eh, too dreadful, let us say, or even too much to worry about. My wife is . . . is . . . is . . . worried about how she will act when she has to have the baby all by herself; and when it cries, if there is something wrong with it and she has to make the (cough) decision, and she had to, to calm it by herself. Eh, part of the reasons that I am not as worried about it as she is, is that obviously I am not there as much of the time as she is, and I think also it is very definitely my view that things always seem to turn out fine. Eh, I mean, I am quite certain now that, eh (cough), I will be able to handle the baby and that, she will and so forth. Well that's about it. I mean, that is all, that there is to it. But, as I say, I noticed again there is nothing new, but I noticed the consistency of the way I tend to view things. (Gill and Hoffman, 1982:69–70)

This discourse can be destructured as follows:

Episode A:   The nurse leaves soon.
Episode B:   My wife is worried about how she will act when she has to have the baby all by herself.
Episode C:   I am not as worried about it as she is because I am not there much of the time
Episode D:   I am certain, however, that I will be able to handle the baby and so will my wife be able to handle the baby.

This gives us a chain: A → B → C → D.

This syntagmatic chain can be transformed into a paradigmatic association:

        A:   Nurse leaves
        B:   Wife's worry
        C:   Self does not worry
        D:   No one should worry;
Summary:   Despite some worries, we will be able to manage.

This discourse can be seen as composed of the following features: an event is introduced, its consequences described, a binary opposition established between the discursant and his wife, and a conclusion reached. In this way a complex discourse is presented and then used by the articulator to make a discursive act. That is, he uses these structures of episodes to indicate to the listening therapist "how my mind works" and to show that in contrast to his wife, he sees the world with "a rose-colored approach."

The transformational process in the discourse cited here is produced by the articulator, who needs to portray his character as clearly as possible and who resorts to a structure of oppositions transformatively to do so:

| self | wife |
|------|------|
| optimist | pessimist |
| competent | incompetent |
| absent | present |

The patient could have simply claimed, in bare terms, that he was a competent and optimistic person. Instead, he presents an elaborate discourse, no doubt, to achieve an intricate and secure effect on the respondent. The contrast that he draws between his own character and that of his wife and the variations he plays on the theme of these contrasts grants the discourse a complexity that leads not only to a fuller presence of the self in the encounter but also to a more precise apprehension of the self by the respondent.

Transformations of a paradigmatic nature are often used to make one's significations more specific as well as to avoid any unnecessary ambiguity and confusion. In order to be tactful and decorous one may begin with a euphemism but find that it must be abandoned if it is to be achieved. Consider the following:

Priest: Tell me my child, what did you do?
Confessor: What you usually do when you're engaged, not more than that.
Priest: Caresses?
Confessor: Yes, father
Priest: Did *he* just caress *you* my child?
Confessor: Yes . . . , well together . . .
Priest: Does he touch you in delicate places? Breasts? Bottom?
Confessor: What is the difference?
Priest: A big one my child, a very big one. Because caresses of that kind are lascivious and have nothing to do with the love you have for one another.
Confessor: Are they sins?
Priest: Of course. Grave ones, my dear child. But do you also touch him everywhere?

Confessor:  Yes.
Priest:     The fact that you caress and kiss your fiance in delicate places is
            not, how can I say, a manifestation of love but an animal excita-
            tion of your senses. And you are not ashamed, I mean, when
            your fiance's hands or mouth explored your nude body, you
            were not ashamed? And then you aggravated that by exciting his
            member.
            (from Valentini and DiMegro, 1973, cited in Goode, 1985:22)

The "caresses" become paradigmatically transformed into touches "in
delicate places," which become "lascivious and that have nothing to do
with love," and so on into "hand or mouth exploring [the] nude body"
and "exciting his member." These transformations are calculated to
elicit by stages the information that the priest needs in order to understand what happened between the confessor and her lover as well as to
reveal his own attitude toward the activities.

The priest also uses a number of syntagmatic transformations. The
question "What is the difference?" is answered by an adjective that is
repeated with another qualifying word: "A big one . . . a very big one."
Further on, one can see the internal contrasts drawn between "manifestation of love" and "animal excitation." This compound sentence
establishes a grammatical parallel between the two phrases, and by
using the adversative conjunction "but" it rejects a moral equivalence.
Together then, the paradigmatic and syntagmatic transformations become effective instruments in the hands of the priest and no doubt in the
mind of the confessor as well.

In another example, we find a patient (B) carefully identifying herself
to the doctor (A) by means of a binary categorical system. She has
forgotten to bring her bill, though she did remember it earlier, and in
fact hand written a check:

A:  Hello.
B:  Hi. I brought your check, but I, I haven't forgotten it. But I forgot to bring
    it. Mmm—I have forgotten it. I just remembered.
A:  Do you feel it has to be brought in the very next time after you get the
    bill?
B:  Well, yeah, I usually do. Yeah. I usually like to pay bills as soon as I get
    them. Right now, we have uh—probably for the first time—so many bills
    (laugh) that, that, uh I am not paying them. I am just letting them sit
    there. The big one being $600 for my teeth. I'll just have to pay part, but,
    uh . . . but yeah, I, I like to get them paid. That is the bills basically—the
    rent and our other bills. That is not—I mean that is not the charge—we
    don't have charge accounts. But, but yes, I guess, I, I (pause) . . . My dad
    is with me, but I haven't sat down and talked to him yet.

                                              (Gill and Hoffman, 1982:118)

The following categories represent the organizing principle to be found in this extract:

1. I do remember that I have to pay your bill today. (I am not one of those careless, inconsiderate or impecunious people.)
2. I did write the check. (I do have money in the bank.)
3. I forgot to bring it with me.

These sentences allow the structures of identity to be seen on the horizontal as well as on the vertical axis; that is to say, on the syntagmatic as opposed to the paradigmatic one. In the passage one can discern an association among remembering to pay, remembering to write the check, and forgetting to bring it, and then remembering that forgetting to bring it is an indication of really forgetting it after all. In these exercises the articulator is seeking to establish an *identity* for herself. Identity's logical and social-psychological referents are coterminous. In establishing an identity for itself, a self seeks to claim features for its character that will be identified as uniquely its own vis-à-vis others in a field of relations.

There is a minimum of self-disclosure in the following piece of discourse, and although there is an absence of complex discursive action, it is nevertheless possible to trace the steps by which identities are being established:

A: I don't know where the—wh—this address is.
B: Well where do—which part of town do you live?
A: I live in four ten East Lowden.
B: Well you don't live very far from me.

(Coulthard, 1985:73)

Malcolm Coulthard (1985) analyzed this exchange [which is really a summary of a more comprehensive analysis by Emmanuel Schegloff (1972) from whose work this example is taken] in terms of embedded elements or what Schegloff calls "insertion sequences." Instead of answering a question, a respondent inserts a question in return, saying in effect, "If you answer mine, I will [then] answer yours." This strategy, Coulthard notes, ensures that "during the inserted sequence the original question retains its transitional relevance and if the second speaker does not then produce an answer it is noticeably absent in exactly the same way as it would be if there were no intervening sequence, and the questioner can complain about the lack of an answer in exactly the same way" (1985:73).

Yet even in this simple exchange various transformational steps are being taken:

| self | other |
|------|-------|
| ignorance | knowledge |
| my part of town | your part of town |
| close to Lowden | 410 East Lowden |

Various details are assembled for the construction of several contrasts and for the definition of a concrete place as well as the relationship of two people to the place. No doubt, as the conversation proceeds, the exact address that the first speaker was seeking to locate would be also defined in terms of the places already defined. Indeed, there is perhaps no more secure and clear way of giving a sense of a place than by comparing it to other known places. This brief exchange reveals the transformational and discursive mapping of an interpersonally relevant territory and various points in it. But the exchange is about more than place. Each of its steps presents a self, albeit a very minimal one, and asserts a presence. In fact, the opening gambit presents a mild sense of diffidence by making a statement that is also a question. The discursive matter indicates the questioner as slightly diffident and the respondent rather dominant. Instead of responding to the question directly, the respondent inserts a sequence, a return question, seeking a minimum identification of the questioner: "Which part of town do you live?" The ability to do this, to parry the initial question and thrust in one of the respondent's own, is a demonstration of control, if not of power, in the situation. The next change elicits a very precise location from the questioner and a rather vague, although relevant response from the respondent.

Consider another example, taken from Carl Jung. He had asked one of his patients to say all that came to her mind when presented with the word *Socrates*, a name the patient herself had introduced. She said:

Socrates — scholar — books — wisdom — modesty — no words in order to express this wisdom — it is the highest groundpostament — his teachings — had to die on account of bad people — falsely accused — sublimest sublimity — self satisfied — that is Socrates — fine learned world [long pause] — No thread cut — I was the best tailoress, never had a piece of cloth on the floor — fine artist world — fine professorship — is doubloon — twenty five francs — that is the highest — prison — slandered by bad people — unreason, cruelty — excess — rudeness. (Jung, 1906, cited in Abse, 1971:57–58)

Jung noted that the thoughts in this text did not flow smoothly and that the articulator suffered from a "peculiar disturbance which can be best designated as a deficiency in the faculty of discrimination between important and unimportant material" (1906, cited in Abse, 1971:57–58). On the contrary, the entire passage is replete with fine discriminations, contrasts, and comparisons. Rather, the most noticeable feature of the text is a lack of clear syntactic ordering. There are few verbs in the discourse. The opening phrase is an assemblage of nouns, followed by a syntactical phrase and a thought that is not sequentially connected to the preceding one, containing also a Joycean neologism: "it is the highest grounpostament." Jung argues that the author is making an identification between herself and Socrates and that her pathology is revealed by the fact that she cannot free herself from it. This identification is undertaken by a categorical transformation:

1. Socrates was a man of wisdom, a scholar, a modest man who was falsely accused.
2. I am a seamstress, a fine artist, and modest, who also has been falsely accused.

A metaphorical association is made between a fine seamstress and a man of wisdom, both artists and both persecuted. Nevertheless, it takes a skilled interpreter like Jung to discern this meaning. Such interpretations are not likely to be made in normal discursive relationships, and so an audience would be hard put to find the narrative line and logical sequence of events leading to the final claim of a Socratic identity. The absence of syntactic articulations and sequential development is what makes a responsive interpretation difficult to accomplish. In the absence of work done by the articulator on his or her own text, the span of attention the interpreter can bring to his or her tasks is limited, and this limits his or her interpretations and response.

## Symbolic Semiosis

Ernest Cassirer developed systematic arguments for the development of what he called "human responses" from "animal reactions." "Animal reactions are signals," he noted, "whereas human responses are symbols. Signals and symbols belong to two different universes of discourse: a signal is part of a physical world of being: a symbol is part of the human world of meaning, signals are 'operators' and symbols are 'designations' " (1967:32). This distinction, in Cassirer's view, leads to a whole new way of living for humans: "Man has, as it were, discovered a new method of adopting himself to his environment. Between the receptor system and the effector system which are to be found in all animal species, we find in man a third link which we may describe as the symbolic system" (1967:24). That is to say, "Instead of defining man as *animal rationale* we should define him as *animal symbolicum*" (1967:26). It was left to Suzanne Langer to describe succinctly how the symbolic facility operates in human acts: "The brain is not merely a great transmitter, a super switchboard, it is better likened to a great transformer. The current of experience that passes through it undergoes a change of character, not through the agency of the sense by which the perception entered, but by virtue of a primary use which is made of it immediately it is sucked into a stream of symbols which constitutes a human mind" ([1942] 1970:42). In the same work she wrote, "Speech is, in fact, the readiest active termination of that basic process in the human brain which may be called *symbolic transformation of experiences* ([1942] 1970:44, italics in original). In a number of works since this was published she has expanded these ideas, seeking to use them in answering a variety of questions about human beings (1967, 1972). Nevertheless, this early statement, representing a fruitful synthesis of Cassirer's view with her own and many others, stands as a nice summary of her views.

The implications of being an "animal symbolicum—of indeed finding itself in the predicament of having to practice symbolic transformation," is that "[m]an is separated from his natural condition by instruments of his own making" (Burke, 1966:13). The operation of this symbolic imperative is manifest simultaneously in conduct and speech. This process of transformation involves the basic material's replacement by a more fully developed and refined or, as the case may be, by a less developed and crude substitute. One feels hunger and eats not just food but various natural substances that have been turned into hamburger or steak, pasta or pudding. In semiotic terms, *a sign selected for an object is replaced by another one before it is presented for the elicitation of an interpretant, thereby controlling the nature and quality of the interpretant and various consequences thereof.* In this method of transformation, human experiences are perceived, defined, and re-presented in such a way that their significance is essentially altered. These experiences are typically carried in linguistic forms. The symbols with which humans experience reality and through which they articulate their experience are complexly and systematically conceived and constructed. These symbolic transformations occur in the most ordinary of discursive acts, though needless to say in the hands of some they achieve a strength and a quality that sets them apart. And every such interaction is undertaken with the systematic use of words and gestures, each deliberatively or habitually selected from a repertoire so as to indicate a more or less finely crennelated pattern of intentions.

In using the repertoire of discursive elements, an articulator is able to create a stylized discourse, which is achieved by the selective deployment of transformed symbols. One of the ways an agent engages in symbolic transformation is to employ one or more of the tropes of the language to embody intentions, present self, characterize his or her texts, and thereby control the responses they mobilize. The major tropes are metaphor, metonymy, synecdoche, irony, paradox, and oxymoron.

Although Kenneth Burke considers only the first four as the "master tropes," his description of the transformations accomplished through their use is nevertheless instructive: "Metaphor is a device for seeing something in terms of something else. It brings out the thisness of that or thatness of this" (1962:503). Describing the uses of metonymy, he wrote, "The basic 'strategy' in a metonym is this: to convey some incorporeal or intangible state in terms of the corporeal or tangible," e.g., to speak of "the heart rather than of the emotions" (1962:506). Synecdoche refers to transformations of "the part for the whole, whole for the part, container for the thing contained, sign for the thing signified" (1962:507–8). Irony occurs, Burke notes, when one tries, by the interaction of terms upon one another, to produce *development* that uses all the terms (1962:512). One may add that irony tries to create a development not only through the interaction of terms, but also of terms and situations. Paradox refers to a symbolic transformation that appears to be contradictory but on examination turns out to contain a subtle signification, as does oxymoron. In using these transformations, an articulator seeks (1) to convey subtle and complex selves, attitudes, and relationships; (2) to enrich and render complex, challenging, and agonistic conversational exchanges; (3) to control modulation and timbre as precisely as the self, situation, and context demand. We will examine the first three tropes here, leaving irony to be discussed later.

Consider the social rule that euphemisms should be used to describe certain bodily functions. Such euphemisms are metaphorical reconstructions meant to achieve specific discursive and semiotic effects. Transformation converts one function into a new metaphor, then transforms that into another, and so on. For instance, in public references to fornication, articulators may say "make love," thus transforming the act into a polite and morally acceptable form. People who use this form for this act often stick to polite forms for other functions as well, thereby defining their style and selves. For others this can be too polite; they will convert the act of fornication into what are in fact referred to as "earthy" forms, thereby defining their selves and their style. Further, the latter earthy forms have many other uses, as verbs, adjectives, and adverbs. They add force and emphasis to one's utterances, decisively removing all ambiguity and prevarications regarding the articulator's intent and emotion. The celebrated four-letter words and expletives are symbolic transformations used in seeking to achieve these effects.

Often the transformational semiosis offered to the other in discursive acts is truly inspired and original. Consider the case of a mechanic giving evidence in a divorce case. Describing an act of fornication by another mechanic to which she claimed to be a witness, she says: "I looked through the window and there he was, tightening her bolts." As a symbolic transformation, this description transcends many levels: lovemaking has often been transformed into screwing, a mechanical metaphor, and the witness in this case creatively transforms the mechanical part of this metaphor into the tightening of bolts.

In the following example, a patient, an actress, is seeking to describe her director's reactions to her therapeutic involvement:

> Patient: We're rehearsing today. And I love to rehearse. And uh. it doesn't seem unreasonable to me to leave for two and a half hours. But I am getting a lot of static from J. He seems to use two things when he wants, when he want to get at me. We had a huge fight. Such a, such a big fight, that I ended up crying in front of, at him, crying and screaming at him . . . Yesterday, he calls up in the middle of the afternoon yesterday, and he decided that G's volunteering to help was an arch-insult and that is full of shit . . . I said "Well, you know, I will be leaving for couple of hours in the afternoon." He said, "Why? Where do you have to go?" And I said, "I'll have to go to the shrink." And then he said "Oh my God." He is always going on like that . . . I call him up and he says "Hello" and I say "Hello" and he said "Well, how is the shrink? I just can't understand what it is that compels you to go up there four times a week. Tell me what is so interesting about it. I only wish I had made a pact with the devil, so that I would do something like that four times a week, like going to the movies."
> (Gill and Hoffman, 1982:49–50)

In this passage both the patient/actress and her director carry a presence and a force because of the way various metaphors are deployed, even though they may be conventional ones. She gets a lot of "static" from her director as opposed to getting scolded by him, teased by him, berated by him, and so on. This metaphor, drawn from radio terminology, is concrete, clear, and brief and, it effectively achieves her intention. "Full of shit" makes its appearance, too. This metaphor is part of the standard repertoire of contemporary speech and is an effective instrument with which forcefully to dismiss, reject, and ridicule someone else's claims. It too is brief, concrete, and unmistakable in its intentionality.

The producer's words also are of interest. He thinks that the patient is being "compelled" to go to the shrink. His choice and use of this word denies the actress initiative, volition, and perhaps even a self. He sets up a complex tripartite metaphorical structure in the next structure, in which the visit to the therapist is a pact with the devil and is like going to the movies. The therapist is equated with the devil, and going to the movies is equated with going to the therapist; both then are equated with a pact with the devil. The foundation of this transformation is the Protestant attitude about work and idleness in which the devil finds work for idle hands and going to the shrink is going away from working at rehearsals, as is going to the movies.

Synecdoche achieves its signifying force in discourse by allowing an articulator to indicate his or her attitude toward the subject at hand in artful and parsimonious ways. For example, emotions are managed, interactions kept "safe," and "face" is maintained by a draftee during the Vietnam war by his saying "I have always wanted to check out the girls of Vietnam." The over all context of the war in Vietnam included a variety of discomforting elements in addition to the danger of death and injury. In synechdochically reducing all this to the pleasant aspect of sexual adventure expressed as a talkworthy element in the discourse, the articulator seemingly seeks to minimize the danger and discomforts as well as to save himself and others from sentimentality.

Paradox achieves the force of emphasis in discourse by calling attention to the complex and extraordinary nature of the articulator's intentions and encompassing an awareness of inherent ambivalence. Consider the following: "I have to punish you for your own good because I love you" (said by a father to his son). "I now have to go home and fight" (said by a man unhappy in his domestic life).

These statements, by presenting a seeming contradiction within the body of the utterances, signify forcefully and effectively the complex and ambivalent nature of an articulator's intentions. They also forestall challenges and questions from listeners who now have reason to understand why the son is being punished and why the husband is reluctant to return to the haven from a heartless world.

An oxymoron, like a paradox, seeks to contain superficial contradictions to be used to make other claims. Here the constructions are more sharply epigrammatic and phraselike, seeking to reveal the contradictory nature of a phenomenon in the world. It seems to possess not only a descriptive function but a discursive and signifying one as well. When someone is called a "thoughtful Tory" or "friendly fascist," the oxymoronic constructions describe the contradictory behavioral and attitudinal features of certain kinds of people and one's feelings about them.

These tropes of discourse typically are not used whimsically or decoratively. Rather, they are present in discourse as definers of the multifaceted intentionality of the articulator. They embody the signifying force the articulator seeks to convey and for all practical purposes are the intentions of the self as they come to be read by an other. The sarcastic remark, ironic intonation or allusion of a sentence, metaphorical, paradoxical, and synechdochic verbalisms are to be read in their own terms and deciphered so as fully to receive the intention of the self. In the event that such a reading is not done, it can be safely said that the intention of the articulator has been lost, or misplaced, leaving his or her act totally or partially incomplete.

## Conclusion

If the intentionalities of the subject are manifested through discourse in interaction, it should be recognized that such intentionalities are complex, subtly varied, and intricately structured, and are always changing throughout the duration of the interaction. These complex and structured intentionalities, or what I call crennelated intentionalities, are embodied as finely textured forms, which *are* discourse. The tropic transformations of symbols give concrete and forceful images that, encapsulated in the often complex intentions of the articulator, not only add the presence of the self and texture, but also give a feeling of genuine commitment to the interaction.

Although there are differences among the transformational processes described by various scholars, they are basically similar. Each process involves a systematic and disciplined change of form, from a simple to a more complex one, or from a complex to a simpler one, or even from a simple one to another simple one, and/or from one complex form into a different complex one. In each case a basic form is changed into another. Indeed, one can use the general thesis about generative grammar as a paradigm for defining the similarities: if there is a deep structure that determines the surface structures of human languages, there can also be a further underlying structure whose function is to convert impulses to forms more accessible to the agent who in turn makes other changes in order to make them available and interpretable to other human beings. Structures are nested in other structures, which may or may not be more complex than the former ones but are nevertheless generated by them. Fecund structures can transform impulses into acts, acts into grammatical, phonological, categorical, and symbolic forms as well as into socially acceptable ones. The *isomorphic* operation of these acts of transformational semiosis is a constant human preoccupation and its products are discursive acts. Discursive acts thus are complex acts of transformational semiosis by which words are assembled in order to represent intentions to be announced to others so as to achieve given effects. It is at the level of the intentionality of the self that all the complex variables present in the discursive act become unified and instrumental in the creation of defined effects in the world. The variables that eventually manifest themselves in the discursive act are the result of systematic transformational operations performed by a minding organism.

It is not that every actor in the human drama is consciously, deliberately, and informedly constructing and undertaking his or her discourses with the foregoing principles in mind. Rather, these principles become features of the *habits of discourse* a human being acquires as a member of a speech community, and these principles are constantly polished and relearned in the discursive interactions of everyday life. It is not enough just to acquire the language; one must also learn to use it in socially, situationally, and literarily appropriate ways. Habit, used here in the Peircian sense, unifies the various elements of a discursive act into a seamless whole wherein universal concepts become particularized in a given situation, functioning as a vehicle of the self and its intentionalities, a vehicle with a tale of its own. This vehicle, this Peircian habit, is continuously reinforced and validated in every interaction a human undertakes. If discourses are ineffective, the person has to ask himself or herself how and where he or she went wrong. If not, then the others in the situations and interactions will enforce the rules of discursive acts, correcting any improper usages and enforcing the rules.[4]

The semiotic process thus is an activity by which signs are deployed and their effects conceived and then achieved through acts initiated by a minding organism. Insofar as there is no initiation or cognition that is not determined by previous cognitions, it follows that signing is a continuous process and that the formation and transformation of signs are the fundamental activities of minding.

## Notes

1.  For an informed discussion of this from a strictly pragmatic standpoint, see the essay by Rochberg-Halton. He wrote, "Neither the extremes of a structuralist 'infernal culture machine' nor a symbolic interactionist 'scientific ludism' can provide the comprehensive theory of meaning that seems to be the goal of the ongoing restructuring of social theory." He also seeks to "trace the parallel threads of situation and structure" by using the concept of sign (1982:457). While generally in agreement with his position, I think he is too harsh in his description of both the structuralist and interactionist position both in this essay and in his later work (1986). The same can be said of Anthony Giddens's critiques in his many publications (1982, 1984). The urge to be post-everything seems to be an indulgence that is difficult to resist. This kind of post-postim has not really been a source of enlightenment.

2.  The notational system used here is reproduced directly from Coulthard. He acknowledges his indebtedness in this part of his work to the studies of D.C. Brazil (1975, 1985) and notes that discourse analysts (and I may add students of all interactional phenomena) ignore intonation as an essential element of the discursive acts, at the risk of a great impoverishment in the understanding of their basic processes. Needless to say, I have merely touched on this aspect of communication here.

3.  Chomsky's revolution in linguistics is unique in that it is an ongoing one. From its beginnings with the publication of *Syntactic Structures* in 1957, Chomsky has continued to expand, refine, and at times abandon or modify its claims and conclusions. It is therefore impossible to pay attention to all the changes that have occurred and are occurring now. Following Neil Smith and Derdre Wilson,

however, I believe that "Chomsky's main contribution has been as a system builder who has constructed a complete picture of the nature of language and the language user. It is the consistency and power of his overall framework, rather than the individual arguments which make it up that we feel makes Chomsky's work revolutionary" (1979:10). It is this system to which I am appealing here. Incidentally, this work by Smith and Wilson is a lucid and comprehensive examination of Chomsky's thought from which I have benefited greatly.

# Acts of Interpretation

## — 4 —

Several generations of social psychologists have been nurtured on the idea that the reading of a sign can be described adequately as a "response." In behaviorist psychology and some forms of social psychology, the idea of response to a stimulus has acquired a central place. In the latter view, the response was an automatic, indeed mechanical reaction controlled by the stimulus. Mead takes the notions of stimulus and response and uses them metaphorically to describe the interactional process. In his work a response to a stimulus is transformed into a threefold one in which an individual's reading of his or her own productions is a crucial activity: one responds to his or her own gestures as he or she produces them and the other responds to them in more or less the same way, thus making possible the emergence of meaning between them (1934:99).

As important and insightful as these views have been in undermining the behaviorists' mechanistic approaches, the concept of response used in Mead's work remains a rather limited one with which to describe the complexity of interactional processes. In many ways the use of the word *response*, as well as many other aspects of Mead's theorizing show traces of the behaviorist milieu in which he lived, thought, and worked. Pursuing a path designed to liberate the study of human beings from mechanistic theories, and enabling several generations of students to keep themselves from being seduced by the easy virtues of behaviorism, Mead himself was nevertheless trapped in many of its features. The notion of response that he shares with the behaviorists is one such feature that needs to be expanded, albeit within Mead's own scheme. The recipient of a symbol of a "vocal gesture," as Mead calls it, does not just give a response. Rather he or she interprets the other's gestures and constructs a complex discursive act as his or her contribution to the meaning of the interaction. Insofar as the symbols, icons and indices that constitute the act were selected to achieve given effects, it follows that the articulator has some initial conceptions of these effects. In his formulation of these transactions, Mead argued "It is of course, the great value, or one of the great values, of language that it does give us control over this organization of the act" (1934:13). Such control over the act is used to guide or direct the symbols toward eliciting the desired responses, and in the event these responses do emerge from the other, a meaningful transaction has been concluded. Insofar as the output from an articulator is hardly ever an isolated sign, the very arrangements of many such signs must be taken into account when interpreting discourse. As Bakhtin puts it, "One might say that grammar and stylistic converge and diverge in any concrete language phenomenon, but if considered in the whole of the individual utterance or a speech genre, it is a stylistic phenomenon. And this is because the speaker's very selection of a particular grammatical form is a stylistic act" (1986:66). To the extent that all articulations are complex stylistic acts, the differential elements that enter their composition must be taken into account in their interpretation. The answering vocal gesture can be a very complex and at times such a recalcitrant, elusive, and studied phenomenon that once the initial act is articulated, the articulator finds himself or herself at the mercy of the auditor's intentions and attitudes. Thus the power of the respondent in the creation of a semantic organization reveals the fact that there are limits to the signified (Perinbanayagam, 1985:12–17). The moment one has signified something, he or she loses control over it (however politically and institutionally powerful he or she may be), and must wait for a respondent to recognize it and define it and so complete the organization of meaning. Insofar as Mead talks about bringing "control" over one's acts through language (1934:13) one is justified in arguing that he in fact was describing a process that can best be called an "interpretive response," or in Bakhtin's words an "active response." Bakhtin argued, "The fact is that when a listener perceives and understands the meaning (the language meaning) of speech, he simultaneously takes an active responsive attitude toward it" (1986:68). In being actively responsive he or she can also be selective and purposeful. Such *pragmatic selectivity* is important to both articulator and respondent and is made possible by shared principles that enable both participants in an interaction to interpret knowingly and conspiratorially.

The discursive act to which a respondent directs an interpretant is a complex entity—assembled and systematically transformed—in which one seeks to elicit commensurate responses. To respond to a symbol, thereby creating "[t]he logical structure of meaning . . . in the threefold relationship of gesture to adjustive response and to the resultant of the given social act" (Mead, 1934:80) is initially to *apprehend* the structures of the sign and then *read* them in an informed and intelligent way. If "delayed action," as Mead said, "is necessary to intelligent conduct" (1934:99), delays of varying durations are no doubt imperative in creating meaningful relationships. To apprehend the discourse of the other is to attend, interpret, and vivify the semiotic, situational, and self/other dimensions of the text that is made available: that is, implicitly to dismantle and reconstruct the material of the text. The signs reach the individual as discursive acts demanding *work* before an interpretant is produced, and the reconstructions and initiatives that elicited them constitute an interdependent whole. They are dialectically and interactionally related, and participate, however tentatively, in defining each other. The initiatives and the reconstructive responses thus are both active and constitutive processes.[1]

An act of discourse is then only one part of the process by which meaningful interactions and relationships emerge. The other part is the responsive act of interpretation that completes the interaction. Such an act is not mechanical or automatic but is creative and constructive. Typically, it takes the material presented and seeks to find the variable and conjoint significance carried therein. To the extent that these processes are ongoing activities, however, there is continuity both for the organization of meaning itself and for the selves of those participating in it. In achieving such an organization of meaning, initiative and interpretation are important, but the latter's quality, perspicacity, and occurrence after the initial move seem to confer a great deal of power on it. The respondent is able to consider the articulated material given to him or her, examining not only its significance at the overt level but at the covert level as well. He or she is able to attend to the full implications of the discursive act and to calculate, to some extent at least, the likely consequence of his or her own response to the articulations of the other. To use Peirce's terminology, he or she is able to consider semiotically the intentional interpretant of the articulator, the effects of the interpretant on the respondent's own self, and anticipate also his or her own intentional effects on the articulator before producing a response. That is to say, responses made in discursive interactions are quite complex, are given to analytic exercises of at least minimal proportions, and are embedded in convolutions of assumptions, interpretations, and anticipations. It is in the fulcrum of the initiator's discursive act and the respondent's acts of interpretation that meaning emerges, and the respondent's interpretation is therefore a *reconstruction* of meaning in discursive moments and relationships. It is a response, but a response that needs an adjective to indicate its complex and active quality.

It is in reconstructing the intention of the other through the discursive text that the other presents that the intentions of the respondent come

into play: His or her interpretations are as full of a self as the articulations of the initiator. The respondent presents as well as constitutes a
self in the course of presenting a discursive act as much as the articulator
does in his or her acts of presentation. The significances presented and
read by each participant thus signify selves and their intentions simultaneously.

The emergence of meaning is founded on the activity of a self that
receives and reconstructs the significance of the structures that the other
has presented to it. The structures that represent the intention are
primarily linguistic ones embedded in systems of human actions. In the
words of Sandra Rosenthal, "Language is the expression of pragmatic
meaning; pragmatic meaning becomes explicit and communicable within the structures of language. . . . [A]t its basic level meaning is embodied in the activity of a *purposive agent* engrossed in the world and
language emerges as the expression of such active engagement"
(1986:27 italics added). Mead, too, noted that the "responses" to the
environment, which include the articulations of the other, are selectively
made by purposeful agents.

In describing the stages of the act, Mead (1938:3–26) went on to argue
that although all perception involves "immediate sensuous stimulation
and an attitude toward this stimulation" such perception is not a passive
response since "the process of sensing is itself an activity" (1938:3).
Mead followed this description of the nature of the act by expanding
these conceptions in ways that seem useful for an examination of interpretations. Discussing the processes of mind in nature Mead noted:

1.  An individual in acting with reference to the environment will be
    acting with reference to himself or herself so that his or her action
    will include himself or herself as an object.
2.  The process of bringing the self as an object into conduct and
    experience implies that the individual indicates things and their
    character to others.
3.  The stimulus of which he or she makes use is one to which he or
    she tends to respond in the same fashion as that in which the
    others respond.

Further, Mead presents another set of ideas that seem particularly relevant to a social psychologist's understanding of the relationship between meaning and the social act. Reviewing the importance of novelty
and the problematic, he makes the following points:

1.  The environment causally determines the organism, whereas the
    determination of the environment by the organism is selective.
2.  Such selections are made by organisms that have a content, i.e., a
    self.

3. Such content always involves the carrying out of the life processes; as such they always involve a future, and a future involves an experience of uncertainty as to what will in fact happen.
4. The existence of futures and the uncertainty thereof creates the possibility of novelty. Such novelty is created by the difference between the anticipatory imagery of the result of the act and the actual experience. Second, the hypothetical structures of future situations where a conflict of tendencies to action exist denote the possibility of novelty emerging in the response itself (1938:3–4).

These constructions of meaning are organizational activities between two or more participants in everyday life, simultaneously involving the linguistic and pragmatic processes. As Rosenthal observes, "Pragmatism, the inseparable mingling of the sensuous and the relational, is the vehicle by which we think about and recognize objects in the world. . . . Perceptual meaning and conceptual meaning involve the same structure" (1986:28–29). Conception and perception as well as articulation and responsive interpretation involve all participants in undertaking the processes of transformational semiosis. In these exercises of semiosis an agent is presented with a more or less consummated discursive act—an act consisting of systematically arranged words embedded in signifying physical and spatial gestures. This signifying act is intended to elicit certain interpretations and responses, and—to the extent that it does—is an instance of a signifying act that has achieved its completion.

The respondent is also an agent, indeed a self-conscious one, and his or her strategies of response are subject to the processes of transformational semiosis as well since he or she has to read and interpret the acts of the other, and he or she can do this best by attending to the structures in which they are manifested. In other words, the respondent has to *reconstruct the intention of the other* from his or her signifying presentation to the best of his or her own ability and with the best information to which he or she has access. Such acts are essentially acts of reconstruction of the intentions of the other. Although interpretive acts begin as reconstructions of the available text, they may be so complex and convoluted as to demand a prior "dismantling" (Derrida, 1976). Such dismantling is, however, a mere strategy soon to be followed by the coup de grace of reconstruction and assembly, or as Jacques Derrida would put it, the acts must be "reinscribed" in some way (1976). Such reconstructions are however, both pragmatic and interactional activities, orthodox deconstructionists notwithstanding.

## Interpretation and Uncertainty

Discursive statements, insofar as they are constituted by words and intonations, can never achieve precise meaning. The articulator's signification will have its own uncertainty. He or she must select and interpret his or her own selections and in such an enterprise will face the uncertainty of meaning. The words and their arrangements by the very fact of receiving attention from an already constituted minding process will be altered. Once the statement is articulated it faces another mind's attention, and this too produces its own degree of uncertainty. The mind of the respondent will be forced to select from among a variety of significations in the articulated text, judging the one selected to be the intention of the other. This given articulation by the respondent demands that the initiator decide whether his or her articulation has been effective, or at least effective enough to allow him or her to proceed to the next response. This can be a continuation or clarification of the original intent in the face of the response it has elicited. Thus the interpretive chain is replete with uncertainty insofar as the very instruments with which significance is articulated and meaning constituted are the same ones with which its degrees of precision can be measured. Typically, these interactional chains of signification and meaning are self-corrective processes: one can clarify one's own statements if they have been mismeasured or ask for clarification from the other when necessary. These steps will then ensure for all *practical purposes* a parsimony of interpretation.[2]

In the discursive interaction of everyday life, significations and the meanings that emerge from them cannot be endlessly deferred insofar as these significations demand immediate action. The resultant signifying act then closes the deferment process, however temporarily, initiating a new series of significations. For example, if one person issues an insult to another, it is not politic for the respondent to defer its interpretation. Similarly, it would be difficult to defer the response if the initial articulation were a question, challenge, or command. *Further, the deferment of an interpretative response will itself be taken to be an act in its own terms and certain responsive steps taken by the initiator.* The same can be said for texts that demand urgent practical action. Consider the following passage from a UN field officer in Sudan to his principal in New York:

> Donor response to the Secretary-General's appeal has been very encouraging. . . . UNICEF has received pledges for some US $4 million, and is awaiting confirmation of contributions amounting to some US $5 million to cover its appeal of US $9 million (please see attached table).
>
> It is therefore important that current negotiations would be urgently consummated. It should also be noted that additional funding will be required to cover increasing estimates for logistic requirements, mainly by WFP.
>
> Moreover, no donor has yet responded to FAO's appeal of some US $2 million for seeds, tools and cattle vaccines. UNICEF has made an advance of US $250,000 towards this amount so that some of these supplies can be ordered and delivered (United Nations, 1989:02)

It is no doubt possible to find opportunities in the textual strategies used in this passage for deferment and assessment of differences and indeed for the construction of alternative meanings. There is, however, in the realm of practice, no time. The reader has to interpret the text parsimoniously so that he or she can take some urgently needed action. He or she cannot go and do further research himself or herself to examine the interpretational acumen of the original author, and even if he or she did, it too would be endlessly deferable. Faced then with the contingencies of deferment and immediate action, he or she will have to consider whatever differences that he or she can perceive in the text, arrive at a plausible and parsimonious interpretation, and act on its basis.

Such parsimony is hard to find in everyday life. Some would overinterpret one's articulations, an extreme instance being "paranoid delusions"; others would habitually underinterpret, as in obtuse, dull, or insensitive responses. One consequence of the uncertain relations between signifying and interpreting is the emergence of an overinterpretation or an underinterpretation, which sets up further links in a chain of interpretations. Both of these can be trying experiences in social life and can become very serious in their implications if the articulator is not given an opportunity to engage in corrective exercises. In overinterpretive responses, the recipient of the communication does not pay either sufficient or informed and intelligent attention to the structures in which the statement is presented. In such interpretations an ironic thrust can be taken for a compliment, a compliment can be taken for an ironic insult, a friendly tease can be taken for a hostile act, and even a mild reproof can be taken for a major insult and offense. Further, a neutral professional interest can be taken to be an erotic overture, and an erotic overture can be taken to be a mere professional courtesy. Or else a joke or pun can be overinterpreted to signify insult and offense to the self of the other, or may not even be recognized as a joke, making the articulator say "I was only joking" or "It was only a joke." Whatever the unconscious significance of these sallies, the claim that it was only a joke retracts the force of the discursive act, seeking to neutralize its overinterpreted effects.

Further, if an interpreter of a text is to have some authority, it will be possible for him or her to use ambiguities in advancing his or her own interests by overinterpretations. For example, a remark meant neither to contain nor convey a racist or sexist slur can be interpreted by an interested self as doing so in order to denounce the author of the text. The respondent may have other reasons to want to bring the author into disrepute and, by taking advantage of an ambiguous text, may claim that the author is a racist or a sexist. An example comes from my own experience. I was giving a class lecture on the racist and sexist subtexts of jokes, and to do this satisfactorily I offered some examples of jokes in their original form. A student given to political zealotry arrived late for class and, quite ignorant of the context of my joke telling, began to get visibly angry. Within minutes of her arrival, she stalked out of the room, threatening to report me to the dean. In deconstructive terms, her construal of my text was legitimate and warranted. But on *interactional grounds*, such an interpretation, and any action based upon it, was surely illegitimate and unwarranted. The respondent invested a text that was being created interactionally and contextually with a particular significance that no one else in the audience would accept. Indeed, had she bothered to wait till the end of the class to discuss the matter with the other students, she would not have made a mistake and encountered embarrassment. (As it turned out, she later came to my office to apologize for her error.)

It is often the case that on discovering that his or her discourse has been over- or under interpreted, the articulator will leave matters as they are because he or she sees some advantage in it. Thus, if an innocent remark taken to convey erotic interest brings a favorable response, the initiator can leave the interpretation intact, proceeding to the next step on the basis of the overinterpretation. An articulator can also deliberately cloud his or her text, inviting the other to select an interpretation, thus leaving his or her own self behind a protective rampart. The meaning in such a development will surely be the *selected* response to the discursive text.

Overinterpretation can result from the fact that words have places in other forms of discourse, and that in the new usage the respondent assumes that the original place is being invoked by the articulator. A wife tells her husband:

A:   You can't do anything right, George, You can be so clumsy and disorganized.

George is made quite angry by this remark, because he assumes that his wife is referring not only to the fact that he has just upset the cup of coffee in front of him but also to his general professional failures. "Getting things right," "being organized," and "being controlled" are locutions that can be applied to any kind of performance. George can interpret them to be offensive and loaded significations. But the fact of the matter is that he does not know whether these interpretations are her interpretations also. A parsimony of interpretation would have waited for further information, while an overinterpretation would single-mindedly view her as in full command of her interpretations and then head into a quarrel.

However, this might not be an overinterpretation if situational and contextual data were taken into account in arriving at an interpretation. If, for example, the wife is in the habit of using mocking sarcasm and double entendres in her discursive strategies, it would be an underinterpretation for the husband to assign a benign intentionality to the articulator. If the statement occurred in the course of a quarrel already in progress, the interpretation would have to take into account all the discursive acts already articulated. Situational overinterpretation leads only to embarrassment, while systematic overinterpretation over a period of time will lead to the disruption of relationships and disorganization of self. However, responsibility for overinterpretation does not always lie with the respondent. The articulator too can be clumsy, thoughtless, imprecise, and deliberately confusing and evasive, inviting overinterpretive responses. Even mere carelessness can do this.

Underinterpretation can occur when the articulator, assuming that the other is a normally knowledgeable and informed person, uses locutions and strategies with which the other is unfamiliar. First, this unfamiliarity may be cultural, in which a member of one culture speaking what he or she assumes is a shared language can make use of complex discursive acts that are not quite comprehensible to the other. Second, the respondent may be either physically or mentally handicapped, deaf, or autistic. Third, he or she may be habituated to a pattern of defensive underinterpretation: servants and other people who lack the power to take action against what is a more or less veiled insult can choose to treat it as a neutral remark. Finally, insofar as responding to the discourses of the other is a matter of training and talent, of cultivated skill in the local dialect and intonation, situations, and contexts, underinterpretation can result from a lack of interpretational competence. Such incompetence can be the result of faulty socialization, cultural and subcultural habits, or individual failings.

In any case, underinterpretation, if it is occasional and situational, can have no serious consequences besides embarrassment. Systematic underinterpretation, however, can have important consequences for the self. The signs it will be able to gather for its own presence and development will reach it in an impoverished and weakened form. The richness and variety of significations, the shades and nuances with which others articulate their significations, as well as the reflected self will be lost.

In responding actively to another, there is always the danger of being trapped in the quicksand of the relations of uncertainty that obtain between signification and the emergence of meaning. In order to control such eventualities, an interactant must be alert and attentive to the structures in which the discourses of the other are articulated and then produce responses that take them into account. The contexts and situations in which the discourse is being articulated become available in relation to the articulated text. Contexts and situations are not signified independently of articulations; thus it is in the relationship between the two that one must find the meaning of the interaction.

This does not mean that a mechanical response is never provided to a discursive act. In specific moments, particular individuals do give simple, unthought, and ill-interpreted responses to the discourses of others. For example, some individuals are dull and witless and incapable of interpreting the discourse they confront. This can include those physiologically impaired as well as those socially deprived. Comprehending a text in all its richness, after all, is dependent on cognitive processes that need neural functioning at optimum levels as well as socially acquired skills of linguistic facility, situational awareness, and cultural knowledge. If these two features are impaired, only a mechanical response is possible, whatever the texture of the discourse the recipient faces. The mechanical response is a feature of impaired facilities. However, a mechanical response can be occasioned by the indifference or antagonism of the recipient of the discourse; he or she cannot be bothered to provide a full, rich, and interpretive response, since the other is not important enough to warrant it. Or the self of the recipient is not intimately enough involved with the articulator to justify the work and attention that a nonmechanical response demands. He or she therefore feigns a dullness of mind, leaving the subtleties of the given text unattended. This mechanical response is purposive and deliberate, a defensive presentation of self. Standard stimulus/response theories of human action and response presuppose a dullness of intellect in both articulator and recipient of discourses.

Finally, a response may be mechanical because the recipient of a discourse, while not impaired in any general way, may be insensitive to certain specific qualities of a text. The prime example of this are those who are insensitive to the *tone of a text*. This does not refer to intonation or the musicality of the articulator but to the signification of the text in all its integrated wholeness. A text obtains its signification in terms of the interplay of its various internal features as well as the roles and selves of the articulator relevant to the situation, the placement of the text in a temporal sequence (i.e., the context), and the situation. All these features must, at a certain optimal level, be incorporated into the responses produced to the discourses of the other. Such an incorporation would produce a response that is sensitive to the tone of the text. Any response substantially below the optimum can be said to be a mechanical response that is deaf to tone. In such tone deafness, a recipient misses one or more of the layers of reflexivity contained in a discourse. Complex ironic passages of discourse, varied metaphors, metonymies, synecdochies, and paradoxes can be lost on those deaf to tone and dull to linguistic nuance.

*Semantic Interlocking*

In producing a discursive act, an articulator can be said to be intentionally *synthesizing* various linguistic elements and presenting a text; the respondent meanwhile should be *analyzing* them, albeit habitually, in order to apprehend fully the intentions of the articulator. Nevertheless, "these two tasks," to quote Chomsky on grammar, "which the speaker and the hearer must perform are essentially the same . . ." (1969:48), not only for grammar, but for other structures as well. That is to say, the articulator composes a complex structure consisting of phonological, semantic, syntactic, categorical, and symbolic variables to represent his or her intentions as well as he or she may, and the respondent has to attend to them in one way or another in order to arrive at his or her own interpretation. Of course he or she may not do this well enough and in such instances will either pay a price for errors or, as is more often the case, the articulator will correct the respondent by persistent insistence on the articulator's own significations. The articulation of a signifying discourse is a complex activity but so is reading and responding to one.

The uncertainty that emerges in the course of a discursive communication does not necessarily forestall the constitution of stable meanings in interpersonal transactions. A sufficient or optimum degree of certainty is assumed by all participants and assessed in terms of the effects they mobilize in the succeeding phases of the transaction. In fact, an organization of meaning is negotiated. Fitzgerald, commenting on the relationship between the pragmatic maxim and Peirce's theory of signs, opined, "One of the motives Peirce had in proposing his pragmatic principle was to eliminate the disputes of traditional metaphysics. Much of the difficulty there seemed to stem from the fact that philosophers proceeded by defining one word by means of another word. It was necessary then to find some non-verbal result which would bring their discussions back to reality" (1966:164). The same principle operates in the organization of a meaning in an interaction. Instead of endlessly defining one word by another word and experiencing the uncertainties thereof, the effects of the words are considered in practical ways that allow meanings to be ascertained. Such an ascertainment establishes what Goffman called a "working consensus" on the situated meanings of the articulated discourse and is predicated on that basis. Some action is in fact predicated on an interpretation that defines the meaning of the discourse until that meaning is challenged by further discourses and actions.

A gesture, verbal or otherwise, together with an answering one that bears at least a minimum of congruence to the earlier one, is the primary unit of the organization of meaning. The initial acts and the returning ones become ongoing organizational activities. That is, the acts connected to each become a *course*; they take on a moving, running character. The acts of one—utterances, moves, gestures—achieve a telic completion in the acts of another and become *semantically interlocked* with that other. It could perhaps be said that there is no more important organization in the life of a human being than this one. If one is able to achieve a congruent semantic interlocking with whomever one encounters in the interactions that constitute a life and is able to hold the other's attention as the other holds one's own, then alienation and estrangement would be obviated—at least for a while.

Each statement in an interaction can be considered as a serve or drive in a game of tennis that both elicits a return to a great extent as well as contours its shape, direction, and position. The return can in turn be killed—that is, no response made so that it falls dead—or the returnee can alter it to some extent, and thus control at least minimally the next response. This tennis formula contains the twin structure of the life of discourse: influenced and controlled by an agent at a certain moment, it then gathers a life and a destiny of its own, only to be brought under some control by the other so that the process begins all over again. Ongoing and uncertain though these processes appear to be, there is yet a method in it, indeed an organization similar to what Sacks, Schegloff, and Jefferson have called the "systematics" of turn taking (1974).

Discursive acts must bear a very strict congruent relationship to the developing sequences that issue from the various participants if a semantic organization is to emerge. Not only does a question demand a reply, it demands a response that fits the question, even if in a rough and ready fashion. Similarly, a statement demands a response that continues it even if the continuity is somewhat remote. The absence of a commensurate response can signal a lack of interest in or competence to continue, or even hostile or unfriendly attitudes. A total refusal of response will nevertheless establish its own meaning insofar as "strong inferences can be drawn from the official absence of an answer, and any member who does not answer does so at the peril of those inferences being made" (Schegloff, 1968). A ready and fulfilling response to a statement immediately establishes an interpersonal organization, and perhaps even a measure of intimacy, solidarity, and commitment. This is well recognized by most people, since refusing to respond in any way and giving irrelevant or sarcastic responses are standard means by which to forestall the emergence of an organization or intimacy between the two actors. Take, for example,

A: Will the No. 7 train take me to Manhattan?
B: Yes it will; but change at Queens Plaza.

This simple exchange clearly has an interlocking relationship that can be called a semantic organization. Such an organization indicates a mutual engagement between the statements, an interactionally achieved structure of entailment between one statement and another. In contrast, consider the following:

A: Does the No. 4 train go to Brooklyn Heights?
B: I am a pencil and you are paper.

The response that has been made to the question is not a commensurate one—no semantic organization has emerged between the statements. And no interlocking relationship could be created between the selves involved in the transaction. Similarly,

> Gosh I don't know what it is. You see—she says—I don't know, I am sure there is Cinderella. There is much better play than that—He is an awful idiot. (Abse, 1971:55)

lacks addressivity insofar it is not possible for an ordinary person to respond to it. In the first case the question has addressivity: it is possible to attend to the structure of the sentence and reconstruct the intention of the speaker. In the second case, the question has addressivity, but interrelationship of the response to the question makes it difficult to reconstruct the intentions of the second speaker. In both cases, the parole becomes meaningful in terms of various features of the language: the interrogative form of the first sentence, and the categorical identification of the train and the destination (in the second case, the No. 4 train differentiated from Nos. 1, 2, 3, etc.; Brooklyn as opposed to Queens). In the third passage, each individual sentence is grammatically sound, but the narrative logic of the paragraph and the categorical logic of the references make it difficult to decipher. The speaker says he does not know what it is and then introduces a female character who says something that is unclear in its meaning. The construction of the next two phrases does not enable a respondent to ascertain whether she or the speaker is saying "I don't know" or whether she is saying there is a Cinderella. The same observations can be made about the next two sentences: what play is he talking about and who is the awful idiot? The signified is neither clear nor precise and its allusions and categories are vague, leaving the fellow parolee in a quandary about his own reactions.

However, there need not be a fully cooperative, fulfilling, and commensurate relationship between two statements for an organization of meaning to emerge. Consider the following:

A: Is this the way to Pace University?
B: I really don't know. But I can show you the way to Jesus Christ!

Here the respondent is not too helpful to the questioner, who wants information regarding directions to a particular place. The respondent, however, has deftly turned the question to his advantage by transforming the word "way" into a metaphor, giving an answer that does interlock with the questioner, giving him new options about the direction of his life rather than for the moment. This answer in turn can at the least elicit one of two retorts. The initiator can now say:

A: No thanks; I have more pressing claims now.

or

A: Really? Okay, Show me the way to Jesus.

Asking a question defines the path the discourse will take and can in fact be said to give direction to the life of discourse. It accomplishes this as follows: it forestalls other questions being asked, questions that may be equally or more consequential than the one asked; the answer may give rise to further questions that are chained to the earlier questions and its answers; these questions and answers open byways that are connected to the earlier question or questions and answers.

## The Limits of Interpretation

Insofar as one's articulations depend on the other's interpretation for completion, the character and quality of the other person will have an important bearing on emerging meanings. The knowledgeability, informedness, and boundaries and horizons of his or her mind will contribute to the reality created by the initial articulation. The other can be informed enough—as in the earlier example of the patient who interprets the therapist's comment on dreams—to interpret an articulation in a particular way. This is an act that carries its own pathos; it limits the interpretation to whatever it is that the other knows, claims to know, or claims is the only important thing to know, thus restricting the emerging meaning to only that interpretation. The patient can interpret a comment about dreams in a Freudian way, as seems customary nowadays. However, if one knows one's Jung, one can add his more elaborate and cosmic theories of dreams to Freud's interpretation. Or else, one can interpret Mead's work as that of a simple-minded behaviorist, rejecting the idea that he was a pragmatist influenced by the behaviorist movement who struggled to incorporate some elements of behaviorism into a pragmatic theory of self act and meaning, and so close further discussion.

Practical affairs can reveal this capacity to define the limits of the acts of the others by exercising one's own powers. In the course of the tense deliberations and negotiations brought on by the Cuban missile crisis, for example, Nikita Krushchev sent two notes in succession, one stiff and uncompromising and the other conciliatory. The latter had come first and in keeping with an operational theory of linear causality, needed to be ignored, making the stiff note the relevant one. However, Robert Kennedy, in a feat of interpretational boldness and creativity, decided to ignore the stiff note and respond to the conciliatory one. The emerging meaning was one of conciliation, understanding, and mutual accommodation (Kennedy, 1969). In short, all interpretations are pragmatic activities although conducted on the basis of a theory that one knows or takes for granted.

## The Process of Reconstruction

### Traces and Ambiguities

Initiatives and interpretations, complex and convoluted as they are, define and give shape to discourses and substance to the selves enmeshed in them. In using these structures of reconstruction, a respondent seeks to create his or her own effects on the other just as the other sought to create his or her own, by using traces and constructing ambiguities.

Consider the following bit of dialogue, part of an ongoing series of discursive acts, in which the participants would be grievously incomplete if they did not pay attention to its multiple textures:

|  |  |
|---|---|
| Friend: | How are things at the office? |
| Husband: | Very well . . . Everything is coming up roses. |
| Wife: | Yeah . . . you can't keep Bill from spending all his time at the office . . . mornings . . . evenings . . . (trailing off) |
| Friend: | Oh yeah? Up to his old tricks again is he? |
| Husband: | Oh come on, you should be ashamed even to think of something like that. |

(Field Notes)

In interpreting the wife's text, the husband has to apprehend a number of its formal features. To begin with, it is an interruption of an interaction between a visiting friend and the husband and therefore implies that the wife wants to convey something more than the husband would in responding to the question. She frames the substantive part of the sentence in the negative, thereby emphasizing the positive; "You *can't* keep Bill . . . " This calls attention to the cultural value of leisure ("official time" versus "domestic time"), in the expectation that one should spend enough time at home with wife and children, and directs a rebuke at him for violating these expectations. The second formal feature of the sentence is the use of *all* to qualify time. This is contrasted implicatively with *some* or *part* as well as *leisure time* and *work time*, thereby adding to the signification of the text. The binary coding here is both reinforced and supplemented by the intonations employed: a playful ironic signification is indicated that simultaneously teases the husband about his recent affair with his secretary and draws the visiting friend into the circle of intimacy because the friend too, as it happened, had an inkling of this. And there is more in this interaction that would contribute to the interpretation it will elicit: the use of the cliche by the husband (the unwitting allusion to the romantic symbol roses) and the wife's allusive "evenings" (play time, erotic time) are also involved in the impact the text will make on the interactants.

These features are not merely stimuli that elicit a response but are interpretively apprehended significations used in the life of an interaction. All the parties in the transaction have produced a very complex text. The wife, in particular, in the course of fifteen words has created a world of expectation, attitudes, presentations of self, and cultural standards for apprehension by the others. Further, the significances they convey, in themselves neither arcane nor obscure, are easily within the grasp of the others. These discursive acts are complex and—loaded with implications and suggestiveness—demand an evaluation and an examination of the various shades of significance before a response is made. Such an examination involves paying some, if not close, attention to the articulation's semantic content, tonal semiotics, and connections to previous articulations. By doing so, a respondent is able to construe subtleties of intention and character, understand irony an sarcasm, and appreciate paradox, synecdoche, and oxymoron. Further he or she can discern doubts and qualifications in the initiator's statements, affirmatives that actually signify negatives and negatives that signify positives, statements that indicate true enthusiasms or the lack of such feelings, and so forth. Indeed, verbal articulations are *typically* so complex that one has to develop analytical habits to respond to them adequately.

The complex nature of interpretational processes is most clearly revealed by an examination of discursive textual ambiguities. In a famous essay on poetry, William Empson wrote that "a word may have several distinct meanings; several meanings connected with one another; several meanings which need one another to complete their meaning, or several meanings which unite together so that the word means one relation or one process. . . . 'Ambiguity' itself can mean an indecision as to what you mean, an intention to mean several things, a probability that one or other or both of two things has been meant and the fact that the statement has several meanings" (1964:8). Ambiguity then makes choosing the intended signification of a word arrangement, i.e., a discursive act, a problem. As there is an articulator and a respondent and, as indicated earlier, each is producing an interpretant in convoluted ways, ultimate meaning selected out of a variety of options is a consensus achieved inside the situation itself. It is a momentary consensus because it itself is subject to the process of ambiguation of meaning. Theoretically endless, the process is limited by application of the pragmatic maxim.

This is the case even in the most laconic and overtly unambiguous of discourses:

A: May I borrow your dictionary?
B: No.

The request is simple enough. A person who has asked for the temporary use of an object has been denied that use. If the requester is a wife who has been quarreling with her husband, his denial has significations above and beyond the denial itself. For instance, his "no" can mean the quarrel is not over, that there is still ill-feeling on his part and that he seeks to further these ill-feelings. Conversely, a "yes" to the question may convey the opposite set of significations. Obviously in the rejection of the request there are *traces* of the earlier quarrel, which may continue to show its influence on further discursive acts. I am using the word "trace" in two senses. One, the earlier usage by Empson in his claim that "whenever a receiver of poetry is seriously moved by an apparently simple line, what are moving in him are the traces of a great part of his past experience and the structure of his past" (1964:xviii). In recent years the idea of traces has been used by Jacques Derrida. The Derridean traces, although more complicated, do not obviate the Empsonian traces. Defining his master-concept, Derrida wrote, "*Differance* is the systematic play of differences, of the traces of differences, of the *spacing* by means of which elements are related to each of them" (1981:27; italics in original). The husband's response in the above example cannot by any means be said to have been uninfluenced by the immediate past of the interaction, and the wife's response to the denial cannot be oblivious to its multiple significations.

In the following text, a patient (B) who had missed an appointment without calling to cancel it talks with his analyst (A) about the unexplained absence:

1.  A:  Maybe you felt that the kind of interpretations I was making on Monday were the same thing and you couldn't come yesterday 'cause you were scared of this faggot here—who was gonna make a pass at you.

2.  B:  It's almost as if I don't want you to get the idea that I am trying to pursue you and the same time, I can almost get an indication of whether you're trying to pursue me or not, you know. Like, if I come in here and you were pissed off, you know, I'd really be afraid, you know, I'd say: "Fuck me, man, you know, this guy's really after my ass or something."

3.  A:  Oh, you mean, if I were pissed off.

4.  B:  Yeah.

5.  A:  About your not having come.

6.  B:  But as long as, you know, nothing changed and you just said, "Well, that's the way it goes," you know.

7.  A:  That means I don't need you so desperately. I am not after your ass.

8.  B:  Right.

9.  A:  I see. So another slight wrinkle that we can add to your not coming yesterday was that you thought Monday I might be too strongly attracted to you . . .

10. B:  Well, Monday seemed to go real well and I really wondered why, you know.

11. A:  That is what you couldn't stand, isn't it?

12. B:  And—yeah.

13. A:  And then?

14. B:  Oh, I thought: "Jesus, you know, why did I come in here so eagerly or why did I open up so well?" And maybe subconsciously, I thought you know—all those maybes and shit thrown in, but I am [sigh]. That I may have reacted in a way—Well, you are really pushin today, you know, or you're really in tune with what's happenin' or you're the one that wants to get back with both feet."

15. A:  Me?

16. B:  Yeah. You've been away for a whole week, you know, and you gotta get back and secure me, you know.

17. A:  Oh yes. I was too eager to recapture your love.

18. B:  Yeah.

(Gill and Hoffman, 1982:102–103)

Each discursive act in this fragment of a conversation between a therapist and patient demonstrates the need for being aware of their complex internal structures if a meaningful transaction is to be achieved. The second act of discourse uses a common metaphorical structure in referring to anger, beginning the allusion to bodily functions or parts that are to appear later. A respondent must not only understand that the expression refers to anger, but also apprehend it as a very earthy, forceful, and concrete form of this anger. The therapist continues in the subjunctive in 5, and the respondent must be able to read this as an allusion to his not having kept the earlier appointment. In the ninth act, bodily metaphors are introduced again in which a wrinkle of the body becomes a wrinkle of meaning. This part of the conversation is about a sexual signification that the patient is said to have *imputed* to the therapist following the earlier discourse that was replete with sexual tropes. The systematic use of genital words synecdochically and metaphorically in a text that is referentially about a sexual misunderstanding makes the interaction sexual again. As the *references* deny sexual intent, the *tropes* affirm the presence of sexuality. Overtly, however, these tropes are being used to display the contempt the analyst bears towards the patient. Indeed, the quoted segment ends on a note of contemptuous sarcasm, made evident in the written transcript by the adjective "too" put in front of "eager," taken in the context of what has been said before.

The therapist is enabled to proceed in this way by the self-doubts, hesitations, and insecurity the patient's text offers. The repetitive "you know" is a supplicatory ritual. The defensive, apprehensive posture of the patient is almost palpable in the text, and is thoroughly evidenced in the description of what was thought. He is apologizing for ambiguously "opening up" so eagerly and throws a sop to the therapist by indicating that he is in the same universe of discourse as the therapist: "maybe *subconsciously*, I thought." Each, then, was not only responding to the other's productions, but reading and apprehending them, thus creating a symbiotic dance of words and attitudes. The defensiveness of the patient, indeed the defensive text that he produces, meshes with the aggressiveness of the therapist and his text, which helps to define each other. This is well attested by the closing pair of exchanges. The therapist produces a text of biting irony, "Oh yes, I was too eager to recapture your love," which the patient misses completely, merely affirming it— "Yeah"—which was the last interpretation the therapist sought to elicit. Once again the therapist appears as an aggressive interactant while the patient seems not only naive but textually and situationally inept. Further, in the developmental sequences of this transaction, each actor, seeking to stymie the ambiguities, tries to create a closure on the significance of the previous statement only to find a new set of significances emerging.

There is no doubt that each participant in this interaction is both producing and apprehending a multileveled text, and that a fundamental analyticity is operating in both of their ongoing attempts to consider traces and settle on interpretations.

*Informed Interpretations and Ignorant Interpretations*

Knowledgeable responses to an articulation can have consequences for a dialogue on simple subjects as well as complex ones. When one asks about the destination of the train approaching the station, knowledge or ignorance of the respondent will no doubt be consequential. But the importance of a knowledgeable respondent for continued and successful communication goes beyond such occasions. Engaging in a continuous conversation for a sufficient length of time is important in life. To do this one must have knowledge about topics of conversations if one is to receive their sustenance. For many people in the world today, sports provide just such a ready topic. Obviously a sporting conversational sally must receive a knowledgeable response if the conversation is to gain vitality and momentum. In the organization of meaning as well as in the organization of a meaningful life, shared knowledge and an ability to bring it to the fore as occasion demands cannot be overestimated. In other words, when initiator and respondent are well matched, conversations become productive and continuous.

Consider the following exchange between a patient (Jonathan) and his therapist (Havens):

| | |
|---|---|
| Jonathan: | Part of the process of therapy is just testing the expectations and finding out which aren't realistic in the first place, and which would be true, which should be sacrificed . . . |
| Havens: | You don't have to give up all your expectations. |
| Jonathan: | No, but if I have no expectations, then I wouldn't do it. |
| Havens: | One is supposed to need a certain amount of grandeur, right? |
| Jonathan: | Well, I think actually many difficulties stem from excess of grandeur. I am very hard on myself and I expect to be a historical personage. |
| Havens: | May be you can be, maybe you can be. That's a good idea. At least we need the right kind of historical personages, particularly right now.<br><br>[The subject of the patient's dreams, the topic now introduced by the therapists, elicits the next lines of dialogue.] |
| Jonathan: | . . . and I sort of feel it's a common dream, especially for people that are involved in performance, that you know they are up there on the stage, and the entire audience is looking at them with rapt attention, but they have forgotten their lines and they don't know what to do next, and for my next trick I am going to . . . you know . . . there's no props or anything. |

(Havens, 1986:151–56)

This patient is clearly an informed participant in his own therapy, he takes up points made by the therapist with alacrity, even in the last quoted passage in which he displays relevant knowledgeability by expanding on the theory of dreams.

This is important not only in successful verbal therapies, but in all sustaining relationships. Although the existence of a universe of such discourses does not guarantee the success of relationships, their absence certainly guarantees their failure. That is to say, discursive acts must be interpreted knowledgeably for an optimum of meaning to emerge and dialogues to endure.

## Barren and Fertile Interpretations

The semantically interlocked sentence begins with an assertion or question, which we may call a statement, that then elicits a commensurate response. The initial statements can be potent, capable of achieving an input into and evoking responses from the other. These responses can be fertile, capable of leading to further productions. Consider a person at a party approaching another who says:

A:  Lousy weather we have been having . . .
B:  Yes; but I just flew in from the West Coast and it was nice there.

A's statement, though not particularly potent, was adequate. B's response, on the other hand, was very fertile and receptive, a commensurate response, combining the matter of the weather and identifying herself as one who comes from the West Coast. Needless to say, A can now ask a series of questions such as "Where did you come from exactly?" or "How long have you lived in San Francisco?"

Person A could also have made potent statements that would have received fertile statements in return, such as a subtly turned compliment or insult, a clear-cut political opinion contravening those which are accepted in relevant social circles or a viewpoint that challenges any conventional wisdom. The simplest and most common indication of such potency is found in a direct question that can be asked in such a way as to elicit the answers one is seeking. Consider this simple example:

A:  Will the No. 7 train take me to midtown Manhattan?
B:  Yes; but change at Queens Plaza to the RR train.

The precise train and the precise point in Manhattan are both contained in the sentence. This establishes the fact that the questioner knows the No. 7 train is different from other trains, and also indicates that A knows that different trains can be used to arrive at different points in the complex New York subway system and in its intricate

Manhattan subdivisions. These features of the text enable the respondent to give very precise answers. Implicitly acknowledging the questioner's information about the train and the Manhattan subdivisions, B offers important qualifications: yes, take this train, but change at a certain point to another train. The question has potency, but the answer too has the distinct quality of what I will call receptivity. And together, potency and receptivity create a good interlocking semantic relationship between participants.

## Internal and External Interpretations

An actor's initial statement typically alludes to a subject matter that is usually a bounded one. Thus, if one makes a comment about baseball the continuing responses can be about baseball or about sports in general. Insofar as these responses remain within these bounds one can call them internal responses. Most ongoing conversations stick to this rule. But one can make a response that is wholly outside the bounds of the initial comment. Such external responses are made to voice a number of signifying intentions. First, they can indicate that the topic announced by the initial comment is not welcome at this moment or by this person. Thus, an external response will serve to kill a topic altogether:

A:   Have you heard from Sarah?

Now Sarah, the sister of the hostess, has eloped with the butler and the hostess does not want that topic to be raised at all. On the other hand, she does not want to snub A either and so she says:

B:   Why didn't you bring your children with you? My son enjoys their company so much.

On the face of it there is neither semantic interlocking nor semantic continuity in the second remark because the respondent has not made an internal response. But, of course, a response has been made at a deeper level, and a complex significance enunciated and with even a minimum of perspicacity, the initiator will read it and make no further mention of Sarah while continuing the interaction.

Second, an external response can be used to indicate that the topic under discussion has been exhausted and that it is time to finish with it, or proceed in another direction. Further, an external response can snub the initiator: you don't know enough about the subject, therefore let's talk about something else.

## Thick and Thin Interpretations

It is possible to distinguish between responses that are thick and rich and those that are thin. Once the respondent has received the articulator's initial statement he or she has the power to answer in a way that adds and enriches its content and range. One way is to take the original statement and, developing its continuity, enlarge on its implications:

A: You know . . . there is this chap Freedman—he has written a book arguing that Margaret Mead faked her data.

B: Yes; I have read the book. It is overheated and quite tendentious. You should see the review in the American Anthropologist by . . .

B's response is an enriching and continuing one, introducing new information into the discourse and addressing a contradiction to the implied approval of Freedman's critique, thereby defining an emotional tone and enabling the initiator to reenter the conversation. By taking A's comments seriously enough to warrant a spirited response, B has also validated and enhanced A's self. If, on the other hand, B had merely shrugged his or her shoulders and said "Yes I have read Freedman's book" and then looked away or introduced the line "Do you think it will rain today?" we would have on our hands an impoverished response that dampened the self of the initiator and dispelled the possibility of a dialogic moment emerging. Such a response rejects the proffered serious and potentially fertile topic of discussion and offers a trivial one in return. The minimum of semantic organization thereby achieved would obviate the emergence of a continuing discourse. However, B might offer another topic, creating another organization that could take the discourse in a different direction. This would, of course, be a new moment in the discourse whereby the respondent has initiated a new line of inquiry that leaves the choice of continuing it or not up to the articulator. For all that, the thin response is a damp cloth that prevents the discourse from bursting into flame.

## Arresting and Continuous Interpretations

The arresting response seeks to undermine the articulator's intention by refuting the arrangement, presentation, and articulation of the discourse. This can be done by challenging the implicit or explicit grounds of the initial statement:

One-eyed man: Haven't you heard that in the land of the blind, the one-eyed man is king?

Blind man: What is blind?

Another example would be:

A:   Why are you late for class?
B:   I am early for the next class!

In each case the legitimacy of the initial statement is questioned, and the ball sent back to the initiator's court without a continuing and fulfilling response. Indeed, the serve is declared faulty and the server asked to serve again. Consider the following:

A:   You are so beautiful, I can just sit here and watch you forever.
B:   Oh! come on . . . that sounds like a line from a soap opera.

These can be contrasted with

A:   Are you a Christian?
B:   Yes; I am a Methodist. Are you?

Unlike the arresting response, this answer completes the initial rally and asking a connected question in return sets up the further development of what could be a long rally. In addition, the forthcoming and fulfilling answer offers validation of the questioner's self, thereby building a foundation for the emergence of a dialogic relationship. That is to say, the recipient of the initial gesture has by his or her response participated in the organization not only of meaning but of a meaningful relationship.

To summarize, discursive acts elicit active and responsive interpretations that to some extent are dependent on the original acts and their constituent features. This rhetorical power of discursive acts is managed and controlled by the structural features of the texts that constitute them and elicit a proper interpretant.

Insofar as the respondent is also a self-conscious and intentional agent, the act of interpretation will give him or her the opportunity to use it to manifest his or her self and construct a character for the interaction in question. The interaction is in fact the site where a respondent can give play to his or her self by providing one interpretation rather than another, and thereby add elements to its structure or enhance the ones already there. He or she can be confident and assertive or subservient and submissive in his or her interpretive acts and define the self and the other in terms of the responsive act. He or she can be fruitful and co-operative in the interpretation and conspire to create a joint act with the articulator and establish a dialogic self and a relationship. Such interpretations can set up chains of discourse that will create a medium in which the selves of those concerned can be sustained and allowed to flourish as ongoing presences. Conversely, systematically hostile or unfulfilling, evasive and slippery responses will make the cultivation of the discourse difficult, thereby forestalling the construction of fruitful interactions.

Failures on this score can be of many kinds. A respondent can deliberately and insistently offer unreasonable and ridiculous statements, leading the articulator to conclude that the other means are impertinent and hostile, or that he is insane. Or the respondent can provide evasive and prevaricatory responses that will lead to a change in the dialogue and relationship, while deception and deviousness characterize hostile and adversarial ones. In any case, veracity and sincerity, as opposed to inveracity, cynicism, and manipulativeness, are not momentary features of social life or only matters of self-persuasion. Insofar as the other is available as a self with various definite qualifications and characteristics of a dependable sort only through discourse, evasions, prevarications and deviations in that discourse will make it difficult for one to encounter a stable other. Discursive deviousness makes for a fluffy and evanescent self with which it would be difficult to constitute continuing intimate relationships. Indeed, such a self will prevent the emergence of a meaningful interpersonal organization.

Further, the respondent's power to interpret the act gives him a certain freedom, not only to give particular meanings to the discourse that is addressed to him or her, but simultaneously to allow or not to allow it to affect his or her self. He or she can, for example, practice the art of "rationalization," as the Freudians call it, and interpret the discourse in ways that are least damaging to the self. Some can even go further and interpret a neutral or even a hostile discourse as flattering to the self and bask in its glory. Meaning, then, is not only in the response but in the particular response that the other chooses to provide and he or she has many options open.

## Notes

1. I am using the word "apprehend" here in more or less the same sense in which Herman Schmalenbach used it. In an essay entitled "Phenomenology of the Sign," he argued for a threefold description of the sign: (1) it is used in the *setting* of meaning, the initial psychological move; (2) it is used in the *notification* of meaning, the signaling of the intentions of the articulator; and (3) it is used in the *apprehension*, the understanding of the meaning by the others. He further argued that the existence of others becomes available to the self only through "signs bearing a signification" from them (Schmalenbach, 1977).

2. The relationship between the generation of meaning in interactions between human actors and the constitution of meaning of quantum phenomena by an observer has been discussed in an earlier publication (Perinbanayagam, 1986). This may sound strange, but it was the physicists themselves who,

confronted with the contradictions and irreconcilable positions within their own experiments and explanations, first turned to theories of meaning. John Wheeler wrote, "Who can ever dream of abandoning . . . a physics hardware located 'out there' and putting in its stead a 'meaning' software located who knows where? And how can the hard won structure of hard science be moved over, solid as ever, on to this new and other-worldly foundation? Yet, despite all the difficulties, and they are great, that must be the task and achievement of the coming Era III physics . . . . 'meaning physics'; we have to seek nothing less than the foundation of physical law itself" (1984:4). Indeed, unbeknownst to themselves they seem to have settled on a pragmatic theory of meaning, putting a closure on endless uncertainties by adopting the pragmatic maxim, via the "Copenhagen Interpretation." (Perinbanayagam, 1986).

# The Dialectics
# of Discourse

## — 5 —

Discursive acts and the social constraints under which they are constituted can be fruitfully examined from the dialectical perspective that
Kenneth Burke used. Having examined the many usages of the term
"dialechical", he summarizes them under three heads:

1. Merger and division [There may be a state of merger, or a state of
   division, or developments from either side to the other].
2. The Three Major Pairs: action-passion, mind-body, being-
   nothing—[as terms that define each other].
3. Transcendence (Transcendence likewise may be either a state or a
   development) (1962:402)

These three features of the dialectic can be used in the examination of
several instances of discursive interaction. The conception of action as
an ongoing series in which there are no stable and fixed positions is one
derivation that can be made from this interpretation of the dialectic.
Such an ontology of the perceptual world can be applied to the study of
interpersonal transactions and to the organizations that emerge from
and sustain them. Indeed, this approach to complex organizations has
been fruitfully developed by Kenneth Benson (1977). He views the
actors in each organization as elements in a dialectical relationship in
which each such element participates in defining the role of the other.

The dialectical character of organization also is realized through the
management of discourse. It is in this juncture between discursive
interaction and dialectical relationships that the theory of "negotiated
order" proposed by Anselm Strauss (1978) and his associates (Maines,
1982) comes into play. The negotiations by which order is created,
conflict resolved, and order reestablished are conducted by the management of discourse. Such discourses are ongoing activities that constitute
what some who study organization have called its "culture." Gary Alan

Fine's summary of this view holds that "organizational managers should be conscious of the expressive or symbolic context of their decisions" and recognize that management is a form of symbolic action. The cultural forms that characterize an organization fall into numerous traditional genres: slang or jargon, jokes, ideology, sagas and histories, rituals, ceremonies, and stories (1984b:243). A dialectical approach to organizations is able to encompass all these dimensions: differentiations and conflict between the various elements of an organization, the negotiations and orderings achieved between these elements, and the discursive processes through which all of this is accomplished.

It is evident that all discourse is constrained by roles and structures of roles—the elements of organizations. Conversely, roles and role relationships are constituted discursively. These are *simultaneous* processes that are dialectically related in which neither can be considered prior to the other. When one eschews a linear logic, it becomes clear that at a given moment in time participants create discourse that reproduces the organization in and through the talk itself, and that the discourse that emerges is influenced by the roles of the participants in the organization. One cannot merely talk an organization into being, nor can one find an organization that is not constituted discursively. Although discursive constitution may be characterized by uncertainty, there is no escape from the necessity of having to use the available media with the available selves.

In producing acts of discourse for dialogic purposes, the articulator presents a self and so enters into relationships with other selves. These selves, as members of other social organizations, are always implicated in relationships other than those of the moment. One common feature of a self's membership in organizations is the status and honor that go with the respective ranks within each of them. These ranks have to be acknowledged and given discursive presence by the articulator in emerging interactions, unless, of course, he or she *means* to insult, challenge, or provoke the other by repudiating his or her rank. These ranks, statuses, and honor are features of small groups like the family and work groups, as well as the larger society. In presenting these discursively, the articulator brings the macrostructures of the society into the microprocesses of interaction. In fact, the macrostructures become active and ontologically real in and through discursive acts. On the one hand, this re-creates the structure of the social order in the text and, on the other, gives the recipient's self honor, thereby validating it. Such validation is never of a general self, but one that is in fact always particularized and comprehended in terms of the very details being discursively created at the moment.

## The Parameters of Discourse

Discursive acts occur in historically located social organizations, and these organizations have a decisive role in the initiation and destiny of such acts. Indeed, social organizations of one kind or another are the parameters within which discursive life is led. It is no doubt true that such organizations are created through discourse. This is to say, since it is people coming together and engaging in acts of talk describing and renewing other acts that constitute any given social organization, it can be claimed that such talk brings organizations into being. However, the talkers' prior history and identity play an important role in the discourses they produce. What one can say and how much one can claim to know are functions of his or her place in a social organization in the role complex in which he or she is situated. Of course, the role that a person assumes in the interactional context will control the nature of the discursive act.

Many if not all of the formal properties of discursive acts will in fact be determined by the roles that parties to an interaction assume. In a father-son relationship in a traditional society, the tempo and tautness will be more relaxed and slower, the characterization of the other will be less volatile, the agonistic presence muted, the topical relevances very limited, just as the tropic expansiveness will be controlled. Seckman and Couch have studied jocular and sarcastic social acts and concluded that there is an "intertwining" of such acts with solidary and authority relationships: "Jocularity is most commonly contextualized by solidary relationships and in turn invites or affirms solidarity relationships. Sarcasm may be contextualized by either solidary or authority relationships." (1989:327). That is, both the particular discourse and authority or solidary relationships characterize and constrain the production of discursive acts.

This is true of all role contexts insofar as hierarchy and cultural variation are essential features of all social organizations. That is to say, while these relations of hierarchy may be accomplished and realized through discursive practices in the course of the interaction, as some have urged, it is equally true that the interaction begins with a ready set of relationships with which the discourse has to contend. Consider the following exchange on the telephone:

First person:  May I know who is calling?
    Caller:  I would like not to use the name, if it is all right for the moment.
First person:  Hold on please . . . Sir?
    Caller:  Yes um.

First person:    Hold the line please.
        Caller:  All right.
Second person:   Hello, Sir.
        Caller:  Ah. yes. I would . . .
Second person:   Vladimir Sorokin speaking. My name is Vladimir.
        Caller:  I am sorry.
Second person:   Vladimir Sorokin speaking. My name is Vladimir.
        Caller:  Vladimir, yes. Ah, I have, ah I don't like to talk on the
                 telephone.
Second person:   I see.
        Caller:  Ah. I have something I would like to discuss with you I
                 think that would be very interesting to you.
Second person:   Uh huh, uh huh.
        Caller:  Is there anyway to do so in, in ah, confidence or privacy?
Second person:   I see. I understand. Uh huh . . . Just a moment. Hold on
                 . . . please.
Second person:   Sir.
        Caller:  Yes.
Second person:   Maybe you can name yourself.
        Caller:  An . . . ah on the telephone it would not be wise.
Second person:   I see.
        Caller:  Ah . . .
Second person:   So may be . . .
        Caller:  I come from, I, I am with the United States Government.
Second person:   Maybe you can visit.
        Caller:  Ah (sigh) O.K. How would I do that?
Second person:   So you know the address.
        Caller:  Yes. I have been there. I have been by it several times in
                 Washington.
Second person:   I see, I see, so you prefer, ah, to speak to somebody in ah,
                 private.
        Caller:  That is correct.
Second person:   O.K.

*(New York Times*, 1986:01)

Both speakers are not only creating the parameters of the discourse as they converse, but are introducing other parameters that will structure it. These, it turns out, are roles and selves from other organizations; that is, there is a systematic introduction of roles and statuses that are temporally prior to the interaction itself. The more powerful second speaker is substituted for the first and he introduces his name as a way of defining his status. Further, in this bit of discourse there is a very careful attention to the systematics of turn taking (Sacks et al., 1974). These systematics are formal rules when there is a presumption of equality between the participants. In the event that such an equality exists, the pattern of order and system in turn taking will not depend on other orders and systems. That kind of equality is absent in many conversations and so is the orderliness.

There is no doubt that the oppression of the larger society is manifest in small conversations. Insofar as conversations are the fundamental instrument for the creation of reality, who talks as well as when, where, why, and how that talk occurs becomes a matter of paramount importance in the study of social life. It is the case in all social organizations that who talks is a matter decided by the disposition of power and status. Before one talks, one has a membership that defines one's place in a hierarchy of power and privilege, and such a power and privilege is significantly defined by the right to speak and the obligation to keep silent. In the patriarchical family, for example, the eldest male had the higher authority, and spoke and defined the selves and situations for all the other members. Further, the others had to keep silent during these definitional episodes, waiting to be given their turn by the patriarch. While the wife was given her turn by the patriarch, children were often to be seen but not heard. The primal form of this organization is the court of a king who had supreme authority, an authority manifested in the belief that the king can do no wrong—hence the king cannot be contradicted or interrupted. Such conversations with kings, however, must be conducted by counselors and advisors, and a formula is put into effect by which the authority of the king is maintained and advice is given. This is accomplished by using the grammar of the language. (The passive voice, for example, and various locutions like "If the king thinks so," when in fact it is the minister who thinks so and has suggested it with an *apparent* tentativeness to the monarch.) The king, in short, is in total charge, or at least must appear to be so, and the rituals of speaking in turn and keeping silent, including the right to speak in his presence, are used to create that impression. This right to speak was transferred to many other organizations, like the military, and in many of them those who are not in charge have to ask "permission to speak," though asking for permission is in fact an act of speech.

If one must ask permission to speak in the presence of an exalted one, it follows such permission can be refused by the one in authority through disacknowledging the existence of opinion, attitudes, or facts that he considers inimical to his or her self. In these cases, one creates a favored reality by denying the right to take a turn at talking. He or she literally does not hear the other. In an organization where the head has the power of life and death, where associates or counselors are too afraid to speak in contradiction to the titular head, this can create serious problems unless someone with the privilege to speak without qualification is available to save the day. In a real court, the king had a jester who, while parodying him, simultaneously helped define his dignity and power by voicing what others were not allowed to voice in this presence. The jester represents disorder, the disorder that, according to Paul Radin "belongs to the totality of life." He continued, "The spirit of this disorder is the trickster. His function in anarchic society, or rather the function of the tales told about him, is to add disorder to order and so make a whole, to render possible within the fixed bounds of what is permitted and an experience of what is not permitted" (1956:185). In a court then, the jester is the categorical opposite of the king. He is everything the king is not, just as in circuses the clown's bumblings and prat falls help to define the precision and technical mastery of the performers on the high wires. In the communicational processes of courtly organizations, the jester represents the opposite of order and balance; jesting and prattling, he enables the king to hear ideas, opinions, and facts that others are not given either the opportunity or the right to say. The one chracteristic that the jester alone had in court was the privilege of teasing and jesting without being held accountable for offending anyone, including the king. Insofar as the king needed more information and advice than ministers were likely to give, the jester became the means by which the king could receive both. In a court, the jester is the one who does not have to wait for or be given his turn; his privilege is to be allowed to speak even when not spoken to, to interrupt ongoing discourses, to speak to anyone without permission. Violating the orderly processes of interaction and communication, he enters a discourse and changes its direction.

Consider the stories about jesters in Indian writings on court life. There the figure of the court jester, called the *vidushaka*, plays the role of the corrector in discursive interactions that are typically supplicatory on one side. Lee Siegel's (1987) fine study of comedy and laughter provides many illustrations of this role. In one, the king of Kanci is returning from a conquest accompanied by his jester and other counselors. Near his palace, he sees some young boys playing with little toy soldiers. In their game, the king of Kanci is depicted as the vanquished. The king becomes very angry and orders the boys tied to a tree and caned. In response to this, the jester asks the king's permission to leave the court. Asked why he is leaving the jester replies: "I am able neither to kill nor to destroy. By the grace of God, all I can do is laugh" (1987:300). This implied criticism of the king's action makes it possible for the king to realize the gross disproportionality of his order and will presumably lead him to change his mind.

The jester's role in rigid communicational structures is even more fully realized in a story Siegal tells about King Akbar, who was given a parrot he came to value very highly. Ordering his servants to take good care of it, he warned them,

> Whoever tells me that the parrot has died, will himself be put to death."
> The servants did their best to care for the bird, but one day they found it

lying dead on the bottom of its golden cage. In fear of the Moghul's anger, they told the jester Birbal of their predicament. "No problem," said Birbal. He went to Akbar and told him how wonderful the bird really was. "The parrot is a veritable yogi. He has entered *samadhi*." The King, anxious to behold the parrot's beatitude for himself, became furious at the sight of the bird on the bottom of the cage. "The bird is not in *samadhi* you fool, he is dead." The royal trickster smiled, "Your Highness must die, according to your own decree, for, telling you that the parrot is dead." The King had no choice but admit his folly—"I sometimes say foolish things—I must laugh the humorous laughter which is directed at oneself, and in that laughter to forgive as well." (Siegel, 1987:309–10)

In both instances, the other members of the court do not have the task of leavening the rigidities of the court's communicational structure. That role belongs to the privileged turn-taker who carries out the discursive responsibility indirectly and wittily.

The great fool of Western literature is, of course, to be found in Shakespeare's *King Lear*. There too he is a privileged communicator who, in his discursive acts, can defy rank and decorum. He first appears in the play (Act I, Scene IV) after King Lear has given his land and power away to his daughters Regan and Goneril and has banished his third daughter, Cordelia. The fool feels himself free and compelled to let the king know what a fool he has been. After a series of discussions about the king's actions, the following occurs:

Lear:   Does thou call me fool, boy?
Fool:   All thy other titles thou hast given away; that thou wast born with.
      [This prompts Lear's faithful courtier Kent to say]
Kent:   This is not altogether fool, my lord.

The fool indeed was no fool, certainly not so foolish as the king, and throughout the play these two antinomies are played against each other with great skill. In the play, as in many courts, the fool has the privileges and responsibilities of speaking when others cannot and tell what others dare not. Lear's enemies also know the fool's importance in the king's life and discourse. Goneril chides him for his excesses, subjects him to harassments, and finally hangs him, a sign of the general disorder represented in the play.[1]

In the everyday life of those who are not kings, it is not possible to have a permanent jester around. This problem is solved by a member of a group who on occasion takes the jester's role. In a patriarchal family, the role may be taken by one of the children or sometimes by the mother, but never by the father, although even in a patriarchal society the father may be reduced to being a fool. The presence of one playing the fool's role enables communication to proceed without the hierarchical roles solidifying into oppressive and monological structures. A pompous and domineering father who leaves no room for contradictions, accountings, or rejoinders can be made to see his actions in a different light when parodied and ironized by a young child.

Systematic turn taking determined by power, privilege, and precedence is formalized in parliamentary assemblies where the main, if not the only, order of business is talking. In such assemblies, strict rules exist that ensure that everyone's right to talk is upheld and protected. However, in times of political extremism or simply because of expediency, the presiding officer can refuse to recognize an inimical member and so define the emerging reality without the troubles and contradictions the recalcitrant would offer. Still, rules that forbid speaking may elicit penalties. The denial of a subordinate's right to speak or be assertive most often means that effective accounts cannot be given or, conversely, accounts given cannot be trusted. The culmination of such practices may create an identity the subject does not feel he or she can accept or a definition of reality that he or she does not recognize.

The result is often the adoption of identities and acts that others will readily define as schizophrenia, as in the case of Maya Abbott. In a now classic study of the emergence of a schizophrenic identity in this young woman, Laing and Esterson described the discursive interactions that may have led to this: "Her parents not only contradicted Maya's memory, feelings, perceptions, motives, intentions, and made attributions that were themselves curiously self-contradictory" (1970:42). The upshot of these continuous interactions, as Laing and Esterson noted, was that Maya "tried to withdraw into her own world, although feeling at the same time most painfully that she was not an autonomous person" (1970:43).

## Discourse and Decorum

The reflexive discursive act is undertaken by a self intertwined with the society or segments thereof in which it arose and wherein it now functions. Such a self can hardly be expected to disregard the sociologistic aspects and implications of its acts. Further, discursive and interactional activity are the means by which institutional, historical, and societal "facts" are created and re-created as circumstances dictate. There is, then, a dialectic between the discourse of everyday life and the order of the society in which the said discourse is being conducted.[2]

An incorporation of the rules that order relationships between members of a society is an essential feature of the emergence of the self, and the discursive practices that create such an ordering eventually become habits. Intonation will code the relative ranks of the speakers and listeners as well as other features of the self of the other. Terms of address as, contents, will be reflective of the ranks (Brown and Gilman, 1960). There are topics appropriate to certain types of relationships but not to others: intimate matters of a "personal" nature are not usually part of one's discourse with those with whom one has only a formal relationship. Care has to be taken even when using categorical structuration, to ensure that the other is put into an acceptable category or offense will be taken or irony suspected. Consider the following:

A well-known gentleman of Winchester was crossing the Potomac into Virginia in a ferry boat with his horse. The ferryman said, "Major, I wish you would move your horse a little forward," which he immediately did, responding to the man, "I am not a major. You need not call me one." To this the ferryman replied, "Well, Kernel, I ask your pardon, and I will not call you so anymore." Being arrived at the landing place, he led his horse out of the boat and said, "My good friend, I am neither a colonel nor a major. . . . I have no title at all and I don't like them. How much do I owe?" The ferryman looked at him and said, "You are the first white man I ever crossed this ferry that warn't jist nobody at all and I swar I will not charge you anything." (Doyle, [1937] 1971:3)

In this description of an interaction one finds a black man constantly using military titles to address a stranger. It is safe, from a black man's point of view, to grant this status to an impressive-looking white; there could be no possibility of offense and such overendowment of status acts as an insurance against being thought too demanding by a potentially hostile person. These are, however, not merely titles in a military establishment but honorifics that define the self vis-à-vis the other by putting each into definite categories of opposition that automatically define superordinate and subordinate relationships. This issue of managing the relationship between members of different castes has been extensively discussed by Gunnar Myrdal and his associates. They observed:

The conversation between whites and Negroes in the South is heavily regimented by etiquette. In *content* the serious conversation should be about those business interests which are shared . . . or it should be polite, but formal inquiry into personal affairs. The conversation is even more regimented in *form* than in content. The Negro is expected to address the white person by the title of Mr., Mrs. The old slavery title of "Master" disappeared during reconstruction and was replaced by "Boss" or "Cap" or "Cap'n" or Miss. (Myrdal, 1962:610–11; italics in original)

It is because of their serious implications that a great number of rules for managing discursive interactions are to be found in different cultures. Rules of etiquette are quite frequent because they regulate the management of discursive interactions. By defining permissible and impermissible conduct, they define and protect the selves of the participants in interactions, selves constituted by signs from a history of interactions each participant accepts as his or her essential self. In caste-structured societies, the superordinate and subordinate selves brought together in interaction carry with them a preestablished style and force that is acknowledged discursively and gesturally by the participants.

Observance of decorum in discursive acts enables relationships and selves to continue on an even keel. Decorum consists essentially of fitting a variety of discursive factors together into a whole, a process subject to evaluative judgments. First of all is the *decorum of topic:* certain topics are defined as too indecorous for most discursive interactions, although special license has been given, for example, to doctors and nurses in medical situations, scientists in scientific discussions, and accountants and priests in their respective professional situations. These topics are typically concerned with bodily functions, sexual functions, and—in some cultures—money and even religion. In addition, topics in which an interactant may have a special interest are likely to embarrass him or her and so are forbidden. Second, there is *decorum of diction*, which covers such a wide variety of activities that only some can be sketched in here. To begin with, there are taboo words, once again related to copulation, defecation, and the organs thereof. Then there are words that, referring to a deity and his agents, should not be taken in vain. Further, in addressing other people the very structuring of words into discursive acts must reflect the relative statuses of the addressee and addresser. Any lapse from this practice would be indecorous. Just as a social inferior should not adopt a domineering structure of words and address, so a social superior must manage to inject just the right degree of condescension into his or her locutions. Violating this rule of decorum could endanger the interaction and the relationship, because indecorousness in this case can elicit not only embarrassment but anger and violence as well. Third, there is *decorum of intonation:* emotional attitudes, degrees of power and status, a sense of imperative or submissive significance can be expressed in intonation. This too has to be articulated with a controlled precision reflecting all the complex intentions and relationships of the discourse. Fourth, there is *decorum of place:* certain discourses between certain selves can be undertaken only in given places. A dialogue between two people on intimate matters is not undertaken in public places, in front of strangers or third parties, etc. One's own living room, when a stranger is present, or a bus or show where others are present or likely to be present, can be considered a public place. Allied to this is a sense of areas within a house that are reserved as "decorous places." In the living room and more frequently the dining room, certain topics as well as certain attitudes are forbidden because that is where people are eating.

The forms of speech decorum that have been sketched here are embedded in the nature of the social relationship in which they occur. In relationships with other selves, every self considers a position in a hierarchical system as its legitimate right, whether in a bureaucracy, a child-mother or child-father relationship, a student-teacher relationship, or one between a young person and an older person. Or, alternatively, the self might only expect to be treated "civilly," in an egalitarian manner. In all these cases, the rules of decorum specify that relative ranking should be recognized discursively. Violation of these rules of decorum can hurt relationships, rouse anger, and if unabated result in violence.

Because ranking systems are culturally variable, there is a great potential for "misunderstandings" to hurt selves and for hostility and antagonism to occur when cultures mix interactionally. In a culture where easy egalitarianism is the norm in public relationships—in shops, buses, and trams, on streets, and in offices—an aristocratic visitor used to ranking systems would discursively claim deference and respect, creating an ambiance truly ripe for dis-ease and conflict. Conversely, if in such a society a person is too subservient, routinely speaking with "cap in hand," the embarrassment caused would make it difficult for others to have interactions with that person. In social circles where easy informality and egalitarian intercourse are the norm, arrogance and servility of speech are equally obnoxious. An instance of this is someone who habitually apologizes. As Lyman and Scott argue, these people "run the risk of exclusion from social circles, since their demand for face is greater than the available supply" (1970:41). More typically, a more or less finely calibrated sense of place and position is manifested in the discursive practices of those who participate in such relationships.

Discursive decorum, then, is related to the social structure and ideology of a society. In monarchical and feudal systems, addressing the monarch, the lord, or social superior in egalitarian terms and tones is indecorous and promotes conflict; in egalitarian societies, not to use it is an offense and an affront that may promote either embarrassment or conflict. Indeed, in cities and social enclaves where people with different interpersonal ideologies interact, one source of conflict may well be the inability of one group to present discursively the accustomed ranking or the absence of ranking that the other's self-esteem demands.

These rules of decorum are manifested in discursive acts as signs. They have a double function: displaying the sign that the self will claim as its own, which will then be used by others to define the self in all its implications. For example, if one uses an array of signs in conducting a discourse with another without bringing a certain embarrassing topic into the conversation, one displays tact and decorum. If one has done this at a public gathering, say at a christening party, giving the other the honor and respect deemed suitable both dictionally and intonationaly, this presented self will be honored and respected by the others, then and later. To maintain poise and help others do the same is to facilitate the selves of all present. These rules of decorum enable an individual to present a self and to define its nature as well as its location in a social relationship. Collectively, the rules "make society safe for interaction," in Goffman's words (1967:123), because they enable participants in an interaction to take account of all the selves involved, their own and those of the others, thereby protecting the value and worth of selves in given social economies.

In responding to the discourse of another it is possible for one to validate that other's self or to repudiate it, for that matter to enhance, elevate, or seriously undermine it. In Goffman's words, "The self then as a performed character, is not an organic thing that has a specific location, whose fundamental fate is to be born, to mature and to die; it is a dramatic effect arising from a scene that is presented and the characteristic issue, the crucial concern is whether it will be credited or discredited" (1959:252–53). One way to discredit the self is to treat a presentation made by it in an offensive manner. As Goffman says, "The person's orientation to face [i.e., the self] is the point of leverage that the ritual order has in regard to him; yet a promise to take ritual care of his face is built into the very structure of talk" (1967:40). Ritual order is the order of decorum designed to protect the self and to preserve social relationships—until it becomes absolutely necessary to damage it. The "orientation to face" also involves the orientation to the face of the other, so that "when one person volunteers a message, thereby contributing what might easily be a threat to the ritual equilibrium, someone else present is obliged to show that the message has been received and that its content is acceptable to all concerned or can be acceptably countered" (1967:38). That is to say, since a discursive act needs a completing response from another, the maintenance of the decorum of a *suitable* response guarantees the self of the person and the relationship. To refuse to respond at all is to deny the other his or her moral worth as a person, to undermine his or her relationships and presence in a world of others. Therefore, the rules of decorum ensure that at least a "polite response" is provided even if the other is disliked.

Since rules of decorum are subject to human agency they can be used to undermine the order of interactions and disturb the order of the self: deliberate choice and use of topics that embarrass or negatively insinuate about the other, offensive intonations, lack of an appropriate relationship between topic and place, and the absence of a proper response are examples of this. Even everyday relationships can demand a rearrangement of the pattern of relationship between the people concerned.

If the relationship in question is between two social equals, termination of the relationship may yet occasion great damage to the self. If the McDonnells chose to "cut" the Vanderbilts and "turn their backs to them," as apparently happened one day in Southampton, it is safe to surmise that it did not cause the Vanderbilts shame and contrition. The offense the McDonnells intended was religious. Mrs. Vanderbilt, one of their own, had married a divorced man, thereby excommunicating herself. Cuddihy, in an unparalleled distillation of the social, religious, and historical significance of a minute event, states, "For neither party, is there one best action. There is no way of *not* giving offense or scandal either religious or social. Giving "no offense" is an unavailable option; taking offense is inevitable" (1978:88; italics in original).

The Vanderbilts' immediate response to the cut given at the unexpected confrontation is not recorded. Although the elder McDonnells shunned their niece, Mrs. Vanderbilt, she was greeted by the McDonnells' daughter, her cousin Catherine McDonnell. Jeanne Vanderbilt remembered this "kindness for years" (Corry, quoted in Cuddihy, 1978:88). It was not a kindness, Cuddihy argues, but a "categorical act: it constitutes in fact the unkindest cut; it makes a new religious boundary, it deconstructs an old identity, it performs an apostasy; it cures, at long last a sub-cultural anomaly" (1978:89). That is to say, a new generation of Catholics was abandoning religious propriety in favor of a different social decorum—the religion of civility. The greeting may not have been meant as a kindness, but it was defined and remembered as one by the recipient. The event described allows one to see a subtle social semiotic and records an important moment of social change. The elder generation was, by turning their backs on the young Vanderbilt, enforcing a *religious exclusion*, while the younger by her acknowledgment of Jeanne Vanderbilt was producing a *social acceptance*. The younger one was, by a process of structural opposition, creating a new category and abandoning an old one.

If Jeanne Vanderbilt remembered this sign as an act of kindness and the behavior of the McDonnells in turning their back on her is an act of cruelty, the two signs probably more or less balanced out in their impact on her self. However, one can envisage others subjected to systematic and persistent acts of indecorous discursive acts suffering worse consequences: anger and rage can be expressed then and there or suppressed and given voice at later occasions. Emotions of this kind are no doubt the result of the offenses perpetrated against the other's self.

Offenses become signs that violate and contradict the maxisign of a self that has already been assembled. If, on the other hand, it has been the lot of the person to have been slightingly and insultingly treated for a long time, it is likely that his or her current self will not feel violated by an additional slight. The maxisign of the self achieves its own power and existence, its own quiddity and reality, after a while developing a chronic inability to become a new self. In any case, the rules of decorum enable participants in social life to use discursive acts in such a way that the order of social statuses and relationships of selves are maintained until it becomes absolutely necessary to violate them. In Goffman's words, "The signs that we give off and exchange are all we have. Communicative acts are translated into moral ones. The impressions that the others give tend to be treated as claims and promises they have implicitly made, claims and promises that tend to have a moral character" (1959:245–50).

## Topics of Discourse

The notion of topic in recent years has been used by ethnomethodologists and discourse analysts. The most celebrated earlier usage of the notion was, of course, Aristotle's. For him, topic figures as a rhetorical trope with which to constitute statements useful for conducting arguments. Arguments are forms of discursive interaction in which various rules are used either to persuade or to subdue an opponent. These discourses must be astutely organized and presented: topics addressed to the other are first used to gain attention and then to hold it so that the task of persuasion can be accomplished.[3]

Topics, to be useful in this regard, must contain a number of properties and in fact it is these properties that define a topic. Aristotle observed that topics properly constituted can be used for "mental training, conversations, and philosophical sciences." That it is useful for mental training is obvious "for if we have a method, we shall be able to more easily argue about the subject that is proposed." Aristotle further observed that well-constituted topics are useful for conversations and for philosophical arguments (1960:227).

According to Aristotle, topics generated for discourses have to be addressed to others as *propositions* or *problems*. "The problem and the proposition differ in the way they are stated. If we say Is not 'pedestrian biped animal' a definition of man? Or is not 'animal' the genus of man?, a proposition is formed. But if we say 'Is pedestrian biped animal' a definition of man or not?, a problem is formed" (Aristotle, 1961:281). A proposition is a statement that admits of no doubt or uncertainty but does not have to be as explicit as either of Aristotle's examples. Indeed, propositions are often implicit and so do not begin in the same form as Aristotle's. "The moon is full today" is as much a proposition as the claim "Is not the moon full today?" The proposition and the problem are two constituent features of topics generated in discursive interactions.

Typically, the choice and presentation of such topics is meant to maximize the emergence of the chances of a dialogue and a social relationship. The importance of making a circumspect choice of a topic meant to carry the intentionality of the self and the signifying force of a communication cannot be exaggerated, because the topic becomes the substance, the very essence of discursive acts. If one does not have any topic or does not have a topic relevant to the situation and to the others present in the situation, then the other elements of the act will not be able to manifest themselves and the selves that are implicated will not have the necessary sustaining dialogue and may well wither on the vine. Topics of discourse are not mere pegs on which interactions are hanged, or an incident and occasion for some people to come together, but rather are the very bases on which people come together and are the means by which selves are meshed. Because of topics, lives can become connected, and it is on the basis of such connections that lives are lived and sustained. If there were nothing to talk about, selves could not sustain themselves in a dialogue, and so moments of dialogue and relationships between dialogues would not emerge. To find another for a discursive relationship also is to find a topic of discourse and to find a topic of discourse is to find a dialogue. Indeed, one can consider the various experiences people gather in the daily course of their lives as a collection of topics that can be used to construct dialogues and to nourish selves.

Consider, as strategic examples, two common modern experiences that are collected with some dedication: going to the movies and going on tours to foreign lands. On the one hand, the lived experiences provide drama and dialogue as they are occurring to sustain the self. On the other, once those brief shining moments are gone they nevertheless persist as data that can be used in the making and enriching of conversations. One may not consciously go to movies or on tours to provide *talkables* for the self; rather, participation in various activities is converted into a commodity, the talkables serving to ensure one's membership as well as providing for the dialogue's sustenance.

In producing propositions and generating topics through discourse one not only presents selves but demonstrates their essential qualities, details, and nuances. For example, a silly, foolish, contradictory, trivial, or senseless proposition will so define the self and the interaction that emerges. Conversely, propositions that are *not* silly, foolish, trivial or irrelevant will readily elicit engagement. Consider the following:

A: I talked to Joe.
B: About what?
A: About his trip.
B: Where did he go?
A: He went to Philadelphia and was mugged, and to New York where he was arrested.

(Covelli and Murray, 1981:382)

A simple enough conversation, which can be examined in terms of its technical features, i.e., about topic, subtopic, and how they are ordered. However, one can find additional points of interest. To begin with, A and B are able to talk to each other and have a common theme, namely Joe. Fortunately for their interaction, Joe has done something *talkworthy*: he has gone somewhere and returned with news. In fact, he has experienced what may even be described as adventures. He has been mugged in Philadelphia and arrested in new York. Clearly all that is going on here is no mere organization of a topic. Rather, the topic has enmeshed two selves, and the introduction of Joe's misfortunes has created a semblance of emotionality. A is not merely imparting information about Joe, but presenting a self through a discursive act and B is responding to it in his or her own intentionality. To appreciate this fully, we need to know more about A and B, and about Joe's relationship to each of them. If Joe were a dearly beloved common friend, the topic would have one significance. If on the other hand Joe was A[nne]e's ex-lover and B[rian] her present one, the acts and the interactions would have an altogether different meaning for the selves.

In any case, whatever identities each may bear, there is no doubt that their discourse, trivial though it appears to be, is one in which two selves were sustained and their relationships constituted by means of a proposition. If A had come in and said, "I talked to Joe," and the only Joe they knew in common and in whom they shared a discursive interest had been dead for some time this would not have worked. B would have had to ask: "Which Joe?" If A had responded "Joe my brother" and if this were the Joe who was dead, it is safe to say that B would have had a certain difficulty that can be identified as a failure to establish a topic for discussion. This failure would not be based on the fact that A and B did not share a formal feature of discourse, but on the fact that the two did not have a common "universe of discourse" (Mead, 1934:89). Of course, if the two were believers in communication with people who are dead and A were in fact a medium for conversations with those on the other side, a structure of plausibility would exist and therefore a topic would be generated. Clearly the topics generated have to encompass propositions that can subsume the structures of plausibility that are held in common by participants in discursive interaction. Failure to do this will bring the self of the implausible utterer into question and disrepute with the implausibility being taken as a sign of the damage and disorder done to the discursive interaction. But before coming to this conclusion, the respondents will continue to seek to establish a plausible commonality by clarification and probing. Consider these opening words between a therapist (A) and a patient (B):

A:   I appreciate your coming here at such short notice.
B:   Fine.

A: How old are you now?
B: I was born in 1939. So I am 32. But I might be younger than that now.

(Spitzer and William, 1984, Audio tape)

The patient begins plausibly enough, but suddenly says something that seems strange: she can be younger than the years she claims for herself. This violates rules of arithmetic and chronological reckoning, which are part of the culture in which the patient and the therapist live. A, like a good therapist, does not pounce on this but goes on to something else:

A: You have been in the hospital, how long?
B: From Saturday up until today—which is a couple of days or more.

(1984, Audio Tape)

Again, one can see a certain haziness about the reckoning of time. However, these conclusions about a disordered discourse are shattered when the patient is given a chance to explain. Ever so gently the therapist introduces the contradiction in her claims about her age:

A: You said you might be younger than that?
B: Yes; In other words, I react younger than that. I am thirty two actually.

(1984, Audio Tape)

Now it can be seen that her remark about age was not about chronology but her reactions, attitudes, and acts, making it a plausible claim. As stated before, the details of topic generation and response must conform to an a priori structure of plausibility conforming to Aristotle's view of a dialectical proposition: "Does it accord with the opinion held by everyone or by a majority or by the wise"? (1961:195). In the excerpt quoted above, the therapist probed the patient's apparent violation of this rule. Implausible propositions are rarely unremarked by others who search for plausibility. When this search is given up, the other's self too is abandoned. In this case the therapist's searches find a very plausible qualification to the earlier claim and so the matter was settled and he proceeded to the next step.

In some discursive interactions a simple preposition is enough to sustain a conversation. But in other interactions, problems in the Aristotelian sense are necessary. As Aristotle says, "No man of sense would put into a . . . problem, that which is manifest to everyone or to most people—for it raises no question" (1961:295). In other words, if the statement made by A to B ("I talked to Joe") was about their son, about whom there was no contentions issue at hand, there would be no problem as far as B was concerned—that A talked to Joe is not a response to any problem A has indicated. A's comment is now banal and undramatic, and the engagement of the selves with each other via a topic will be somewhat stalled by this bit of talk. In fact, statements like A's are likely to create boredom, leading either to the termination of relationships or a reluctance to engage with those who produce this kind of discourse. As Kierkegaard noted, "boredom depends on the nothingness which permeates existence; its dizziness is infinite like that which comes by looking down onto an endless abyss" (1986:82). One form of this nothingness is the *discursive nothingness* that comes when the other does not bother to produce an effective text.

Besides propositions and problems there is the narrative form of topics that emerge as talkables in interactions. *Narratives* are stories about others or about oneself that are brought forth as discursive material. These have a structure of development from one point to another as well as a grammar. A number of theories of narrative have been forthcoming in recent years. Structuralist theory has a version that seems parsimonious and relevant to our purposes here. This theory suggests that a narrative has two essential parts: (1) the chain of events or happenings, the characters, and the setting, which can be called the *story*, and (2) the *discourse*, which consists of the means by which the story is communicated (Chatman, 1978:19). The interactions and relationships between the characters in the narrative and the problems they are made to face, however truncated they may be in the telling, must have sufficient import, to borrow a word from Suzanne Langer (1953). Import, which is more than the sum of the literal meaning of a narrative, is achieved by the management of the various meanings of the narrative's different elements in order to formulate a delimited emotionality. In giving import to narratives, "Structure, diction, imagery, the use of names, . . . [and] allusions" become the "creative devices that someone's imagination has seized upon in making the image of life that was to express his 'idea' " (Langer, 1953:281).

In everyday discourse, one introduces narrative in order to elicit an engaged response from the other. However, the narrative is also a presentation of self, with the story and the nature of the dénouement becoming features of what the other will take to be expressions of certain features of one's self. That is to say, the telling itself offers moments in which a self is presented and validated or rejected, as the case may be.

That the narrative will bear signs of the self is certainly true, but few would have come to see this so lucidly as a man who was to become a famous American psychologist did on one occasion. Only twenty two, and visiting Vienna, he had asked Freud to let him come and see him. If one goes to see a famous person at one's own urging, it is best to have a topic ready for discourse. Gordon Allport had apparently not done so, and he tells us, "He [Freud] did not speak but sat in expectant silence [waiting] for me to state my mission. I was not prepared for silence and had to think fast to find a suitable conversational gambit. I told him of an episode on the tram car on my way to his office. A small boy about four years of age had displayed a dirtphobia. He kept saying to his mother 'I don't want to sit there—don't let that dirty man sit besides me'. To him everything was *schmutzig*. His mother was a well-starched *Hausfrau*, so dominant and purposive looking that I thought the cause and effect were apparent" (1968:383).

Allport had introduced two characters to Freud, well described for the purposes at hand, and had recounted an event between the two and examined its import. It has no standard denouement but does have an ending—the child moving from one place to another. However, Freud was ready with his own analysis, readily seeing the narrative as a presentation of self. Allport continues, "When I finished my story, Freud fixed his kindly therapeutic eye upon me and said 'And are you that little boy?' Flabbergasted, and feeling a bit guilty, I proceeded to change the subject" (1968:383).

This piece of interaction contains three elements—a story, discourse and, import. The story can be described thus: a boy, who had a dirt phobia. A mother who is a well-starched *Hausfrau*, dominant and purposeful looking. The boy protests about a dirty man near him and moves to another seat. The real cause of his phobia is the attitude and character of the mother herself. Once these elements of the story are presented, there is a denouement: Freud's quick and unexpected analytic observation, which serves as a climax to the story. The discourse is the systematic way by which the story is conveyed to the audience. There are descriptions of the boy and his mother, capsule characterizations, a direct quotation of the boy's words, and another from the auditor coming at the end and giving a dramatic closure. The import of the story is the emotionality of varying colors that the story-telling is able to generate. There is the initial embarrassment at having nothing to say. Then the rather triumphant display by Allport of his awareness not only of his surroundings in the tram, but of the significance of what he had observed and then the final embarrassment of being identified by Freud as the little boy in the story.

The little boy may or not have been his own self to Gordon Allport, but the telling of a story is a discursive interaction in which a self is presented by means of a narrative structure. In addition to the self that Freud saw in the narrative, Allport also disclosed a perspicaciously selected event that had import, contained characters, and displayed his knowledge about German or Austrian culture. Brief though the story was, it nevertheless had enough material to elicit interest and serve as

an opening gambit. Further, when the telling was over, Allport under-
took a change of topic when he felt threatened by the line Freud was
inclined to take.

In addition to narratives of this kind, interactants introduce erotic
stories, shaggy dog stories, ethnic jokes, all of which are narratives, as
well as "true" stories about their friends or themselves. These all fulfill
the demands for a narrative text, which is that they must function as
instruments with which to elicit the *engrossment* of the other and to work
efficiently at sustaining a self through discourse. Often when dealing
with propositions and problems, one becomes intellectually engaged in
creating narratives, whereby emotional identification and disidentifica-
tion are made to emerge in order to elicit the engrossment of the
participants. It is not that propositions and problems have no emotional
components or that narratives are free of intellectual ones. Rather, it is
that in the former two intellectual and rational properties are dominant,
while the latter is dominated by emotional ones.

The chief instrument by which narratives achieve engrossment is by
providing hearers with one or more characters with whom to identify or/
and disidentify. This may be called *engrossment in character*. If the story is
logical and consistent, one gets *engrossment in plot*, and if the ideas
presented in the story are significant and clear enough, one may get
*intellectual engagement* as well.

Propositions or/and narratives enable a self to enter the consciousness
of the other and the other self to enter the consciousness of the articulator. That is, topics with these features allow people to interact, and thus
the topics become the ground and field of discourse. Pragmatic and
instrumental as well, these topics serve various purposes for the self and
the other. They are emotional in nature in that they bring people into
contact with each other, and intellectual in nature in that they allow
people to occupy their minds with each other's inputs and outputs.
Finally, to the extent that they possess certain internal features, discourses enable a mind to be occupied with them. Indeed, if the discourse presented to a mind is not capable of occupying the mind top-
ically, the mind becomes preoccupied, gets "away," and may even in
Goffman's terminology, show a tendency for "occult involvement"
(1963:75–79).

## Irony and Interaction

The fundamental feature of human communication is that human
minding is not only capable of constructing discourses with great flexibility insofar as it uses a flexible medium, but can also effectively
interpret and anticipate the effects discourses will bear before they are

given voice and as they are being given voice. Having arrived at this moment of construction, a self may even anticipate its own responses to the anticipated responses of the other. Discourse, then, can be *reflexively layered* in terms of the significance meant to be conveyed and the meanings meant to be elicited.

By changes of one sort or another, elements along the entire gamut of the discursive act can in fact either be transformed into their opposites or altered so as to indicate varying shades of significations. The reflexive and reflexively reflexive nature of self, language, and discourse can be performed in a way that will either enhance the act, magnifying its significance, subtly undermine, or convey multiple and at times contradictory significations.

Irony most clearly displays the reflexively layered nature of discourse. Kenneth Burke has written "We cannot use language maturely until we are spontaneously at home in irony" (cited in Boothe, 1974:xii). And no theory of meaning, interaction, and social relationships can be complete without an appreciation of the uses of irony. Irony's presence, capacities, and power in discursive communication reveal the essential nature of language, minding and, interaction. A displaced word, a subtle alteration in tone, a misplaced interpretation and response and the entire meaning of assembled words is radically changed. Icons, indices, and symbols do not mean anything except through human intentionalities and in human interactions, and these intentionalities *play with each other* by transforming them categorically, phonologically, syntactically, and socially in ever expanding parameters of signification.

In a comprehensive study of irony, Wayne Boothe notes, "Every good reader must, among other things, be sensitive in detecting and reconstructing ironic meanings" (1974:1). This is no doubt what every reader must do and, I venture to say, what every listener must do as long as he or she lives and suffers in a speech community. Still, Boothe notes, it is possible either to miss the irony or to see it where there is none, but in either case, the response gives rise to definite consequences in social life. One must therefore be alert to the possible ironies of discursive productions, and Booth provides a guide to their detection. His "marks" of irony, ironic significations:

(i)  are all *intended*, deliberately created by human beings to be heard or read and understood with some precision by other human beings; they are not mere openings, provided unconsciously nor are they accidental statements allowing the confirmed pursuer of ironies to read them as reflections against the author.

(ii)  are *covert*, intended to be reconstructed with meanings different from those on the surface, not merely overt statements . . .

(iii)  are nevertheless *stable* or fixed in the sense that once a reconstruction of meaning has been achieved, the reader is not then invited to undermine it with further demolitions and reconstructions.

(iv)   are all *finite* in application, in contrast with those infinite ironies. . . .
       The reconstruction of meanings are in some sense local, limited.
       (1974:5–6)


Ironies, (ii) to be constructed and reconstructed with the above considerations in mind, are used to signify intentions, but with style and
grace as well as with attention to the self of the other. Nevertheless, we
must distinguish between irony that is playful and whimsical and that
which is hostile and contemptuous. Consider the following: A man is
frantically at work in his apartment setting things right for the evening
party. Only his woman companion has arrived, and she is sitting se-
renely on the couch. The man says: "You do not have to help, really."
She laughs, and gets up to help clean the apartment.

Another Booth sample draws attention to the importance of alert
interpretation:

> As my family recently walked toward the cathedral, highly visible before
> us, in Angers, a cement worker looked at us and said, at first without a
> smile, "The Cathedral is that way"—pointing to it—"and the Palace of
> Justice is there"—pointing out the sign on the building right before our
> eyes that read "Palais de Justice."
>   I knew he intended an ironic stroke, though I could not at first be sure
> whether we were to be excluded as mere victims—stupid American tour-
> ists who would not recognize the deliberate absurdity of such obvious and
> uncalled for direction. But we were clearly webbed within the circle of
> ironists as soon as I said, "Oh yes, and the workers are *here* (pointing to
> them) and the Americans are here (pointing at us)." His laughter told me
> he now knew that I knew that he knew that I . . . The circle of inferences
> was closed, and we knew each other in ways that only extended conversa-
> tion could otherwise have revealed. (1974:30–31)


The situational and contextual nuances and subtleties common to the
language and the community enable the articulator to project ironic
force into his or her discourses. Indeed, without some mastery of these
various features of the language it will not be possible to be a full
member of the community in question.

In presenting an ironic discourse, a self achieves a variety of purposes.
Sometimes, the purpose is to deflate the other's pompous or smug self-
presentations. Boothe provides a relevant story:

> Student    Things are turning up good all over. I got my scholarship, I got a
>    A:       date with Jessie for tomorrow night, my dad just wrote and said
>             I could have a car.
> Student B:  You know what, you lead a fine rich life.

Student   Oh well, things aren't always good for me . . . (He looks up and
A:        sees scorn in the other student's eyes. He blushes.)
          You know what, you are a real prince, a real prince.

(Booth, 1974:5)

The irony here seeks to undermine the smug self of the other by a remark that is a little awry: fellow students do not typically pay such compliments to each other and when they are in fact paid they indicate a covert significance. The respondent here is momentarily taken in but sees the irony only after reading the other's gaze. The "scorn" in the other's eyes signals the irony in the discourse and ensures that the intentions are correctly interpreted. The response that student A provides, once he has read the intention correctly, is interesting in its own right. It is an example of sarcasm, and signals that this time he has read the remark correctly. If student B was seeking to reduce the smugness in the other, student A with his sarcasm seeks to redeem some of his esteem by remarking that the other is being anything but "princely" and has been cruel to a friend. In cases of both irony and sarcasm, there is a covert significance to the text that is intended, stable, and finite. The irony and the sarcasm were both used to assert and define a self and to defend the integrity of the interaction and value of the relationship by eliminating the threat of an excessive pride and smugness. At each stage of this simple and ordinary episode, a symbolic construction of a very precise significance had to be achieved, reflexively anticipating its overt meaning and then its covert meaning with the recipient having to do the same. The significances in the discourse could be said to be dialectically layered with the recipient having to unravel them as he or she went along.

## Notes

1.   It is, of course, not the case that jesters in all courts function in this way. Nevertheless, the complex roles that they do play in court life are essentially connected to the power structures of the court and the influences they have on communication. For example, the king in his exalted position cannot be easily humorous and friendly with his counselors, nor certainly they with him. However, the jester can joke with the king and the king can talk freely with him in turn—indeed the king can experience easier dialogic moments with the jester than with anyone else. Fools and jesters have similar roles in the theater: a dramatist can use the fool as a foil to advance the plot, the fool's presence giving the king opportunities for discourse that cannot be addressed elsewhere. The serious function they fulfill in courts should not, however, obscure the fact that they are also entertainers who enliven the business and art of the court. The jester and the fool have been the subject of many studies. Enid Welsford's survey of the fool in history and drama remains a classic ([1935] 1966). In recent

years William Willeford has undertaken a phenomenological analysis of the clown, the jester, and his audience (1969). Empson offers a critical examination of the fool and the jester in "The Praise of Folly," "Fool in Lear," both in *The Structure of Complex Words* (1969). (Quotations from *King Lear* come from *Shakespeare: The Complete Works*, edited by G. B. Harrison. New York: Harcourt Brace & World, 1952.)

2.   For an excellent examination of the use made of discursive practices to establish honor and to claim status in medieval European society see Frank Whigham's *Ambition and Privilege*, particularly the last chapter, "The Rhetorical Semiotics at Court" (1984:32–62).

3.   See Coulthard (1985:79–88) for a summary of the views of the ethnomethodologists.

# Forms of
# Discourse

## — 6 —

Discursive acts typically are constituted in such a way that certain formal structures that influence and inform the nature of the interaction that emerges can be seen in them. A discursive act by itself offers the possibility of varied responses and interpretations from an external world, which creates for the self the opportunities to enmesh its life with that of others. In the web of discourses in which humans live, every moment is constituted by the use of one form of discourse or other. These forms may be nebulous and defy classification. However, it is possible to delineate some of the forms by which this web is constructed and to specify the consequences for self and interaction. These forms of discourse—analogous to Bakhtin's (1986) *speech genres* and Lyotard's *modes of discourse* (1989)—have elicited discussion in their guise as speech acts. Lyotard himself, discussing what he terms the "pragmatic aspect" of language use, following J.L. Austin describes utterances as being either "performatives" or "prescriptions." The former are described as acts in which the effects of the utterance "coincide with its enunciation" (1988:9), and the latter, "modulated as orders, commands, instructions, recommendations, requests, prayers, pleas, etc.," as acts in which "the sender is clearly in a position of authority, using the term broadly: that is, he expects the addressee to perform the action referred to" (1988:10). Lyotard adds certain refinements to Austin's positions and Wittgenstein's thesis about "modes of discourse being language games—that is actions defined by specific rules of practice and usage." First, the rules that define a language game "do not carry within themselves their own legitimation, but are the object of a contract, explicit or not between players." Second, notes Lyotard, "even an infinitesimal modification of one rule alters the nature of the game." Finally, he argues that "Every utterance should be thought of as a "move" in a game" (1988:10).

There is however a major problem: neither Austian's nor Wittgenstein's view on the uses of language has a place for the character and quality of the performer–user. Lyotard goes very far from the *deperson-*

*alized* theories of Austin and Wittgenstein but not far enough. He writes, "A *self* does not amount to much, but no self is an island; each exists in a fabric of relations that is more complex and mobile than ever before. Young or old, man or woman, rich or poor, a person is always located at 'nodal points' of specific communication circuits, however tiny these may be" (Lyotard, 1988:15). The self may or may not amount to much, but a reflexive self is all a human actor is, and a self is that which exists at the nodal points of communication and that which receives the communication. Discursive forms are used by such selves to elicit certain responses from other selves and do not exist as depersonalized and suigeneris phenomena.

By acting discursively, a person enters a life with others, opening himself or herself up to all manners and possibilities of responsive acts. The act projected can be rebuffed, rejected forcefully, or ignored; or it can be accepted forcefully, subtly, ambiguously, politely, encouragingly, or tentatively, thus providing sustenance to the self of the articulator and the interaction. To some extent the nature of the response can be predetermined by the nature of the discursive act that is proffered. And, of course, there can be no meaningful response before a signifying act is offered in one or another form. In everyday life a person articulates and encounters a number of such acts, each having particular social and structural features. To the extent that the dialogic self exists, it exists in and through very specific discursive processes used in their constitution. The particularities of these acts, and the types they represent, become the instruments by which the emotional and intellectual features of the self and its essential integrated quality are created and sustained.

One can attempt at most a partial classification and description of such acts, based on the functions they perform in interactions and social relationships and in the manifestation and maintenance of selves. My focus will be on the interactional function of the discourse as it seeks and elicits its effects by manifesting specific structural characteristics. While some forms may resemble others, such a resemblance is overridden by a different function in the interaction and in the maintenance of the self. The descriptions of the various forms of discourse and their likely function in interactions and constitution of self offered here are brief, and a chapter could be written on each of the forms.


## Demands and Requests

Interactants often have to ask for certain specific responses. These askings contain a definition of the self relevant to the particular context and to the nature of the relationship that is envisaged with the other.

Forceful imperative askings may be called *demands*; prayers, importunings and invitations may be called *requests*. When a person makes a demand, he or she defines his or her self and that of the other, and also establishes the parameters of the ensuing relationship and dialogue. A demander indicates an unequal power distribution in the relationship, and forestalls the emergence of a friendly and affable interaction by creating a relationship of an adversarial nature. To the degree that he or she has the socially defined right to make this demand, he or she has also asserted his or her self, and to the extent that the demand is complied with, the self is validated. However, if he or she overlooks the right to make the demand and instead makes a request, a more complex and subtly varied relationship is created with the other. Even in this case, the self of the articulator is validated by the emergence of a commensurate response, but at the same time the self of the recipient gets protection and is perhaps even enriched by the act. Nonetheless, that the articulator is the self who selects the nature of the act, by demand or by request, endows him or her with an extra measure of power and authority, which confers a special complexity on the relationship. The recipient can feel grateful for not having been subjected to authoritarian humiliation but nevertheless acknowledge that the power to either enhance or diminish his or her self rests with the other.

Consider this in the following extract as President Nixon (B) and his legal advisor John Dean (A) are conversing. A secretary intervenes:

A: Good morning, Sir.
B: Oh, Hi.
A: How are you?
B: I wanted to talk with you about what kind of a line to take. I now want Kleindienst on the—it isn't a matter of trust. You have it clearly understood that you will call him and give him directions and he will call you, etcetera, and so on, and so on. I just don't want Dick to go off—you see, for example, on executive privilege—I don't want him to get off and get the damn thing—get us—
A: Make any deals on it—
B: Make a deal—that is the point. Baker, as I said, is going to keep at arms length and you have got to be very firm with these guys or you may not end up with many things . . .
A: Yeah.
B: (To Secretary) I sent some notes out—a couple of yellow pages—something on the teachers' thing that I am not doing today—just send it back to me, please.
Secretary: Alright, Sir.
B: So you see, I think you better have a good, hard face to face talk with him and say, look, we have thought this thing over. And

you raise the point with him that this cannot be in executive session because he is likely to float it out there and they will grab it.

A: That's right, and as I mentioned yesterday he is meeting with Sam Ervin and Baker in this joint session and that is probably one of the first things they will discuss.

(Woodward and Bernstein, 1974: 43–44)

In this conversational interaction, the president of the United States is asking his assistant to undertake certain acts. In the course of asking, he is apparently interrupted by his secretary to whom he then gives an order. This order is couched in structures of politeness and decorum: "just send it back to me, please." This elicits a response from the secretary that includes a titular salutation, "Alright, Sir." Similarly, his orders to Dean are couched in the language of requests: "have a hard face to face talk" with someone, "raise the point with him," etc. Irrespective of the intonations used, the formulation of the intentions does not bear anything else but politeness and consideration for the self of the other. In this interaction, the president is, in terms of status and power, clearly superior to both his secretary and his legal assistant. Nevertheless, he handles the relationships with a presumptive equality that protects the selves of the subordinates. Indeed, it can be said that the superordinate has been providing his subordinates signs with which their selves can be constituted or refurbished. This equalitarian mode performed here routinely and matter-of-factly is prescribed by American culture, so that only when these routines are violated does the significance of these signs for the selves become apparent, as in the cases of rejection, hostility, worthlessness, incompetence, and unlovedness.

These askings may be couched as demands in other relationships. In the following excerpt, made famous in sociology by Erving Goffman (1961a: 17), Brendan Behan (C) is subject to a number of demands from his prospective warden Whitbread (A) and his assistant Holmes (B) at an institute for the juvenile offender:

A: And 'old up your 'ead, when I speak to you.
B: 'old up your 'ead, when Mr. Whitbread speaks to you.

. . . . . . . . . . . . . . . . . . . .

A: What are you looking at, Behan? Look at me.

. . . . . . . . . . . . . . . . . . . .

C: I am looking at you.
B: You are looking at Mr. Whitbread—what?
C: I am looking at Mr. Whitbread
Mr. Holmes looked gravely at Mr. Whitbread, drew back his open hand and struck me on the face, held me with his other hand and struck me again. . . .

B: You are looking at Mr. Whitbread,—what, Behan?
I gulped and got together my voice and tried again till I got it out. "I sir, please sir, I am looking at you, I mean I am looking at Mr. Whitbread, sir."

(Behan, 1958:40)

The structures of demand in this conversation are varied. The initial statement is without prefixes and suffixes—no names, terms of address, or titles, but a short staccato set of words asking for a particular action. The structure of the sentence and the sense are well matched here: the sense is a demand to look at the face of the other, to face the words he is about to utter, and an interference with the freedom of the person to choose how he wishes to hold his head. The same values are carried forward in the next series of words and actions. Short imperative sentences are matched by slaps on Behan's face and together these constitute a structure of demands that will make Behan submissive and contrite, which will lead him to provide the mandatory deferential salutation at the end of every sentence. These words and moves by Whitbread and Holmes are calculated affirmations of their respective selves and of the collective identity of their professional selves that thus become the signs of their self-constitution subject to interpretant responses culminating into a maxisign. The same can be said for Behan, although in his case the demands are for an alteration in his conduct. The demands make him a captive, and his consequent submissiveness and docility become signs he must interpretively absorb into his self. The manner, style, and particular contents of the demand reinforce these signs and begin a turn in the career of the self that, depending on what happens in the thereafter, may or may not breed a number of consequences. In fact, the upshot of these demands and the consequential humiliation of a self might well be the emergence of bitter and resentful habits of the self, making it a habitual "malcontent" and "criminal."

## Instructions

The instructor as a discursive actor typically has both rhetorical and political power as well as the knowledge the other wants or needs. By definition the instructor has an awesome status because he or she can fill the mind of the other and shape his or her self.

The inequality of the discursive structure contributes signs to the selves that are interacting. Consider this excerpt from a conversation between a teacher (A) and her pupil (B):

A:   Well, suppose I let you tell them what has happened recently that I dislike.
B:   I been talking out of class at school and acting up.
A:   And did I teach you how to do that?
B:   No mam.
A:   What did I teach you to do?
B:   To sit on my seat.
A:   And?
B:   And don't say a word until the teacher tell me.
A:   And you failed to do that.
B:   Yes mam.
A:   Well don't you think it would be a good idea for us to sit down and talk this over with Marge and maybe she'll give us some of her ideas about this some other time as to whether you should be doing these things or not.
B:   Yes, mam.

(Loman, 1967:57)

This conversation is instructional in its own terms and in its references to instructions given earlier. But the sheer volume of words and the length of the sentences the superordinate produces carries their own discursive weight, which constrains the recipient to short, and at times, disyllabic answers. The content of the discourse defines one participant as possessing knowledge about proper deportment of self in a particular situation and the other as a transgressor. The entire passage has a stance: one can imagine the teacher, tall and imposing, standing over the pupil engaging in her discursive act. The final summary reinforces her authority and power and incorporates a third party as an ally in her act.

This exchange has many facets. The teacher's self is embellished by acts of instruction and enlightenment—signs that enhance her self. She brings her pupil to submission and recitation of proper class deportment and allows the entire performance to be witnessed by an outsider, who further validates the teacher's self. Of course the pupil's dependent, subordinate, recipient status is reinforced by the structure of the interaction as well as the discourse: the signs that the child gathers defines him as a miscreant and subordinate who must, in the future, incorporate some further signs into his self if he is to receive approbation and validation from the teacher and Marge.

The dialogue is an extreme example of this kind of discursive act. Often the signs generated in such interactions are more subtly wrapped in fabrics of politeness and courtesy, or irony and sarcasm. But these too provide effective signs of the self.

## Compliments

Compliments are signs of an evaluation, a judgment about an aspect of an other's self, about that self's performance in a given context, and its comparative standing with other moments or with relevant others. Overt, direct, obvious, and pointed compliments, for example, "That's a beautiful dress you are wearing" or "This is a very fine research paper," are acts that build the self in obvious and clear ways. Of course, the respondent's own evaluation of the articulator is crucial. If the articulator is one who pays compliments too freely and loosely, their value will be low as compared to compliments offered by one given to considered and "measured" comments. Status and power also play a part in a self's evaluation of a complimentary sign. For example, praise from a respected professor about a research paper would have more weight for the self than the praise offered by another student. The emotional power inherent in complimentary discursive acts connected with love and loving is twofold. (1)  The content of the discourse reveals the conceptual form of the articulator's ideas of the recipient. For example, a favorable comment about a dress can imply good taste, good investment, a good figure or perhaps even overall approval of the other's erotic and esthetic presence. (2)  Such signs define the significance of the whole discursive encounter. Clearly, complimentary signs contribute to the constitution of the self of the recipient and can accumulate into patterned aspects of the maxisign of the self. However, there is always a danger of inflation: too many compliments, uncritically and too easily issued, or rendered without warrant and justification make them valueless. Flattery is a systematic set of compliments about another, but to be effective they must be seen to be sincere, and not cross the razor's edge over into the manipulative. And because not everyone can make the distinction, many find that discursive acts that they believe were well-meant turn out to be manipulative.

An articulator paying a compliment often feels a duty to set the limits of the value to be placed on it. Free-floating compliments leave their valuative bases vague and unspecific, a practice not always politic or wise. For instance: "You write well—for a foreigner." The first part is an unabashed compliment, and if said by a professor to a student in whose life writing well matters, it becomes a positive contribution to the self. However, the tail of the remark, like that of a scorpion, packs a sting: you are a good writer only by particular standards. The context within which a compliment is given can transform it into an ambiguous force.

However, in intimate relationships as well as in merely friendly ones, a compliment can put the self of the articulator on the line. For example, a compliment may be ignored; the recipient simply chooses to *unhear* it:

A:   You are indeed looking lovely tonight.
B:   Aren't you going to dance with Eunice?

This is gentle rebuff that has given the self of the articulator another shape at least for now, vis-à-vis his relationship with this person. There are, of course, stronger rebuffs:

A:   You are looking very lovely tonight.
B:   What? You shouldn't be saying things like that to me Harry. It makes me wonder what you are up to.

In sum, by means of compliments a self is proffered and the responses of the other help define that self. Such definitions enable the interactants to define the moment and their relationship, and so pass on to the next stage.

## Insults

If we can praise others we can also devalue them. Insults are discursive acts that undermine and refute the self of the other. They are issued with appropriate tonal, linguistic, and symbolic characteristics, and are constituted by signs directed at both the other and the articulator's self. An insult must be understood by the other to be effective, and so it must be related to the self of the other to find its mark. An insult, then, challenges the maxisign of the self, seeking to undermine or tarnish it. For example, to call a man a woman is an insult because he has carefully constructed an integrated and coherent text of "manhood" as his self. Such a self has a cognitive form and a cognitive structure limned with culturally induced anxieties and tensions. However, calling a transvestite a woman might be considered a compliment.

Insults may be distinguished by their degree of power. Those that "cut to the quick" elicit strong reactions, while those that are mild can occasion repartee rather than anger. The power of an insult depends on the capacity of the signs deployed to undermine that aspect of the other's self considered to be dominant or important. Further, insults to superiors as opposed to insults from superiors have different signifying values. In medieval Italy, a canon who insulted another was fined twenty lire, but if he insulted a chaplain the fine was only five. Peter Burke in his study of the anthropology of early modern Italy writes, "Generally speaking, insults by inferiors to superiors were taken very seriously. In fourteenth century Venice 'verbal violence' against the doge or lesser officials of the commune was severely punished (sometimes by cutting off the offender's tongue)" (1987:99). In these cases, punishment for violating the social status of a self is provided for by the city state's legal code.

All forms of insult attack a cherished aspect of the self. Whether true or false, the discursive act's metaphorical and tonal qualities create umbrage and hostility, and can bring an audience to question the victim's reputation. Immediate reactions cover a varied spectrum embracing counterinsult, sullen silence, acceptance, indifference, refusal to acknowledge, or violent physical response from recipients who have neither patience nor capacity for self-defending or self-asserting words. Insults to an absent person are slanders that can be taken up by the victim only at a later time. Nevertheless, these too are meant to produce signs that undermine the slandered's self.

### Retorts

Many diverse discursive strategies besides the insult can be used to injure a self in one way or another. Complaints and contradictions are forms for doing this directly, and many other forms of discourse used ironically achieve similar effects. A self's defensive measures, such as rebuttals, rejections, counter complaints, and denials, can be subsumed under the title of retorts. The classic rhetorical analysis of the retort as a discursive strategy is Touchstone's speech in *As You Like It*:

> Jaques: But for the seventh cause, how did you find the quarrel on the seventh cause?
>
> Touchstone: Upon a lie seven times removed . . . as thus, sir. I did dislike the cut of a certain courtier's beard. He sent me word if I said his beard was not cut well, he was in the mind it was. This is called the Retort Courteous. If I sent him word again "it was not well cut," he would send me word he cut it to please himself. This is called the Quip Modest. If again "it was not well cut," he disabled my judgment. This is called the Reply Churlish. If again "it was not well cut," he would answer I spake not true. This is called the Reproof Valiant. If against "it was not well cut," he would say I lie. This is called the Countercheck Quarrelsome. And so to the Lie Circumstantial and the Lie Direct.
>
> (5.4.69–86)

The beard, subject of Touchstone's insult is, or course, the sign of the self. It is the self that is offended, and it is defended by a simple detail of the charge at stage one, by a modest affirmation of one's right to determine his own beard in stage two, and in stage three by challenging the other. In the next three stages the rhetorical style becomes grave: the insulted self is more assertive now, indeed more valiant. This is followed by a return insult that calls the insulter a liar, setting the stage for a quarrel, and is followed by the retort of the circumstantial and direct lie. Touchstone's discourse does not tell us what the last two are for, but they can obviously be used either to augment or modify the previous claim that the insulter is a liar.

> Touchstone:   . . . All these you may avoid but the Lie Direct, and you may avoid that too, with an "If." I knew when seven justices could not take up a quarrel, but when the parties were met themselves, one of them thought but of an "If," as "If you said so, then I said so," and they shook hands and swore brothers. Your "If" is the only peacemaker, much virtue in "If."

> (5.4.101–8)

So in everyday interactions retorts are used to defend the self. As we have seen, the insulter makes a charge directed to a socially valuable and cherished aspect of the self that an effective retort needs to disarm. We see this in the following:

> Michael J.:   I bet you a nickel.
> George J.:   What?
> Michael J.:   Gotta see some money . . . bet you a nickel that I am looking sharper than you.
> George J.:   No you wasn't.
> Michael J.:   No you had your play clothes on (laughter).
> George J.:   I ain't have my play clothes on.
> Michael J.:   You had your Batman socks on too.
> George J.:   I did (laughs) did not.
> Michael J.:   You did (laughs) so.
> George J.:   a? a?
> Michael J.:   Got something else to say?
> George J.:   Wait a minute—let me tell you something. Greg Barker look better than you. You come in here with your clothes hanging down all the way down to here (laughs).

> (Loman, 1967:1)

George's last statement introduces a challenge and then a retort: "You come in here with all your clothes hanging down all the way down to here." George's initial retort, denying Michael's claim outright with a "No you wasn't," is followed by the reason why George cannot concede that Michael looks sharp. The boys insult and retort, but it occurs in the context of a bantering brotherly relationship and does not lead to the crossing of swords.

If an insult or a charge is made and no retort is made, the charge is left as a label for the self in question. The insulter will be able to take the charge as having been accepted by the other and the recipient will either have to accept it publicly or smolder indignantly in secret and face the consequences. Retorts do not always repel the charges made:

Maya: Well, why did I attack you? Perhaps I was looking for something I lacked—affection, maybe it was greed for affection.
Mother: You wouldn't have any of that. You always think that is sloppy.
Maya: Well when did you offer it to me?
Mother: Well, for instance if I was to want to kiss you, you'd say, "Don't be sloppy."
Maya: But I have never know you to let me kiss you

(Laing and Esterson, 1970:36).

In this interaction we find charges and retorts made by both parties: the mother responds to the daughter's charge by claiming that she had only been conforming to the daughter's standards. Although this particular encounter has not resolved the issues, the mother's retort has protected her self to some degree.

Although a system of insults and retorts can become play in most lives, they are instruments with which selves are presented, their claims asserted, and boundaries defended. To be slow in the production of retorts or inexpert in their construction is not only an instance of social failure at the fulcrum of an interaction, but an acceptance by default of the insinuations contained in the insult. A talent for ready retorts, suitably constructed and delivered, is an indispensable skill in all social encounters. In the verbal games called the "dozens" frequently played in black subcultures (Abrahams, 1974), the object is to continue insulting each other until one of the parties either loses his or her temper or calls the game off. In the game, both insults and retorts are acts of originality, wit, and stylish verbal constructions. No doubt such games teach both poise and self-control to members of a community who have need of these qualities in their relations with members of the dominant community.

## Commands

Commands are acts that bear a strong signifying force that reflects and defines the self of the articulator within a formal structure. They are given and accepted within organizations constituted by a system of roles, relationships, and rules and therefore are readily accepted as long as the relevant roles, relationships, and rules are in force. Typically, therefore, they do not require force or verbal abuse in order to be obeyed. One finds the command most systematically used within military establishments, because military roles, relationships, and rules are not only clear-cut, but are fundamental to the organization. But the command does not belong only to the military. Leaders of patriarchal families and authoritarian management structures often control their subordinates by means of commands. In bureaucracies of the type discussed by Max Weber, (1958:196–240) the written instructions that must be given to other officers are, in fact, discursive acts. Although on the horizontal level, written instructions are disguised as requests, on the vertical level they are orders. A command, then, is a discursive act that represents the articulator's power and status in a particular social structure, affirming his or her self and constituting a sign that refers inwardly and becomes a facet of the articulator's maxisign. Conversely, by complying with a command the recipient defines himself or herself as an appropriate participant in the organization.

## Assertions

Assertions are statements voiced in a manner that implies that they stem from an authoritative, privileged, and knowledgeable foundation, and thus become signs of the self making the assertions.

Here are John Ehrlichman's words, spoken in a conference with then president Nixon and his assistants, Bob Haldeman and Ron Ziegler on the afternoon of March 27, 1973:

> We have three very serious breaches. One was the whole Szulc group; one was the Pentagon Papers and the other was the Pakistan-India situation; but there were leaks all through there and so we had an active and ongoing White House job, using the resources of the Bureau and Agency and the various departmental security arms with White House supervision.
>
> (Woodward and Bernstein, 1974:191)

This is a series of interconnected and developmental assertions containing statements of facts judged to be serious, together with a description of the steps taken to meet the contingencies the facts created. In making these assertions, the articulator has presented a self—an informed, perspicacious, and responsible observer. Of course, there is always a danger that others will produce claims counter to these asserted. In the situation described here, it was possible for one to challenge Ehrlichman's list, his judgment of its importance, the quality and value of the precautions taken, and even the veracity of his claim that those steps were taken. By challenging these assertions, the self of the articulator is challenged, making him defensive and apologetical or even mobilizing new assertive signs.

Consider another example from everyday life. In Schegloff's (1972: 101) study of the formulation of place, in which is found an everyday conversation containing the following discursive act. A and B both live in the same town and A has offered B a job as a nurse and B asks:

B: Where is it?
A: Out in Edgartown, on Strawson Road.

In this exchange, A, who has earlier indicated that there was a job available for the recipient, formulates place by giving the name of a precise location in a town. These assertions, one a knowing and definitive claim about an important issue (a job for the respondent) and the other a claim about knowing a place with some exactitude, are presentations of signs that define a self: I know about a job, maybe I even have inside information about a job and I am savvy about places, addresses, and locations.

But, imagine two possible negative responses to these claims: (1) "You're always boasting about things like these. Remember the time you sent me to Allentown for a job?" (2) "Oh, come on—there's no Strawson Road in Edgertown—I used to live there. You must mean Swanson Street." The refutations of A's assertions are new signs that cannot but define the self of the articulator, who now has the option of admitting that he is an unreliable braggart or that his knowledge of places and locations is not as precise as he had claimed. But whether the assertions made are affirmed, qualified, or refuted by the other's silent or vocal gesture, signs have been presented, their resonance experienced, and their varied effects are fated to become part of the maxisign of the self.

## Rebuffs

A contradiction challenges and refutes claims made by proposing or implying an alternative. By making an assertion or a simple claim, the self becomes committed in varying degrees to what has been stated, and a contradiction refutes that self predicted in the dialogue. Such contradictions may be almost imperceptible:

Wife: Are you going to walk Rufus?
Husband: Did the bloke come about the TV yet?
Wife: No.
Husband: He will have to wait then.

(Wardhaugh, 1985:155).

The wife's question is a strong request that intrudes into an apparently unrelated topic, and the husband replies that since he will have to wait for the TV man the dog too will have to wait. The man's contradiction of the wife's assertion that the dog should be walked was done as indirectly as the request. The initiative and the response were clothed in the accoutrements of tact and sensibility to the selves of the two parties. The irritation roused by this, however mild, is nevertheless clearly displayed in the developing sense of the conversation leading to the construction of the short, pointed last sentence, by the use of the future tense, and particularly by the placement of the temporal conjunction *then*. The emotionality of the sentence is a powerful negative that resolves the question with an air of finality, and we can infer that Rufus will not get his walk until after the TV bloke has come and gone.

## Accounts

In a justly famous paper, Marvin Scott and Stanford Lyman stated: "Talk we hold is the fundamental material of human relations" having the "ability to shore up the timbers of fractured sociation, . . . to throw bridges between the promised and the performed, . . . to repair the broken and restore the estranged" (1968:46). "An account," they assert, "is a linguistic device employed whenever an action is subject to valuative inquiry. . . . By an account, then, we mean a statement made by a social actor to explain unanticipated or untoward behavior" (1968:46). These accounts, then, are discursive acts offered by a damaged self in an effort to reconstruct itself. Interactions and relationships between people are based on the presumption that each has a particular kind of self, a self conceived in terms of various details, such as punctuality, veracity, decorum, or loyalty. These are signs that others attribute to a person that he or she seeks to use in his or her own definition of self, but during everyday interactions and relationships, events can transpire that challenge these presumptions and so call for reconstructive discursive work. Following J.L. Austin's (1970) ideas, Scott and Lyman divide accounts into two types: excuses and justifications. Excuses "are socially approved vocabularies for mitigating or relieving responsibility when conduct is questioned. We may distinguish initially four modal forms by which excuses are typically formulated: appeal to accident, appeal to defeasibility, appeal to biological drives, and scapegoating." Justifications, on the other hand "are accounts in which one accepts responsibility for the act in question, but denies the performance quality associated with it" (1968:47). These accounts are presented as discursive acts by a self that has been questioned and they seek certain effects in others. These effects are usually recognized, although people may seek clarification and details before fully accepting them.

In spite of an elegant formulation, Scott and Lyman's account seems to be concerned exclusively with the maintenance of the *integrity of the interaction*. An account is demanded and it is given and honored, and everybody concerned is satisfied, at least for the moment. In an ongoing *relationship*, one must not provide merely an account, but one that is *defensible* in the long run and the short run as well. If an account is later discovered to have been unveracious, more accounts will have to be furnished, and if one systematically continues offering accounts that are later found to be false, they will become signs that define the articulator's self as a liar and manipulator.

Accounts are signs that indicate self, and the content of accounts—their quality and character, their sources and implications, their roots in one ideology or another, the goals they foster—allow that self to be read by others. Excuses that invoke a god or a devil indicate a self different than one that draws excuses from theories of a random universe, just as heroic and patriotic ideological justifications present a self different from one claiming only to be doing his or her duty. Accounts, like other interpretive responses are thus indexical of other systems of meaning and are used to make inferences about a self.

## Disclaimers

Hewitt and Stokes (1975) introduced this concept into the study of the interactional management of selves and identities. Such management they argued, must be based on what one says and does in attempts to control the ways others might cast them. One can forestall a particular casting or "typifying," as Hewitt and Stokes call it, by disclaiming some of its overt effects. In other words, the initiator of a disclaimer, conscious of the fact that the ensuing statement could create an unwelcome interpretation, seeks to prevent that response. Controlling another's response to one's own productions, directing it away from a particular responsive interpretation, and defining the limits of one's own discursive act seem to be the essential features of disclaimers. Meaning may be in a responsive interpretation, but there is no need to leave such interpretations under the other's total control.

Hewitt and Stokes describe four types of disclaimers:

1. Hedging: "I am no expert, of course but . . .," "I could be wrong on my facts, but . . .," "Let me play devil's advocate . . ."
2. Credentialling: "I am not prejudiced, some of my best friends are Jews," "Don't get me wrong, I like your work, but . . ."
3. Sin licenses: "I know this is against the rules, but . . .," "What I am going to do is contrary to the letter of the law, but not its spirit."
4. Cognitive disclaimers: "This may seem strange to you . . .," "This may sound crazy but I think I saw . . ." (1975:4–5).

While the different types do not seem to be as watertight as might be desired, they are nevertheless very revealing about this kind of discursive action. Such action can be used with some precision to define the boundaries of the self by seeking to establish a priori the "real" significance of one's remarks, its apparent meaning notwithstanding.

## Programs

These are verbal definitions of contemplated activity that is being arranged for execution or realization, and are discursively offered to social circles and significant others. They define a line of action as well as a goal. Thus, they become elements of one's identity and to the extent they are accepted and validated by others, they are signs of the self. They signal inward to the mind of the articulator and outward to the others, and as they gain validation they become an aspect the self of the articulator. These programmatic discursive acts can be constructed poorly or well, tactfully and circumspectly, or smugly and offensively. Such work demands close attention to the various features of language and its transformations, as well as to the social context. A smug and offensive act of programming may prevent validation and bring unhappy consequences for the selves or the interaction itself.

Programs are not always given in simple declarative sentences or statements; often they are contained in descriptions of the contemplated events and activities; sometimes they occur as disjointed remarks, offhand comments that when pieced together constitute a definition of the self and an announcement of its program. The latter can occur in social circles such as the family or friendship groups, and may even become a running theme of the self and its relationships to given others over a long duration. The more often programs are asserted and validated, the more secure will they become as signs of the self, helping to give it shape, substance, and presence (Perinbanayagam, 1985: 101–134).[1]

## Jokes

Jokes, a very common feature of social relations, have received little attention from those who study discursive interactions. The profound contributions of Freud (1905) Freud focused on the unconscious meanings of jokes and Radcliffe-Brown (1961) has focused on the structural implications of jokes. Eye-opening as their work is, they nevertheless leave the interactional and semiotic implications unattended.

Radcliffe-Brown argued that a joking relationship is one "between two persons in which one is by custom permitted, and in some instances required, to tease or make fun of the other, who in turn is required to take no offense" (1961:90). The joke is then a discursive act meant to elicit a very particular kind of response. Radcliffe-Brown notes further, "The joking relationship is a peculiar combination of friendliness and antagonism. The behavior is such that in any other social context, it would express and arouse hostility; but it is not meant seriously. There is a pretense of hostility and real friendliness" (1961:91). The joke referred to here is an immediate and creative act making the present moments of an interaction ones characterized by both mirth, mild hostility, challenge, refutations of identity, innuendo and ambiguity, allusiveness, and even obscenity and profanity. These acts are *addressed* to the other directly, and implicates the self of both the addressor and the recipient. The joke becomes an instrument by which a dialogic moment is created and a dialogic relationship reinforced.

Radcliffe-Brown describes the various implications of a joking relationship in terms of the patterns of avoidances and alliances found in all human societies. That is to say, people who live together are obliged to ally with certain of the others in his or her circle with varying degrees of intimacy and commitment. In the various African and Oceanian communities Radcliffe-Brown described, these kinds of relationships are based on the kinship system. For instance, he notes that "one of the first tasks that strikes the sociological inquirer is that the custom of 'joking' with the wife's brothers and sisters is very commonly associated with a custom of strict avoidance of the wife's mother, frequently of the wife's father and more occasionally of the wife's mother's brother" (1961:106). Joking and avoidance are "polar opposites," and we can explain the one only by explaining both.

The joking relationship is a "form of familiarity," permitting disrespectful behavior. "It is for example a relationship in which, in some cases, obscenity may be freely indulged in . . . [O]bscene talk, in all or most societies, is only permissible in ordinary social intercourse between persons standing in especially familiar relationships" (1961:107–108). It appears that either by joking or avoiding joking between two sets of others an articulator is defining differences between relationships—one of afference, the other of deference. These jokes constitute what may be called "playful insults," whereby friendliness and antagonism, acceptance and *schadenfreude*, are delicately blended and balanced and become a "method of ordering a relation which combines social conjunction and disjunction." (1961:97).

As for societies where kinship is not a dominant form of social or interpersonal relationship, or where acquaintanceship and friendship with those outside the kinship circle are equally important, Radcliffe-

Brown's observations require some modifications. In such societies the joking act is also a means of achieving two social effects; (1) giving expression to certain already established relationships, clearly defining them, claiming the rights and privileges that accompany these relationships, and fulfilling the obligations that go with them; (2) creating and/or expanding a particular relationship by making joking acts to elicit desired responses. At any moment in the assembly and presentation of such an act, the other can refuse to respond as anticipated. To refuse to take a joke is, in effect, to refuse to accept a relationship and thus to deny the identity that the content of the joke may define and attribute. *In creating this act the articulator needs to calibrate, with varying degrees of precision, the cautions, liberties and licenses that he or she can take in the relationship.* When jokes overstep these marks they can undermine the self of the other, and if done deliberately and systematically, they become mocking acts rather than playful games intended to present a self and define a relationship. The balancing of conjunction and disjunction is not an easy task, particularly in modern societies where relationships are ambiguous and parameters are uncertain. Nevertheless, joking relationships abound in modern societies, too. They can be found in families, particularly between siblings and cousins, in peer groups, and in friendship circles. In each group, jokes of a particular type are deployed as forms of play, and their varied insult-quotient is used to define relationships.

The varied power that can be carried in insults, and the fact that as a form the insult allows for the display of verbal skill and mastery of situations, enables it also to become a form of play. This has been fully recognized in dramas of many kinds, from Shakespeare's jesters and comic figures to the studied and cultivated witticisms in the plays of Richard Sheridan, Oscar Wilde, Bernard Shaw, and many others. In black American society, as previously mentioned, insults are used deliberately in interactional and discursive playing. Variously called "the dozens," "signifying," or "joning," such playing consists of offering insults of increasing pungency to the other, eliciting retorts until one party gives up. This is a sort of discursive duelling in the presence of an audience, which acts as judge and evaluator. Ulf Hannerz writes, "Joning is an exchange of insults. . . . The boundaries of the concept are a little fuzzy; there is some tendency to view joning as an exchange of insults of a more or less jocular type in sociable interaction among children and adolescents" (1969:129). When the moment comes that one participant has had enough, the statement "I don't play that game no more" constitutes an act of surrender, meaning that the other's jibes have "gone too deep." Insulting a player's mother seems to be one that is considered too deep. William Labov (1972) has shown, there are rules for ritual insults that specify which liberties can be taken with the self of the other and on which occasions. These rules also specify those signs with which discursive acts are to be constructed so as to have only effects that, while teasing and provoking the self of the other, *maintain* rather than undermine a relationship.

Domination over another by means of joking is typically accomplished by the systematic serial deployment of jokes over a period of time. These jokes are challenges and refutations of the present self, and when the relationship between joker and recipient is a continuous and uneven one, such as between father and child or husband and wife, the continuous jokings, or "running jokes," become instruments of domination that can be countered, if at all, only by severing the relationship.

## Teasings

Opposed to joning, where there is always an intent to test limits and cut deep, is mild, playful teasing. In this form of the discursive act there is no fundamental contest of selves. Rather, there is shared goodwill and a sense of mutual trust that one's "real self" is not in question. Consider the following interaction between two brothers:

M.J.: I bet you a nickel
G.J.: What?
M.J.: Gotta see some money . . . bet you a nickel that I am looking sharper than you
G.J.: No you wasn't
M.J.: No you had your play clothes on. (Laughter)
G.J.: I ain't ha' my play clothes on
M.J.: You had your Batman socks on too
G.J.: I did (Laughs) not
M.J.: You did (Laughs) so. You did so.
G.J.: a? a?
M.J.: Got something else to say?
G.J.: Wait a minute—let me tell you something. Greg Barber look better than you. You come in there with your clothes hanging down all the way down to here (Laughs)
M.J.: What?

(Loman, 1967:1)

In this interaction one brother establishes a teasing relationship about the younger brother's childlike self-presentation (play clothes and Batman socks). The costume's inappropriateness and therefore joke-worthiness is acknowledged by G.J. In his half-hearted laughing denial of the charge. M.J., clearly winning this contest, challenges G.J.: "You got something else to say?" G.J. certainly has and in pointing out an inelegance in M.J.'s own clothes, wins back points lost in the first round. Laughter punctuates this exchange, even occurring in the course of a denial of a charge, which indicates the bantering nature of an already established dialogic relationship.

This kind of teasing cannot be initiated by a social inferior and certainly cannot take place between strangers or mere acquaintances, because suitable discursive teasing strategies are affirmations of already existing relationships. Whereas the joning joke is a "put-down," which is a deliberate attempt to question and undermine the self of the other, the teasing discourse is only a mild shove.

In both joning and teasing, a fundamental mastery over intonations, categories, and symbols of discourse is of great importance. In the absence of such mastery, the recipient will not be able to interpret the joke as a joke, will over interpret, taking more offense than was intended, or under interpret and so not take the offense that was in fact intended. The proper timbre and tone for the playful teasing in the interaction between M.J. and G.J. lies in the mildness of the offenses against the "collective consciousness" with which each accuses the other. Further, the imposition of laughter at the correct places in the discourse defines the bantering, playful, and whimsical nature of this discourse.

## Deceptions

In relating to another, a self is presented through discourse, and this disclosed self claims implicit or explicit veracity. To the extent that a person allows the other to take these claims at their proclaimed value, a commitment has been made as to their veracity, and both the proclaiming self and the other are bound by them. Questions are raised if and when these claims are discovered to be untrue: Why were they made in the first place? What happens after their inveracity has been discovered? Michael Gilsenan investigated the relationship between lying and honor in a Lebanese village and noted, citing George Simmel, "A lie by X about X is a classic instance of 'creating the self,' of purposely fashioning a social personality 'out there' for one's own contemplation, of making an object—for his own aesthetic self regard—but lying in the every day world is also a conscious act directed at another; it is always part of social meanings and social relations" (Gilsenan, 1976:191). That is, deceptions are practiced in order to construct certain signs of the self that are addressed inward and outward. By enticing the other into accepting certain definitions of the self, the articulator may also come to accept them and so gain new signs for his or her maxisign. Such signs may be invested and articulated to meet a significant other's expectation, to fulfill the demands of a social circle, or to defend a self against attack.

Deception can also be practiced for the protection of the other. Information and attitudes inimical to the self of the other may be filtered, and articulated signs that the initiator and recipient come to have in common will be maintained and defended. This process will hold while the relationship lasts or until the signs are discovered to be false, at which point deception can be used or an account offered that explains why the earlier statement was presented. But, whatever the motive for the act, deception damages a self and a relationship deeply, often irreparably.

Unlike deceptions that are not meant to be discovered, playful deceptive tricks perpetrated on another are meant to be explained soon concluding with everyone having a good time. Gilsenan describes *kirzb* in detail as practiced among young Lebanese men. In this form, notes Gilsenan, "[t]he essence of it consists precisely in the liar's ultimately *revealing* the lie and claiming his victory: I was lying to you, you ate it. In the laughter there is a sense of superiority, the fleeting dominance of A over B" (1976:192 italics in original). The fact that the point is to disabuse the recipient of his or her beliefs on a later occasion makes this temporary lie radically different from an outright deception. Nevertheless, it calls for skill in verbal construction and performance, and coordinated and interdependent activities with others, and certainly has implications for the development of a self. Playing *kirzb* leads the trickster to the mastery and deployment of various verbal and performative skills, and the ability to coordinate one's acts with those of others. The victim of the trick, besides learning lessons about giving trust too readily and the importance of skepticism, is above all presented with opportunities for maintaining poise among friendly insiders and preparation for the world outside friendly circles, where poise and skepticism are of major importance in maintaining social relationships.

### Scoldings

Scoldings, are those interpersonal discourses one party addresses to another indicating a failure to meet certain standards and expectations, and are typically given by those whose structural position in a relationship defines their right to administer them. Examples include mother to child, supervisor to subordinate, warden to prisoner, husband to wife, wife to husband, and sibling to sibling. The content of a scolding reflects the nature of a relationship. The scolding a mother gives to her child would be radically different from that a supervisor gives to a subordinate or that a teacher would give a pupil. Such scoldings in their very construction and articulation seek to convey both the nature of the relationship within which the scoldings are being presented, the self that is doing the presentation, and the degree of emotionality involved. A mother can be curt, short, and pointed when talking to her child. Jules Henry reported the following incident:

> Mrs. Wilson wants Norma to get two chairs so Norma and Abby could put their towels on the chairs while they are in the pool, but Norma says, "You are the one who said we should go swimming."
>
> Norma is being given an instruction about a trivial matter but in her eyes, because earlier the mother had prevailed upon Norma to go swimming with her friend Abby, it becomes a continuation of her mother's attempts to control her behavior. Her mother scolds her for her resentful remark, adding a threat as well:
>
> "Well if you think that's the case, then you can put on your shoes and you can't go swimming." The effectiveness of this scold depends on Norma's relationship to her mother, and her true feelings about swimming: she may want to swim, while not liking to be controlled by her mother. (1973:215)

A supervisor would not normally adopt the tone and structure contained in this act. He or she may have to be a little more indirect and circumspect, insofar as he or she is talking to an adult co-worker. In such scoldings by the supervisor, the act would reflect a *relative inequality* of status rather than an absolute one. Consider the following:

> A: Susan, you were late again. This can't go on, you know. You were late twice last week . . .
> B: I know—I was held up . . .
> A: (interrupting) Don't do it again.

This is a scolding administered to a subordinate by a supervisor, in particular to a secretary by the chairman of a department at the university. At the simple utilitarian level, the scolding is meant to ensure the availability of the secretary at the right time and is designed to promote as well as the discipline of the workers and thereby the efficiency of the office. But it has further uses, too: it gives an opportunity for the supervisor to assert his self, present and define his authority and performance as a supervisor, and show the errant secretary and her office mates that not only is he the titular head of the department but also a functioning one. The listing of late comings, the interruption, the raised voice, and the announcement of a lack of interest in excuses are all designed to define the relationship of superordination and subordination as well as a certain indifference to the esteem of the other's self. Clearly the chairman would discipline a fellow professor in a radically different manner. In such cases some deference and consideration would be shown by the discursive acknowledgment of the other's self and relationship to the scolder.

Beratings and rebukes are two forms of scolding differentiated by degrees of seriousness and intent. A berating is a strong and sustained verbal assault on the self of the other. Blasphemy and obscenity would be one way to deliver a berating; a second would be to undermine the other's professional or occupational self; and a third way would be to question another's ancestry, a man's wife's fidelity, or a mother's chastity. In all cases, a systematic verbal undermining of the other's claims to self in certain cherished areas of social life are used to define the other.

Rebukes and chidings, although milder forms of scoldings, do put the self of the other on the spot for having failed to meet certain fixed standards. Consider the following:

> While the three of us were in the kitchen, Harriet was crying in her room. She cried and cried and neither Dr. nor Mrs. Jones made a move nor said a word to her. At last Mrs. Jones said to her husband, "If you happen to be passing the bedroom, would you glide in there and do something about your daughter?" He asked laughing, "Why didn't you simply say, 'Go in and take care of Harriet?'" She said, "You know what you would have said if I had done that," and he replied, "What would I have said?" and she answered, "You would have said, 'Go to hell.'" He laughed and replied he would have said "Okay" and she repeated "You would have said 'Go to hell.'" (Henry, 1973:51)

Mrs. Jones has couched her request in an elaborately polite style. Her explanation for so doing amounts to a rebuke to her husband regarding his habits of response to her requests and about taking responsibility for caring for their child. The rebuke calls attention to his failings and by implication suggests a change of attitude.

By means of such discursive acts, the self of an articulator is asserted and the boundaries if its tolerance defined. The acts therefore establish the limits of a relationship. Further, the scolder indicates a number of claims on the other and defines them with little possibility of ambiguity. When scoldings are infrequent or occasional, they will restore the relationship to the keel of what one of them desires. If on the other hand the rebukes or scoldings or beratings continue in a relentless pattern, the relationship will be completely dominated by bitterness, and the selves of both recipient and articulator will be fully influenced by these acts and the signs they generate.

## Complaints

In relationship with another, a self has various rights and privileges defined as expectations to be fulfilled by the actions of the other. If these are not met, the disappointed self can articulate dissatisfaction by means of whinings, expressions of pain and anguish, or by requests and demands. Complaints are made against a background that the self and other share and accept, and thus complaints appeal to a common standard. When the self can legitimately complain that these standards are not met, the other can be expected to respond favorably. Without such acts the other would be at a loss to ascertain accurately the expectations of the self and the extent to which they have been fulfilled. Indifference to, negligence of, ignorance of, forgetfulness of, and doubts about the other in a relationship with a self need to be countered and obviated by discursive action and complaints in order to do this. Children complaining to parents communicate and establish the standard they expect. Although it can be about a small matter, for example, "the blanket is too scratchy," the consequences can be anything but small. By asserting itself in this manner, the child has created a sign for itself, namely, "I am not one who will sleep under a scratchy blanket and I will ask for a change." The fate of this sign depends on the response it elicits. If the mothering one can accept the child's standard and change the blanket, a number of other messages will be conveyed; to wit, "I am a responsive and loving mother"; "I can be talked to by my child"; "I accept its standards of comfort here, and perhaps elsewhere too"; "I am willing to listen to my child and so validate the presence of its self." The child, too, by making a complaint and so enabling the other to produce responsive signs, has created the data for the constitution of its self. A mother, whether providing hostile and rejective signs or affectionate and supportive ones, contributes to the emergence of the maxisign of the child's self. A child or adult who does not complain has surely abandoned the relationship and may even be "depressed."

## Rebuttals

These are responses to charges, rebukes, complaints, insults, and other similar acts that challenge or seriously undermine certain aspects of the self. An effective rebuttal, forceful in its own terms, specifically answers the semantic content of the offending discourse. To begin with, signifying force is given to rebuttals by the tonal qualities of the discourse. If the charge is made with a raised and loud intonation, the respondent produces a rebuttal of equal volume and pitch. The content of the rebuttal will address the charge directly. Sometimes the rebuttal is a mere denial:

A:  You were drunk last night.
B:  No, I was not.

This must be considered a feeble response that can be made stronger by further sentences. Consider an alternative:

B:   No, I was not. What are you talking about? I don't even touch the stuff.

This does not stop at a mere denial but adds details likely to provide a certain verisimilitude to the rebuttal. In some circles, to be drunk is considered an offense against certain rules of conduct and so the charge has to be rebutted forcefully. A mere complaint of inconsistency against a self on that score is perhaps not a serious offense, but if made against one whose self is under a cloud to begin with, it demands a detailed rebuttal. In the following, a mental patient, Joseph, and his therapist, Barnham, are having an exchange:

Joseph:   Worse this last week than ever. I suppose we've been in the hospital too long. Everybody's wanting to go home. Everybody's fed up and we're getting on each other's nerves. We're sick of the place and we just want to go home.

[He offers a critique of the hospital and claims to speak not for himself alone but for the other as well. The therapist offers a mild contradiction and rebuke.]

Barnham:   And yet last week you were saying . . .
Joseph:   I know, I've changed my mind, I just want to go home. I don't want to be in that place for another week. I have changed my mind. I have been in there too long. I am going round the bend, I am getting headaches. It just confuses you somehow in there. They are marching around that much. The racket, the marching.

(Barham, 1984:109)

The rebuttal consists of explaining the change of mind in terms of commonly accepted standards: (1) home is where one likes to live; (2) one stays in a hospital only for a given duration, and one cannot stay there too long; (3) the routine and the noise are too confusing. In other words, the change of mind is justified and does not indicate any failing on the speaker's part.

Rebuttals, true or not, assert an equality of stigma between initiator and the respondent. They save the situation and the face of the responder, and they restore a certain equilibrium to the relationship. When this reflexive responsive act is not readily available, one can retreat to other standard ones such as curses, obscenities, or attacks on the honor and chastity of the other's mother. When verbal rebuttals become inadequate, an offended party takes to physical force.

Rebuttals are constructed in terms of certain social parameters of discourse: the power and influence of the person being rebutted and the cultural meaning of the role relationships between the participants playing a part, as well as the style and content. In the official environment, subordinates have to recognize the hierarchy of the system and rebut in a respectful manner. This can be termed the *bureaucratic parameter* of discourse. In some societies, according to a code that can be called the *chivalric parameter* of discourse, open and forceful contradictions or challenges to charges and assertions made by women are forbidden. In both the above circumstances of discursive rebuttals, the implication is that forceful and brutal ones will do even more damage to the self of the respondent. Needless to say, those entitled to claim these discursive privileges can abuse them, and/or employ them, to advance their own interest. Most typically, however, rebuttals are instruments with which a self defends itself and *controls* the signs by which it is to be constituted.

## Interruptions

In their pioneering essay, Sacks, Schegloff, and Jefferson (1974) argued that everyday conversations are characterized by a systematic taking of turns by each speaker. As one speaker finished, another starts, and this proceeds in easy minuets of discursive acts. When this system fails, there are two developments: an *overlap* and an *interruption*. Schegloff defined these as follows: "By overlap we tend to mean talk by more than one speaker at a time in which a second one had projected his talk to begin at a possible completion point of the prior speaker's talk. . . . If it is projected to begin in the middle of a point that is in no way a possible completion point of the turn, then we speak of it as an interruption" (1973, quoted in Bennett, 1981:171). These two kinds of inputs into ongoing conversations are not merely conversational practices, but are discursive acts in their own right that bespeak of the selves of the participants and the nature of the relationship the conversation is sustaining. Research has been reported purporting to show that interruptions are frequently made by men in a conversation when a woman is speaking and that this is an aspect of the oppression of women in society (Zimmerman and West, 1975). No doubt one of the situations where women are oppressed is in conversations, but it is surely too simple to claim that this occurs through interruptions. The point is that it is not "men" or "women" who engage in conversations, but selves and roles in various relationships with each other. These "men" and "women" who talk to each other are indubitably husbands and wives, senior and junior colleagues, sisters and brothers, domineering and submissive role-players, people with bad, overbearing manners, differing conventions about conversational interactions, and so on. Further, some speakers have special claims to speak on certain topics and occasions. That is to say, they are endowed with selves that are relevant to these variable factors, and their interruptions will be made and accepted within these parameters. Such selves may be acting in loving, hostile, friendly, affectionate, bureaucratic, or collegial relationships. In these relationships and with the selves that characterize them, when the articulator says something it carries his or her self with it. A respondent has to listen without interrupting if it is an authoritarian relationship in which he or she is the subordinate, but in egalitarian relationships he or she can interruptively present his or her self and mix it up with the other who is speaking. Dominant selves in relationships can be men or women and, as Stephen Murray wrote, citing earlier work by Frank (1979), "To recognize an instance of interruption either as a conversationalist or as a conversation analyst inevitably requires interpretation of the prior history of the interlocutors' relationship within both the particular interaction recorded and analyzed and the preceding interaction" (Murray 1987:102).

Interruptions can be acts that challenge, refute, and assert a position that differs from the ongoing discourse. These, however, have to be distinguished from acts that in a strict turn-taking sense are interruptions, but that function as continuation, confirmations, or completions of the point being made. Consider the following interaction between President Nixon (A) and John Erlichman (B):

A: Tell me. Can I spend a minute? That's the thing that I wanted to know. I knew about the New York Grand Jury. What in essence is that? Vesco—
B: It's a, it's a runaway Grand Jury.
A: Yeah.
B: It started out as an SEC action against Vesco for violations of the Securities Act. They then lumped into this two hundred and some thousand dollar donation to the campaign.
A: Right.
B: They have been on to that.
A: Right.

(Woodward and Bernstein, 1974:264).

The president changes the direction of the conversation with his aide with a question asking permission to do so: "Can I spend a minute?" He does so, seeking certain information in a very paradoxical way: "I knew about the New York Grand Jury. What in essence is that?" He knows something, but not its essence, and by uttering only a single word presents a key stimulus to his aide, who, without waiting for the sentence to be completed, proceeds by answering: "It is a runaway Grand Jury," an explanation elaborated further in the succeeding pieces of discourse. The interruption of the president's discourse is really a run-on sentence, *a shared line* that continues and completes the preceding one, not an introduction of power and assertiveness by the other but a sign of support, obeisance, and compliance.

Overlapping conversational points seem to arise when a miscalculation about when the speaker is going to stop is made, or when, because of a conviction that the other is not going to stop soon, a perceived interregnum is seized for throwing one's own self into the act. The overlapping of inputs seems admirably suited for turning a flowing conversation into a dialogue. In letting one's words overlap and continue the other's line, some equality of status, time, and turn taking in conversations is claimed, and by virtue of placement in the midst of the ongoing activity, the self is itself defined vis-à-vis the others. In contrast, complete silence in the face of an interaction obliterates a self, at least for the time being. Insofar as selves exist and survive as manifested discursively in interactions, it is imperative that one enters an ongoing conversation.

Interruptions and overlaps, although discursive acts in their own right, are at times parts of discursive acts by which selves enter interactions. They can be instruments for the presentation of domination by selves, not on an a priori basis of gender, but in terms of the roles the selves are called upon to play, in particular, interactions and relationships. They can be used to indicate total commitment and dedication to the ongoing proceedings; they can be challenges to and refutations of the points made in the conversation; and they can be rejections of another's right to tell a story, hold the floor, etc. Furthermore, they can be announcements that a more urgent matter has come up since the other started speaking, e.g., dinner is ready, a fire alarm has sounded, or war has been declared. That is to say, in Stephen Murray's words (1987:101–110), interruptions are at times demonstratives of power and at other times of solidarity.

## Narrative

Narrative is a form of discourse that is comprehensive in scope because all other forms can make use of the narrative form for achieving their effects. Chatman (1978), discussed earlier, has argued that a narrative consists of *story* and *discourse:* story is the structure of events, incidents, and characters, and discourse is the verbal matter with which the story is presented. Gerard Genette has suggested that narratives have five essential elements: order, duration, frequency, mood, and voice. By order, he means the temporal order of a narrative and the relationship it bears to the actual ordering of the events in the story. The former need not bear a direct relationship to the latter insofar as it is a rearrangement made to achieve certain effects. Duration refers to the time actual events of the story take to occur and what relationship this has to the telling of it. It is clear that the telling can be altered by reordering events or alluding to them over again—this is frequency. For example, an event repeated, like a leitmotif, in an artful way achieves certain effects, but if it is clumsily done, it may have a totally different effect. Mood is defined by Genette as distance and perspective: "Distance and perspective . . . are the two chief modalities of that regulation of narrative information that is mood—as the view I have of a picture depends for precision on the distance separating me from it, and the breadth on my position with respect to whatever partial obstruction is more or less blocking it" (1980:162). Finally, voice is given to narratives by the willful presence of a narrator of an action and a subject who has a relation to the events being told: "the subject here being not only the person who carries out or submits to the action, but also the person . . . who reports it and, if need be, all those people who participate, even though passively, in this narrating activity" (1983:213). In other words, the voice of a narrative vividly indicates the self of the narrator as well as narrator's relationship to the listener. While Genette uses Marcel Proust's *A la recherche du temps perdu* to illustrate his method of analysis and to support his conclusions, any narrative can be seen to contain Genette's structures. Consider the following:

> I went to see my father today, you know Jim. I am so crushed—he was so cold and indifferent—I told him that I would like to come and see him, lunch twice a month at least—now that I am alone and need some support—But he just put me off—lunch time, he has to spend with clients, he says. (Field Notes)

The narrator has achieved certain effects by the different *ordering* of the temporalities of the first two sentences: the first is in the past tense, the second in the present. The first sentence is about the time and the event that is the subject of the narrative, while the second is about the time of the telling itself. This ordering is followed by a sentence that is a report in the past tense of something that was told about the future: "I would like," followed by a description of the present continuous state: "I am alone . . . ." The narrative ends with a report of the continuous activity of the father: lunch time is spent with clients, always. It is a story with a short *duration*: the conversation it reported is short, as is the reporting itself. The symmetry between the thing told about and the telling is important to secure the realization of the effects sought. Overelaboration and too much of an investment of time in its telling would slacken the narrative and dilute its strength. Moreover, the story, simply and directly told with no repetitions and iterations, comes directly to the point. That is to say, it is governed by the rules of parsimony. These arrangements of the narrative, leading to the creation of a certain *mood*, seek to achieve the necessary distance between the character in this story and the narrator and listener. A kin is introduced whose existence and relationship is known to the listener as well as the particular situation and context in which his companionship was sought. The information given by the narrator, just enough to make the story effective, establishes the perspective from which it is to be viewed by the listener: She called her father and made a simple request, one easy to fulfill, and even then, and knowing fully her particular circumstance, he rejected her. Finally, the story being told has a very distinct presence as a production with a particular *voice* addressing another.[3]

## Notes

1.   Accounts, disclaimers, and programs have received extensive commentary and are being presented here only in the most elementary form.

2.   For a review and discussion of the ethnomethodological approaches to the analysis of "cutting out operations" see David Helm (1985). He makes the interesting and convincing claim that "cuts" need not always be "mean" operations. For example, if a mother finds that her still conversationally incompetent child is unable to respond to a question, she may appropriate his turn and reply, saving him from embarrassment. For a critique of the ethnomethodological position see Murray (1985), Murray and Covelli (1982; 1987)

3.   I am indebted to the work of Robert Scholes (1982) for this discussion of narrative. This work is an admirably parsimonious and creative integration of the work of Tzvetan Todorov (1977), Gerard Genette (1980), and Roland Barthes (1974). For a recent work that embraces both classical and contemporary theories about stories and storytelling see Robert Georges, "Towards an Understanding of Story-Telling Events" (1969).

# Emotions in Discourse

## — 7 —

It has been properly argued that emotions are "embodied"; that is, they have a physiological correlate. The claim also has been made that emotions are "situated self-feelings," that they arise from "cognitive social acts," and that "they are directed towards the others" (Denzin, 1985). But to the extent that emotions are communicated as well as experienced within the social act, they are also aspects of a signifying discourse. It is thus within the terms of social acts that emotions more often than not exist and manifest themselves (Shott, 1977).

Ongoing social acts are typically part of a social relationship, and emotions of varying degrees of intensity are brought into play through them. The emotions are put into play by the use of signs and are subject to systematic and intentional transformational processes. Goffman puts these points very perspicaciously as follows: "The human tendency to use signs and symbols means that evidence of social worth and of mutual evaluations will be conveyed by very minor things and these things will be witnessed, as the fact that they have been witnessed. An unguarded glance, a momentary change in tone of voice, an ecological position taken or not taken, can drench a talk with judgmental significance" (1967:33).

They are drenched with significance because they constitute emotional attitudes. These actions are the means by which emotions are put into play. The presence of emotions in the gestures and expressions of the people present recognized and read by the other and, in turn, read by the self, thereby constituting an interactional resonance. While knowledge of their presence may be difficult to demonstrate clearly, their absence will be evident to any and every participant. Such absences can be seen in the conversational encounters with those who speak "without affect." Indeed such encounters and the responses to them make participants who do speak with affect uncomfortable. They feel incomplete because they are unable to participate in the creation of the resonance necessary to maintain and continue the interaction. Emotional resonances need not be verbalized in any particular way, though often they are, because they are inescapable presences in the entire gamut of moves and gestures, of statements and interjections, by which social acts are conducted and interactions maintained. Such emotional resonances are also made visible when discrepant and mutually contradictory emotions are resolved. An interaction dominated by the emotions of joy, affection, and mutual regard is very quickly changed by the entry of another party who brings not only news of fearsome events but the emotion of fear itself. The new circumstance must be absorbed and, whether rejected or accepted, will change the emotionality of the interaction.

Emotions, according to Norman Denzin, have temporal phases or moods. As he puts it, "A mood is never temporally free, and moods always accompany states of mind. . . . But prior to the mood or a feeling, is the person's state-of-mind which reflects their cognitive, moral and emotional attachment to themselves and their situations" (1984:16). But then how do these "states of mind" that bring the self face to face with itself and its situations become available to fellow interactants? Or, in the words of J.L. Austin, "How do we know that another man is angry?" which raises three other questions relevant to any answer:

1. When to all appearances angry, might he not really be laboring under some other emotion, in that, though he normally feels the same emotion as we should on occasions when we, in his position, should feel anger, . . . making displays such as we make when angry, in this particular case, he is acting abnormally?
2. When to all appearances angry, might not he not really be laboring under some other emotion, in that he normally feels on occasions when we in his position should feel anger and when acting as we should act if we felt anger, some feeling which we, if we experienced it, should distinguish from anger?
3. When to all appearances angry, might he not really be feeling no emotion at all? ([1961] 1970:111–112)

Austin notes that these questions are "special cases occasioning genuine worry." We may worry, "(1) as to whether someone is *deceiving* us by suppressing his emotions or by feigning emotions which he does not feel; we may worry, (2) whether we are *misunderstanding* someone (or he us) in wrongly supposing that he does 'feel like us', that he does share emotions like ours; we may worry, (3) as to whether action of another person is really deliberate or perhaps only involuntary or inadvertent in some manner or other" (1970:112; italics in original).

These difficulties are handled, according to Austin, by using established procedures for dealing with suspected cases of "deception, misunderstanding or inadvertence" (1970:112). *Certainly one does that; but the interesting question is not how a respondent handles deceptions, but how he or she reads the ordinary indication of attitudes and intentions—the nondeceptive and purposive ones.* Austin's answer to this question is very instructive: "It seems . . . that believing in the other person's *authority* and *testimony*, is an essential part of the act of communicating, an act which we all constantly perform" (1970:115; italics added). That is to say, by assuming that the other person has control over his or her productions, one then can accept and use them as tokens of his or her intentions. In dramaturgical and dialogic terms, the answer to Austin's questions about anger is that for *all practical purposes* the subjective experience of feeling or not feeling anger is not relevant at all. What the recipient *takes* to be the other's subjective feeling is relevant, because this is what elicits the responsive act that achieves ontological and behavioral status. Typically, members of a society, using the word in both a narrow and broad sense, are expected to make use of a common idiom when displaying intentions. Emotions, like other attitudes, become semiotic achievements rather than acts of intersubjective clairvoyance. They are signs that mobilize intentional as well as effectual interpretants. The semiosis of emotions includes the various signs that define and convey them to the self, the body, and the other. The initial point in the chain of semiosis (sign → interpretant → sign → interpretant →) may be the body as often as it may be the self. The body's impulses are transformed into concrete and separate signs by the mind and then given to processes of *self*-presence and *other*-incorporation. Conversely, the self's intentions are reproduced as bodily responses. Subtle, soft, and gentle emotions are often transformed into gross ones, and, perhaps more frequently, gross ones are transformed into subtle ones. Whatever the origin of such emotions, a semiotically minded organism sooner or later ontogenetically or phylogenetically transforms them into socially recognized and recognizable signs.

To understand the play of emotions on the self, its conceptualization must be redeemed from an excessively fluid form it has been given in nearly all interactionist theories. The self is no doubt created by social relations and is sensitive and responsive to ongoing social processes. As Herbert Blumer wrote, "I wish to stress that Mead saw the self as a process and not as a structure" (1969:62). Process can be best, indeed fully and accurately, described only as one of transformational semiosis. The idea that the self is a completely amorphous, insubstantial and evolving entity and is totally and discontinuously tentative and formless is surely unacceptable. Rather, it is constituted and reconstituted by signs in ongoing processes. Far from being in a *continuous emergence*, the self is to a degree bounded by rules concerned with the definition, management, and presentation of cognitions and emotions and their interrelationships. Cognitions, of course, are subject to ordering rules such as those of logic and grammar in all societies, and although emotions are subject to those rules they are also subject to additional rules that apply only to them.

In the normal course of everyday life, these rules are routinely embedded in social circles and communities and are observed by one and all with varying degrees of fidelity. When they are violated, accounts of various kinds are given to protect the self and to ensure ongoing self-maintenance and interactional commitments. These rules arrest potential anarchic processes and help in organizing the maxisign of the self, so that even emotions become features of the mind that are related to the self. A self, then, is constituted, formed, and in part bounded by rules about feelings regarding how and how not to experience and express them (Hochschild, 1979).

Emotions are not to be contrasted with cognitions and understandings, because they are inseparable aspects of human being, seeing, and doing. As recent philosophical work on emotions argues, "an emotion is partly cognitive, but this part is not so much a source of knowledge about the world as an evaluation or appraisal of some part of the world in *relation to oneself*" (Lyons, 1980:71; italics added). The arguments Lyons provides for his view that emotions are cognitive and evaluative phenomena are many and varied. The more important of these arguments include the following. An emotion is based on "certain judgments correct or incorrect, cursory or well-considered, irrational or rational as [to] what property something possesses. It would be contradictory to claim for example both that one loved X or was angry with X, but new nothing about X" (1980:71). These properties include

> the cognitive aspects of emotions, the knowledge or belief about properties, is the basis of an evaluation. . . . So, for most emotions if not all, what emotion, if any, will well-up in a person will depend on how he sees the object he has apprehended or believes he has apprehended. A man is afraid because he "sees" the object or situation as dangerous. A man is angry because he "sees" the situation as offensive or insulting. A man is embarassed because he "sees" the situation as one in which he has lost face. A man is in love because he "sees" the person as appealing. (1980:77–78)

As emotions become lived experiences, they also become cognitively understood, linguistically labeled, socially situated, and ethically and pragmatically evaluated. That is, they become elements of social acts. In pragmatic terms, such "seeings" and "evaluations" are responses made by a minded organism, and are indeed interpretants of signs. In Averill's words, "Standard emotions are as much a product of complex cognitive processes as are such other cultural products as religion, art, science, and the like" (1980:67).

## The Vocabulary of Emotions

Since emotions occur as cognitive features of a minding organism and are achieved semiotically, they demand a vocabulary logically connected to previous cognitions. Peirce wrote: "If a man is angry he is saying to himself that this or that is rude and outrageous. If he is in joy, he is saying, "This is delicious". If he is wondering, he is saying "This is strange". In short, whenever a man feels, he is thinking of something" (1935, volume 5:292). Insofar as a person cannot think of anything without the help of signs, emotions also have to be thought of in signs and are made available to humans as "vocabularies of emotion" (Geertz, 1959). These vocabularies are not just lists but are relational systems of words that indicate differences of kind and degree among the emotions. Vocabularies of emotions are initially used to socialize a child, Geertz found in her study of Balinese socialization practices, and are involved in teaching how emotions are to be experienced and how people are to indicate them semiotically to the self and others. Jules Henry's early study of the "linguistics of emotion" makes the same point. His work enables us to see how particular definitions, identifications, and labeling of emotions have consequences in the prosecution of social acts. Consider his study of usage of the expression for anger in an African community:

"If we turn to an analysis of the expression *to nu*, we will be able to understand certain peculiarities of its use and the emotional response elicited by such use. The element is a post position meaning "direction toward" and *nu* is the element that expresses anger. In this case *nu* is treated as a verb. The element *nu* also occurs alone, however and means "dangerous." thus a sentence with the expression *to nu* means "(he is) dangerous." thus *to nu* has in it something of directed danger, and *nu* has in it something of undirected anger. Hence, the statement "I am angry with you" suggests "I am dangerous towards you." In line with their use of indirect speech in difficult situations, conspirators in a murder plot do not say "Let us kill them," but say instead "Let us be angry with them." When Tuli asked his father-in-law to be "angry" he was asking him to commit murder. (1936:250–356)

It is obvious that the state of affairs Henry described is not unique to this community. In every linguistic system there are expressions to cover emotions of one kind or another that determine the acts that will follow as a matter of course. Indeed, in Henry's example, to get angry or be angry is not to describe a state of mind but to indicate an incipient act. Emotions are indisputably incipient acts because they are available to the self and others who will demand further signs. Citing Mead's (1934) work on the subject, Burke pointed out that these incipient acts are either substitutes for acts of one kind or "first steps towards an act" (1962:236). For example, anger can be manifested as verbal abuse, a physical attack, or both. Discursively articulated emotions, then, are acts in two senses: they are themselves acts, and they are the beginnings of further acts in the form of verbal or physical signs. In American society, an expression of love toward an eligible partner is a prelude to actions of one kind, while an expression of love toward one's mother is a prelude to actions of a different sort altogether. Similarly, an expression of hate demands further congruent actions such as the termination of further relationships, a thrashing, or perhaps murder. In other words, emotions do not merely reside in the body or mind, if they ever do, but are vocabularies used in the definition of situations and for describing procedural steps about to be taken. Just as motives, they are "typical vocabularies having ascertainable functions in delimited societal situations" (Mills, 1940:904).

The legitimate reduction of the mass of feelings a human child may possess or be exposed to is a structure of signifying terminologies. As they become familiar to the self and its social circles, those feelings can be put to use in either proposing new lines of action or in sustaining lines already in progress. Insofar as such a familiarity and usage is inseparable from self-consciousness, it is pointless to wonder whether or not people really feel the relevant emotions. If actors are content to base their justifying vocabulary on the language of feeling, others are obliged to take them at their word. However, the discrepancy between claiming to experience an emotion and really feeling it is not likely to be too frequent. Even without having to take galvanic skin responses or pulsations of the heart, the other will be able either to validate the self's presentational emotions and complete the social act, to look for further evidence of the emotion being presented, or to reject the emotions and go forward to the next step.

Once transformed into vocabularies, appropriate performances through which emotions gain their standing are learned. In other words, emotions are presented in ritualized form so that control, management, and proportions are maintained. Human performances are always subject to esthetic considerations, and in the management of emotions one is trained to maintain proper ratios between situation, identity, and audience. *These ratios cannot be maintained without a vocabulary of emotions embodying variations being used with some precision.* For example, adult males in American society, when publicly confronted with grief, are expected to perform in a stoic and restrained manner, while American women are granted greater latitude and can express their grief by means of tears. However, under no circumstances is the injunction relaxed that requires that certain ratios be maintained between the situation and the emotions expressed: grief or joy, love or hate, shame or fear are each subject to a disciplined form of expression. Since such disciplines reflect social boundaries of expression and control, they also take part in controlling what and how one feels, and for this reason, though the overlap may not always be perfect, one feels as one expresses and expresses as one feels.

An excess of any emotion in a given social act or a series of acts is a threat to any normal self, situation, and society. One can protest too much, love too well, hate too deeply, or be shamed and frightened to the point of death. In fact, excess of emotions in terms of the culturally determined ratios is one of the standard signs by which mental illness is judged. An adult who takes a rebuke as a suicide-worthy event, who claims to have no emotions, or who celebrates the death of a loved one is suspect in both moral and pathological realms and is thus open to varying labeling procedures. The prototypical literary example, of course is Hamlet, who let "the clouds still hang" on him, though he should have known that his "father lost a father; that father lost, lost his, and the survivor bound in filial obligation for some term to do obsequious sorrow. But to persever in obstinate condolement is a course of impious stubbornness, 'tis unmanly grief" (1.2.89–94). Indeed, the whole speech by Claudius, Hamlet's murderous stepfather, is a statement regarding the rational and proportional experiencing of grief and orderly display of same. No doubt he had his own reasons for wanting to stop Hamlet's brooding. His argument, however, has the stamp of authenticity and universality: Do not violate the rules of propriety and proportionality—sensing grief too deeply is dangerous to the mind, and displaying grief wantonly is inimical to social relationships.

## The Degrees of Emotions

The fact that there are standard vocabularies for emotions enables one to conceive them in structural terms. Indeed, the main thrust of the rules for the classification of emotions is based on the principle of quantity, and so the terminology of degrees of comparison used in grammar can be profitably used here. Terms such as positive, comparative, and superlative can be used because emotions, like adjectives, can be so classified and used as the logical and social situation demands. In terms of the relationship between conduct and emotions, then, humans are socialized into an understanding of the different *degrees of emotionality* appropriate to different situations. Let us attempt a tentative classification of at least part of what may be termed the normally used vocabulary of emotion. Since comparisons are not always involved in these usages, the implication of the table below, as one progresses along the rows, is that they indicate increasing degrees of emotional intensity. These words can be transformed in various ways and used to indicate various *gradations* of emotion.

|     | Positive | Comparative | Superlative |
| --- | --- | --- | --- |
| 1. | Timidity | Fear | Terror |
| 2. | Like | Love | Passion |
| 3. | Qualm | Apprehension | Anxiety |
| 4. | Antipathy | Dislike | Hate |
| 5. | Embarrassment | Disgrace | Shame |
| 6. | Fancy | Desire | Lust |
| 7. | Regard | Veneration | Awe |
| 8. | Irritation | Anger | Rage |
| 9. | Disappointment | Frustration | Dejection |
| 10. | Satisfaction | Joy | Ecstasy |

Of course, these terms are not related to each other in a strict linguistic sense but are used in such a way that logical relationships are posited in the discourses themselves. Similarly, for words that are not easily compared, modifiers are used. For example, one can speak of angry, very angry, and extremely angry, just as one can speak of a casual liaison and a grand passion. These words and the words in the table can further be qualified by adjectives and adverbs: antipathy can be qualified, for example, on both sides by the words mild and strong. One can feel great shame or slight dishonor. Thus, it will be seen that though there are three columns to the table, there are interstitial spaces between them in which many logically related emotional descriptions can be fitted.

A second structural arrangement of the emotions can be approached with the oppositional terms of standard emotions and hyperemotions. Standard emotions, those typically occurring in the two left-hand columns of routine everyday activities and self-conceptions, are features subject to the control and discipline of self and other. Hyperemotions are those that are grouped in the superlative column—lust, passion, terror, anxiety, etc. Their presence in social acts and selves is usually disruptive, and they promote acts inimical to the self or body of their enactors. These acts, usually referred to as "uncontrollable fits," "fits of passion," "moments" of terror, hate, or anxiety, are the antecedents of panic and many violent acts, in sharp contrast to the routine acts of everyday life.

Indeed, the very definitional feature of hyperemotions is that they do not lend themselves to reflection, analyses, or systematic verbal programming. Typically, their influence on conduct is described in terms of the bursting of bonds and the breaking of restraining influences. They are said to gush forth, sweeping aside the self in their wake. In durational terms, the difference between hyperemotion and consequent lines of action is so short that no vocabulary emerges to guide and control it.

Blumer's description of the behavior of "expressive crowds" and the "acting crowd" leads him to talk, for example, of the emergence of feelings of "ecstasy," "exaltation," "excitement." These feelings have consequences, in Blumer's view, centering around the "loss of customary critical interpretations," and he excludes the acts that follow such a loss from the category of symbolic interaction (1955:184). These forms of emotionally driven action are beyond the controlled vocabulary of emotion. Because the evidence is clear that the routine acts of everyday life are undertaken in programmed ways, the existence of the hyperemotions confirms the overwhelming importance of submitting our feelings to the control and direction of signs and rules for our identification and for response in and to social situations.

## Discursive Emotions

In the primal encounters of the human species, there is an imperative to convey both *sense* and *feeling* to the other and to use them in establishing interactional relationships and maintaining selves. In the discursive acts of everyday life, sense and emotions are inseparable and intertwined and intermingled, they define and delineate the full signifying force to the other. In seeking to assert, announce, or indicate an intention then, an agent has recourse to verbal forms usually arranged as sentences. In an instructive paper, Michael Root sought to extend this theorem to all forms of rule-governed behavior. Such behavior, he writes, "displays a pattern of organization that is characteristic of language. . . . Language behavior is most often offered as the clearest example of rule-governed behavior. However, one result of our discussion of rule guidance is that the ability to speak and understand a language turns out to be more like our other abilities than first thought. Rules guide speech but they guide many of our other performances as well" (1975:323).

The arrangement of sound that results in music, the arrangement of color and form that results in painting, and the arrangement of form and shape that results in sculpture (and the many other arrangements derived from these) are used by humans as social acts. In such enterprises, as Suzanne Langer puts it, there takes place "the symbolization of vital and emotional experience for which verbal discourse is peculiarly unsuited" (1967:80). What are the essential properties of such symbolization? The essential process involved in undertakings usually described as artistic is the creative utilization of symbols, albeit symbols of a special sort, for establishing a transaction with an audience. As Langer noted in an earlier work, what is involved in a work of art is a "projection of a feeling," a projection accomplished by the choices the artist makes. She continues, "Every choice the artist makes—the depth of color, the techniques—smooth or bold, delicately suggestive like Japanese drawings, full and luminous like stained glass, chiaroscuro or what not— every such choice is controlled by the total organization of the images he wants to call form. Not juxtaposed parts, but interacting elements make it up" (1953:370). Verbal discourse may be, as Langer puts it, "peculiarly unsuited" for the symbolization of certain forms of "vital and emotional experiences," but people nonetheless do use them for conveying emotional attitudes in everyday interactions. They do this by using the linguistic and rhetorical features of language for given purposes and effects in the same way that painters, sculptors, and musicians use their media and techniques.

## The Discourse of Anger

In everyday life, emotions are embodied and conveyed in discursive acts. As in other forms of social acts, these allow one to understand and appreciate the emotional attitudes that the other is projecting and, conversely, to project verbally one's own emotions when they become so pronounced that they need to be expressed to others in striking and unmistakably clear ways. For example, in many interactions there occur moments in which quick, decisive, and unambiguous assertions have to be made in order to protect the self, affirm a value, and/or define a situation and a relationship by expressing anger. Because such responses have to be quick and decisive, there is no time for reflection about original constructions or poetically rich ones. Nevertheless, they must be forcefully and insistently presented in the discourse in order to elicit a desired response from the other.

When Brutus and Cassius quarrel in *Julius Caesar*, Shakespeare provides both Romans with a series of effective discursive acts:

Cassius: Urge me no more, I shall forget myself;
         Have mind upon your health, tempt me no farther.
Brutus: Away, slight man!
Cassius: Is't possible?
Brutus: Hear me, for I will speak
         Must I give way and room to your rash choler?
         Shall I be frighted when a madman stares?

Cassius:   Oh ye gods, ye gods! Must I endure all this?
Brutus:    All this! Aye, more. Fret till your proud heart break.
           Go, show your slaves how choleric you are,
           And make your bondmen tremble. Must I budge?
           .  .  .  .  .  .  .  .  .  .  .  .   By the gods,
           You shall digest the venom of your spleen,
           Though it do split you; for, from this day forth
           I'll use you for my mirth, yea, for my laughter,
           When you are waspish.

                                                        (4.3.35–49)

Although the metaphorical vigor and rhythmic manipulation are truly
striking, a modern quarrel can use the same form. Brutus's short, staccato dismissal of Cassius: "Away, slight man," indicating contempt and
derision both in the words and the shape of the sentence, is paralleled
almost exactly in the modern version, "Go screw yourself." Both are
abrupt, short, and final dismissals. Of course, the content of the act
indicating the irresponsible, socially useless, noninteractional, and often
frustrating character of doing things by oneself is insult enough: You are
not good enough to interact with, either in society or in a loving relationship. Similarly, the allusion to digestive processes as metaphors for self-
pollution is paralleled by references to sodomic practices. Shakespeare's
Brutus also alludes to undesirable features—Cassius had a "lean and
hungry look"—and so the pun in *slight* achieves a double effect. Further,
social stratification is brought into the terms of abuse: I am not your
inferior, so you cannot make me "tremble"; your slaves and bondmen
will be impressed by you, but I will not be.

If one cannot come up with original metaphors and creative formula-
tions as poets and dramatists can, one can draw on a common fund of
obscenity and blasphemy. Obscenities and blasphemies are richly allusive forms that depend on one trope or other for signifying force. They
are peerless in their capacity to evoke cultural anxieties and signify
defiance of conventionalities. They are generally able to indicate both a
wantonness of form and content and a certain emotional profligacy.
When using elements from this tropic bank, a person typically seeks
either to assert or to defend his or her self when the contingency arises.
A fine example comes from a study reported by Seckman and Couch
(1989). In this exchange the common four-letter word achieves a series of
transformations as it is used by both parties. The exchange is between
two workers, one of whom had reported the other for some infraction
and who is now confronted by the victim:

A:   Doesn't it make you feel good when you report others for fucking off?
     [Delivered with a biting tone of voice, while glaring at B.]

B:   Fuck You, I am here to work. [Looked down at his machine and began
     tinkering with it]
A:   No. Fuck you. You fun-loving son of a bitch. [The "fuck you" was
     delivered as a challenge, the "fun loving" was sarcastic.]

(1989:337)

Here, manifested in and through the discursive form of obscenity,
anger is subtly transformed as well by the use of sarcasm—"fun-loving
son of a bitch," as Seckman and Couch observed.

The confrontation between unequal selves, differentiated from each
other on one basis or another, is handled by the norms of civility. These
norms recognize hierarchy and have built into them the "civil" ways of
talking and relating to subordinates and social inferiors, superordinates
and social superiors. In ongoing social life, however, several contingencies can occur where the subordinate self is ignorant of these norms or
misidentifies the other as a social inferior when he or she is not, or the
subordinate refuses at that point in time to acknowledge the status
relationship. In any of these contingencies, the one can address the
other in ways that the other considers demeaning or make requests,
suggestions, and demands that are insulting. Some articulations of this
type will be considered by the recipient as not only inappropriate, but
outrageous. Confronted with such responses a recipient can find himself or herself unable to produce the perfect squelch, the appropriate
bon mot. He or she can typically come up with only a more outrageous
blasphemy or obscenity. In such interactions, emotions well up and
demand manifestation in verbal form either as expletives or addresses.
Feelings of resentment and irritation lead to a certain anger that expresses itself in standard obscenities. In these locutions, a human being
is synecdochically reduced to a constituent part of the body, and the
force of the remark is executed by the implication that that is all the
person is: merely a copulatory or excretory function. In addition, these
locutions also subsume what I will call an emotional paradox: the sexual
organs are both desirable objects and feared ones, at once capable of
giving both pleasure and shame. Displaying them is shameful, but
wittingly and appropriately using them is pleasurable.

At other times and occasions, as a means of articulating one's anger,
incest is brought into the discourse. William Labov (1972) has described
in detail how the suggestion of intercourse with a mother or relative is
used as a vehicle for insults traded in the inner-city, albeit in the "play
form of the socialization of joking." The suggestion of incest from an
incensed and inflamed enemy invests the insult with great emotional
power, even if these locutions are conventional ones. On these occasions, an articulator can draw from the tropic bank stock of recurrent

situations, in this case, cutting words used to defend a self and protect esteem. This most ubiquitous of anxieties incest with a mother, is indicated as the equivalent in effrontery to the affront just given. Of course, one can say this only to a man. If one wants to respond to women who affront one's self, the feeble "bitch" is the only recourse men have, the intimation of incest between daughter and father somehow not available as an effective riposte. Perhaps this means that in patriarchal society this kind of incest is not considered as seriously as the maternal one.

Sometimes the outrage is so extreme or repetitive that words will not suffice and one has to resort to violence, either the ritualized violence of the medieval duel or the instantaneous response of a punch or knife in the body of the offender. I suspect that the reason that a switchblade knife is such a common adornment of an alienated urban young man is that there is constant threat to his self-esteem from members of the oppressor community who have not yet learned the vocabulary of civil esteem the young man has learned to expect. In the face of repeated offenses to his self, of persistent outrageous conduct, verbal and nonverbal, cutting words seem woefully inadequate to repair the damage and thus a knife becomes an imperative. Here the offense goes *beyond rage* and beyond being handled by words. Considered etymologically, *outrage* refers to an excess of rage, meaning also beyond normalcy. Similarly, *effrontery* has connections to front and is allied to barefaced, meaning bold. The word is derived from the Latin word *effrontatus*, which means unattested—i.e., claims made without sufficient warrant. One's claims made about self or the "front" (Goffman, 1959) that one puts forward should be warranted, just as one's claims vis-à-vis others should be, i.e., they should be not "effronterish" nor should they affront. Nevertheless, failure to recognize the frontiers of the self leads to rage and the construction of effective responses.

## Frustration and Catharsis in Discourse

Frustration, though not recognized as an emotion by many, is another emotional response that occurs in the course of an interaction. One engages in a variety of social acts that demand completion by another. In addition, there are acts that demand completion by inanimate objects such as cars. Often these do not cooperate, leaving the act and the acting self hanging. These experiences are emotional, and can be called frustrations. In the course of daily life, the experiences vary. Some are totally frustrating, while others may only be partially so. In either case, a pervasive sense of ill-being, a feeling of inorgasm, begins to limn the self, which will seek to overcome it by one means or other. Such overcoming can occur as forms of catharsis.

Thomas Scheff's (1979) version of the structure of catharsis stresses "knowledge and ignorance" as successive and developmental stages in an ongoing process, and he attributes cathartic effects to this particular form. The concealment of information by one person entices another to seek to unravel or to trap the concealer into subsequent acts of discovery. A discovery or a revelation, made available in small doses in a series that appears to have a logical sequence, elicits further commitment and search, increasing what may be called *interest* in the searcher, leading him or her to further acts of search for understanding, which leads to a final denouement and a satisfying sense of release and completion. In Scheff's view, this release is both psychological and physical. In addition to the psychological release, the emotional self releases various bodily fluids, which also leads to the release of tension. Games of various kinds as well as the normal theatrical and cinematic fare can be considered as possessing the structure of catharsis that Scheff has described.

Scheff's theory of catharsis has a certain commonsense appeal. The knowledge and ignorance form that Scheff describes, or as I like to call it, the revelation and concealment structure, is designed to create an *agonistic situation* (Huizinga, 1964) or a *problematic situation* (Mead, 1938), which thereby elicits and maintains the commitment of the observer or participant. Still, it is a fundamental error to think of the events in the cathartic process as leading to a release of the emotions. The implication of such a view is that one accumulates emotions in the mind and body and then when they reach a certain point of saturation they are voided in one way or another. This view ignores the processes that precede the denouement in the cathartic event, and also incorporates the notion that emotions are somehow substantive—things in themselves that can be acquired and stored in some cavity of the mind or corner of the body. On the contrary, as we noted earlier, emotions are felt experiences that achieve their ontological presence as cognitions and performances created over a temporal sequence. Hence, the emotional stifling or incompleteness a person feels is not caused by an accumulation of certain mysterious substantives in mind and body, but by cognized and felt emotions that are not *given play* at the right time and on the right occasion. Emotions are therefore not *released*, but at the point of catharsis, unexpressed emotions are *transformed* into other signs and expressed in new patterns. These new patterns are found both in the routine activities of everyday life like talking, or in occasional activities like participating in religious ceremonies, viewing games or movies, reading, or playing games.[1]

In daily life, humans systematically seek to overcome their frustrations mainly by cursing and swearing, and, because the use of obscenities achieves a cathartic effect, excretory and copulatory acts are used as expletives. Those most frequently used verbs—*shit, fuck, piss—*

as verbs are forms of conversational excretion and copulation. Indeed, their use can be called verbal forms of defecation and copulation— shitting and fucking linguistically. Expletivism is in every way a doing, an act, overt, external and declamatory, with a necessary connection to subvert, internal, and secretive processes of selfhood and conscious- ness. Insofar as the human is a symbolic animal, he or she is also a symbolically transforming one; insofar as excretion and orgasm are cathartic, literally, so is the act of naming them in a rapid, staccato fashion, *enacting the said acts* in the very form of the sentence. Indeed, if selves are symbolically constructed, then catharsis can be achieved not only by physiological but also by symbolic processes.

## Love and Jealousy in Discourse

In contemporary Western societies a self produces various positive emotional attitudes in its relationships with another, and it is important that these attitudes be distinguished from one another. The misuse of love, desire, like, and lust, for example, in discursive acts can imperil a relationship. In the course of interaction, it is often necessary to move from one to the other, define one attitude, gently retract it, express another, and so on. Consider the following conversation between a patient and a therapist:

P: Good morning.
A: Hi.
P: [pause] Well . . . I really can't tell you why I didn't come yesterday. Like, uh, I had every intention of coming but then, uh, this guy at school said, "Hey, you want to go out for a ride in my boat," you know, and I said, "All right," and, uh—'cause it was a real nice day out yesterday—about 70, 75—at least, it felt like it. And, uh, so he was ready to go at 11, you know, and I said, "No, I can't make it until 12:30," you know. And he said, "Oh, yeah, cause you gotta go down to the shrink." And I goes, "Yeah." I said, "But I might cut the shrink today," and he says, "Well, if you cut, come on over. I'll be waiting for you." So I did. And—I don't know. I thought about calling and then I said, "Naw, I won't call." Uh, I figured, you know, it'd be . . . Well, it'd be like, you know, I was gonna do it deliberately, you know; if I didn't call I might give you the impres- sion that . . . aw, "I just can't come today," you know, "it's just too much," you know. SO I thought: "I'll give him that impression and I won't call." [pause]
A: I want to be sure I understand that. You mean, if you didn't call, then I would assume that it was not deliberate.
P: Yeah. Right, you know, I said, "Ay, I just can't help it," you know.
A: But you obviously knew that when you came you would tell me it was deliberate so I would know.

P:   Yeah. But, uh, at least here I could assess your reaction, you know. Nil anyway. [laughs] But, at least, I wouldn't wonder about it, you know. I didn't want to worry about—oh, you know, "What are you thinking now?" you know.

A:   So what's your assessment?

P:   Oh, I don't know. I don't know if I was assessing or just I didn't want to worry about it for the day.

A:   No. I mean today.

P:   Oh. I don't know. I didn't, I got the impression already you didn't think it was any big thing, you know. I mean you weren't pissed off or anything when I came in, you know.

A:   What gave you that impression?

P:   Just . . . Well, maybe that's the impression I want to see.

A:   Oh.

P:   Seemed like nothing had changed or . . .

A:   "Well, I was so terribly relieved. You hadn't come yesterday and you were late today; I thought you were never coming anymore." [patient laughs].

(Gill and Hoffman, 1982:92)

The patient is explaining why he didn't keep his appointment with his therapist. The therapist himself considers this session "a good example of the explication of important issues in the transference as a result of the analyst's exploration of the meaning of an overt event in the therapy," as Gill and Hoffman note (1982:93). The patient has initially to produce a discourse that makes sense, and he does this by providing some information: he didn't keep the appointment because he went boating with a friend. He next has to explain why he didn't call to cancel the appointment: the ambiguities involved, within the psychoanalytic universe of discourse, in a patient calling or not calling to cancel an appointment are suggested. These sensible explanations that no doubt make sense to the therapist are articulated in a style that intertwines the sensible words with emotions, thereby strengthening both elements of the discourse.

The patient begins his discourse with a significant contradictory statement:

"Well . . . I really can't tell you why I didn't come yesterday. Like, uh, I had every intention of coming but then, uh, this guy at school said, "Hey, you want to go out for a ride in my boat," you know, and I said, "All right," and uh—'cause it was really nice day out yesterday—about 70, 75—at least it felt like it." While beginning with a clear refusal to explain his absence, he proceeds to explain it in the succeeding sentence. But this is a contradiction only at the level of sensible communication. On the emotional level, it is anything but a contradiction, since the two sentences constitute one discursive act that amounts to a flirtation, indeed a coquettish move. "The nature of feminine coquetry is to play up, alternately, allusive promises and allusive withdrawal . . . to attract the male, but always stop short of a decision, and to reject him but never to deprive him of all hopes" (Simmel, 1950:50). This strategy can be used by males to flirt with one another as well, and need not always involve the erotic emotions. In his essay, Simmel went on to observe, "Coquetry that unfolds its charms precisely at the height of sociable civilization has left far behind the reality of erotic desire, consent, or refusal; it is embodied in the interaction of mere silhouettes, as it were of their serious imports" (1950:51). In this case, however, the erotic element is strongly present and the therapist is aware of it. He noted, "The session illustrates the very common phenomenon of the enactment in interpretation of the very issue which is being interpreted . . . since what is being interpreted is homosexuality, while what is being enacted is domination and submission" (Gill and Hoffman, 1982:91).

This game of coquettish emotionality is continued in the next sentence of the discourse: the patient describes the relationship with his friend in terms of rejecting the invitation to the boat ride and then accepting it. The same theme is replayed in the next set of sentences: he wanted to call the therapist, didn't want to call him, and "figured, you know, it'd be . . . Well, it'd be like, you know, I was gonna do it deliberately, you know . . . so I thought, 'I'll give him that impression and I won't call' " (Gill and Hoffman 1982:92).

The welling emotionality of this discourse that allows the sense elements to achieve their varied potencies is reflected in the very structure of the text. The significant pauses, intonations, particularly the inclusion of the quotations from the other, the juxtaposition of affirmative and negative statements, and the systematic usage of contradictions in a dialectical way conveys its emotionality. The artful assembly of discursive strategies, even if they become habitual, gives force to the signifying processes. In such processes, the self is presented and defined simultaneously: the self of the articulator as a flirtatious homosexual seeks to display both his coquettish moves and the fact of his companionship with another man. The coquettish presentations and the revealing construction of the text are designed to convey and elicit certain emotions: love and jealousy, or at least a little lusty interest and pique.

## Joy in Discourse

Joy, and all related emotions, can be aroused by a variety of strategies. Often this emotion is discursively produced by enacting or recounting events said to be humorous. These events can occur as emerging sequences in ongoing experiences or in the course of a conversation.

Consider the following dialogue: the participants are the researcher (G), his research assistant (M), and two black teenagers (W and B). Several other black teenagers are listening in. The interview begins with the question:

1. G: What do we talk about?
2. W: Oh you guys pick a subject . . . any old subject you know.
3. G: Any old subject.
4. B: Any old thang . . .
5. W: Are you opposed to . . . to the draft?
6. M: Yeah.
7. W: Are you? (laughter)  . . .  opposed to the draft?
8. G: Yeah. Well I can be, I can afford to be opposed.
9. W: Tell me about your life—I mean about your military service. Was it interestin'?
10. G: Oh, it wasn't very interestin' . . . no.
11. W: Tell me . . . what part of the service did you go into?
12. G: I was in the army.
13. W: Well . . . what war was you in?
14. G: Second World War.
15. W: Second . . . did you . . . how you . . . you . . . where did you go?
16. G: I was in Europe.
17. W: That's the only place?
18. G: That's the only place.
19. W: Um hum.
20. G: England, France, and Germany.
21. W: Oh . . . well
22. G: In those days . . . well . . .
23. W: I mean was you really in action?
24. G: Oh, once or twice.
25. W: Did you kill anybody?
26. G: I don't know. I shot a couple of times.
27. W: You busy shootin' huh?
28. G: I don't know. I never saw anybody I killed . . . I saw some dead people.
29. W: Yeah. Ah . . . have you ever got shot?
30. G: No . . . I got hurt one day we were out . . . out in the morning and I got hurt . . . they put me on KP . . . they made me get up at four o'clock and peel potatoes . . . choppin' potatoes and I chopped off this part of my finger. (laughter)
31. W: Oh?
32. G: That's my "war wound."
33. M: It's a french fry.
34. B: That was the first time you tried smokin' that weed huh?
35. W: He's trippin' . . . you peelin' potatoes.

(Hansell and Ajirotutu, 1982:87–88).

The initial set of questions and answers establishes a subject without any difficulty, and the conversation proceeds apace with further questions and answers. Precisely which of the "primary emotions" (Kemper, 1987) or "gross" or "subtle" (Scheff, 1977) emotions are present in this passage would be difficult to demonstrate, except for the laughter. Nevertheless, there is a continuous emotionality in this exchange between people who were initially strangers. The emotionality is discursively created by the management of various linguistic and social strategies, and the emotionality undergoes various subtle changes as the conversation proceeds. That is to say, emotions are not discrete variables in everyday discourses but are wavelike patterns of continuously changing resonance between participants.

The interviewer begins the dialogue by asking for a topic for conversation (1) The respondent issues an answer indicating indifference: "Any old thing." (2) This indifference is certainly not a primary emotion and cannot truly be derived from one of them. Yet there is no doubt that it has a definite presence and lends emotional color to the interaction. The coloring functions as a signal that the conversation must be developed so as to obviate the indifference. The teen-aged respondent (W) saves the situation by presenting a question that seems to have the capacity to elicit an emotion other than indifference: "Are you opposed . . . to the draft?" (5) The suggestion that he may be against something, indeed be in conflict with or against an established institution or practice, introduces antagonism into the discourse. The answers from both research assistant (M) and from the researcher (G) are affirmative. (6, 8) This answer from adults to a question by a teenager, adults typically taken to be supportive of established institutions, elicits laughter from the teenager, and henceforth the emotionality of the passage is one of good humor accomplished by a variety of strategies. The teenagers express curiosity about the adult's war record. (9) After eliciting his attitude to the draft, the teenagers continue to establish a character for the researcher. He was in the army, he served in Europe—to be specific, in the second world war in England, France, and Germany; he may have killed people, but was wounded only in the finger while peeling potatoes. He was both heroic, in having actually fought in a war, and comic in having been wounded only in the kitchen war. The humor is continued by the allusion to the "war wound" which is wittily (metaphorically) transformed into a "french fry," with a final note delivered in the idiom of an entirely different war: he must have been smoking marijuana to have cut his finger while peeling potatoes. The teasing allusion to being high on drugs functions as a nice coup de grace to the interaction. The teasing itself has a subtle double effect; it is the youngster who is accusing the adult of having been irresponsible, thus reversing the usual roles. These roles were in fact the ones that were being established by the delineation of the adult's character: the adult was more experienced, had fought in a war, and was now in a position of responsibility, while the others were teenagers, raw, inexperienced, and playful. It is the reversal of these roles that is accomplished by the final remark, which adds whimsy to humor. The systematic pattern of contrasts drawn between the interviewer and the teenager's establishes a pattern of agonistics involving character, experiences, roles, and even dialect defining its emotionality. The emotionality of this exchange that began in indifference and ended in laughter had to be discursively cultivated. Such cultivation successfully creates a dialogic moment: the humor and the consequent emergence of a shared joy rose spontaneously from the character of the participants and the discourses they produced.

## Shame in Discourse

Shame, with its variant forms of embarrassment, loss of face, and disgrace, is a common emotion that results from an action that somehow violates certain rules. Gross and Stone wrote, "Embarrassment exaggerates the core dimensions of social transactions, bringing them to the eye of the observer in an almost naked state. Embarrassment occurs whenever some *central* assumption in a transaction has been unexpectedly discredited for at least one participant" (1970:176; italics in original).

In the following excerpt, an exchange between a therapist (A) and a patient (B) that occurs before the "real" therapy begins represents a very complex discursive rendering of shame. A discursive act is presented, its claims found to be unwarranted, the recognition of the full meaning of this claim adding further embarrassment:

A:  Hello.

B:  Hi. I brought your check, but I, I haven't forgotten it. But I forgot to bring it. Mmm—I have forgotten it. I just remembered.

A:  Do you feel it has to be brought in the very next time after you get the bill?

B:  Well, Yeah, I usually do. Yeah. I usually like to pay bills as soon as I get them, Right now, we have uh—probably for the first time—so many bills (laugh) that, that, uh, I am not paying them. I am just letting them sit there. The big one being 600 dollars for my teeth. I'll just have to pay part, but, uh—but yeah, I, I like to get them paid. That's the bills basically—the rent and our other bills. That's not—I mean that is not the charge—we don't have charge accounts. But, but yes, I guess, I, I. (pause) My dad is with me (pause). I, I haven't sat down and talked to him yet.

(Gill and Hoffman, 1982:118)

Recognizing that she has to pay for the services of the therapist and that she had forgotten to do so in the past, she claims that this time she has not forgotten, and then realizes that she has not remembered to bring the check with her. The systematic play of meanings in the use of the words in her opening sentence shows the contradictory nature of her attitudes: "I haven't *forgotten* it"; "I *forgot* to bring it"; "I have *forgotten* it." "I just *remembered*." These meanings seem to reverberate against each other, each signifying a different shade of meaning, with the second usage of *forgotten* indicating her awareness of the Freudian significance of her act. Her understanding of the significance of her act, i.e., the violation of the central assumption of her relationship with the therapist as well as the several implications of her act of forgetting, is captured in the variety of transformations to which the word is subjected. The shame becomes clear and well defined in the ensuing words: the broken rhythm of the sentences, the repetitive punctuations of the text with "yeah," the laugh, the revelations of personal habits regarding the payment of bills and certain financial problems (indeed often called "financial embarrassments") are all discursive manifestations of shame.

## Malice in Discourse

The idea of discrete emotions becomes quite useless when we consider malice, envy, derision, and other similar feelings. In gossip, for example, they seem to occur together. Patricia Spacks, in a very insightful study of gossip from a literary angle, notes that there are two kinds of gossip—malicious and serious. Malicious gossip "plays with reputations, circulating truths and half-truths and falsehoods about activities and sometimes about motives and feelings of others" (1986:4). Serious gossips "use talk about others to reflect about themselves, to express wonder and uncertainty and locate certainties to enlarge their knowledge of one another" (1986:5). In both forms of gossip, certain narratives are introduced into an ongoing discursive interaction, their significance for a system of values indicated, and an implicit or explicit judgment about the individual involved is made. These systems of ideas are depictions of moral prescriptions or expectations regarding propriety, mores, and other rules and regulations. These stories depict an act and elaborate a character against a backdrop of normal conduct, but the telling, done in appropriate tones and forms, "distill malice," to borrow a phrase form Spacks (1986:4) into the narrative. Such distillation is accomplished when a contrast between normal and abnormal conduct in given situations is voiced, and a friend or acquaintance is held up as having behaved in the latter way. This malice, discursively presented, is aided and abetted by the telling details contained in the narrative delivered to friend or acquaintance, and it is this other who is the focus because the discursive act creates a dialogic moment and so reinforces intimacy. Such interactions consisting of a shared and appreciated set of values, events in the life of another, and collective feelings of dominance over the victim of the malice, is filled with emotionality. The establishment of the other as different makes the sharers of the story and the values into a solidary unit.

Another way malice can be entered into interactions through discursive acts is by means of jokes. Jokes frequently play a role in the emergence of joy and as frequently they are used as conveyers of malice or envy. Two of the ways malice can be presented in discursive jokes are (1) as a joke about a third party who is not present; and (2) as a joke or witticism "at the expense" of a person who is present.

Malicious jokes are an attempt to separate one set of values from another and simultaneously to disidentify with another person or sometimes with an entire ethnic group and its values. Attributing certain definite features to a group enables the teller and receiver of malicious jokes to disidentify themselves by means of narratives. Such devices give the malice wholeness and concreteness and thereby emotionalizes the interaction between the participants while at the same time enhancing the dialogic moment.

## Conclusion

Emotions permeate everyday life and as articulated phenomena can be found in all human acts. In some acts they are dominant presences; in others they are subtle and discrete. In either case, they are manifested in and conveyed by signs and, they typically appear in discourses composed by a minded organism who uses language in all its variety and complexity of features for the articulation of acts and emotions.

Students of emotions have always been confounded by the mind-body problem, and indeed, to read current theories of emotion is to be struck not so much by their incapacities and contradictions, but by the theorists' inability to arrive at the proper *language* with which to describe and explain emotionality. Some begin their theories with concepts that imply that emotions are substances or entities acquired and possessed by actors; others seem to view emotions as wild animals that need to be tamed and kept as pets. Or else they are thought of as entities that begin as bodily states and end up as cognitive ones or vice versa.[2]

These theorists of emotion have a very fundamental problem. The language they have used in their discussions is, naturally enough, the linear language of cause and effect; and thus the analyst is forced to put one before the other. However, emotions are simultaneously cognitive and physiological events, interpretive and felt, and it is our entrapment in a Newtonian ontology that makes us seek to find primary or causal significance in one part or another of the above pairs. Emotionality and the physiology of the self are complementary phenomena. Further, emotions are not individual and separate, to be parceled into neat categories complete with analogous descriptive terminologies. Here, too, the concept of complementarity applies: emotions are waves that become more or less pronounced as they develop temporally. Thus, irritation completes itself in anger, and anger completes itself in irritation or even in peace and calm. Emotions are moments in a continuing chain, and only the social occasion, the self, and language allow us to label them for discrete use as needed.

Social acts, then, are not calculated efforts, routinely based on rational and purposive considerations. Rather, they can be said to be limned with emotion. Indeed emotions limn all social acts, both circumscribing and delineating them. They prevent social conduct from being mechanical and overrehearsed, rendering them varied, multiform, and unpredictable. The intensity and importance of emotions in social acts, however, vary. One can find acts that are suffused to a maximum and others that have only a minimum of emotion. Emotions thus are not to be contrasted with cognitions and understandings. Instead, they are inseparable aspects of human beings and doing. One can differ about the nature of the emotion present in such states, and about their intensity, but not about their presence either as traces or dominating features.

## Notes

1.  The practice of transformational catharsis is truly endemic in all human societies. Countless institutions are established to ensure that catharsis occurs as a matter of course and, indeed, as a matter of discourse. Ritual ceremonies in temples as well as domestic rites have this capacity to transform private pain and suffering into public activities shared by others. In modern times, games of various kinds have taken the place of some of these rites. These rites and games are *textured* in similar ways and are designed to elicit certain responses. It is imperative that attention be paid to the basic form in which the catharsis-producing events are made available. To begin with, it is the narrative structure that is common to each of these events: baseball games, football games, dramas and movies, novels, cock fights, wrestling matches, voodoo, and other religious ceremonies. The narrative structure is what makes these forms work toward providing cathartic experience: eliciting one's attention, creating anticipation, establishing a past for future uses. In addition, narratives simultaneously elicit emotional involvement and a commitment of the self, developing these systematically over a period of time and then providing an ending that either fulfills the self or defeats it. The dramatic structure parcels the emotions into neat units and

allows them to develop into a crescendo toward a finale. One can consider these features of games and rites parallel in every way, albeit in shortened durations and tightened plots, to the experiences of life. That is, life experiences are synecdochically transformed into games, and opportunities for catharsis of a complex and structured nature are provided to all who can take them. They do provide a form of catharsis that can no doubt be called a release, and may even elicit the cooperation of the body. Nevertheless, the fundamental structure of the processes that lead to this are symbolic, ones to which involving the self in the activities of participation and committing the self by identification, are central.

2.  It is no doubt true that emotions have a physiological base or correlate. At least, they often do. Thomas Scheff has noted that grief, fear, embarrassment, and anger "are physical states of tension in the body produced by stress" (1977:485), and argues further that "the symptoms of acute fear—pallor, chill in the extremities and rapid, shallow breathing—are caused by tension: constriction of the blood vessels, which interferes with the circulation of blood, causing pallor and chill in the hands and feet, and constriction in the bronchi, interfering in oxygen intake leading to rapid shallow breathing" (1977:485). Kemper (1987) too has argued for a foundation in a physiological autonomic process for a selected set of emotions—in fact, the four for which such autonomic processes have been claimed by some researchers. However, it turns out that the same physiological reactions can be produced by other stimuli as well and hence cannot be used to *delineate* and *distinguish* an emotion. Rather, the emotion seems to have been created by the definition and understanding of the situation in which certain events occurred, and the consequence of such understanding for the named emotion. If a stranger slaps one's face, as Scheff (1977) noted, one may experience a combination of emotions: grief, fear, embarrassment, and anger. But it is the interactional event of the slap by another rather than a branch of the tree under which one was walking, and the fact that it was a stranger that did the slapping rather than a mother, spouse, or teacher, that is consequential. Even when physical action (a slap) leads to emotions as well as physiological responses, it cannot be gainsaid that the identity of those involved will have the main effect on the emotions aroused.

Physical tension must not be confused with emotions, as Arlie Hochschild noted in a comment on Scheff's paper (1977:494). Emotions are, rather, symbolic constructs that are descriptions of a current interactional situation or of consequences of an earlier one. Such symbolic constructions may accompany bodily sensations, but the relationship is one of "cooperation," rather than of identity or causation, in Hochschild's happy obviation of the Cartesian trap. She observes: "I define emotions as bodily cooperation with an image, a thought, a memory—a cooperation of which the individual is aware" (1979:551).

# Drama in
# Discourse

## — 8 —

The presence of drama in everyday life, defined in Kenneth Burke's words "as a fixed form that helps us discover what the implications of the term act and person really are" (1968:445), is truly ubiquitous. The use of the fixed form of drama is imperative for the study of human relations, argues Burke, because "man is defined literally as an animal characterized by his special aptitude for symbolic action, which is itself a literal term" (1968:445). Dramatism, the term that Burke used to describe his method for the study of discursive forms, consists of five key terms: act, scene, agent, agency, and purpose. In a later essay, Burke suggested that attitude be added to the five, making a hexad of his scheme. He summarized his reasons for the selection of these terms, as the elements of a grammar of motives, as follows:

> Dramatism centers in observations of this sort: for there to be an *act*, there must be an agent. Similarly, there must be a *scene* in which the agent acts. To act in a scene, the agent must employ some means, an *agency*. And it can be called an action in the full sense of the terms only if it involves a *purpose*. . . . The pattern is incipiently a hexad when viewed in connection with the different but complementary analysis *attitude* (as an ambiguous term for *incipient* action undertaken by George Herbert Mead [1938] and I. A. Richards. (1968:445).

Even then the generating grammar remains incomplete, in my view. Acts, conducted in given scenes by a self with an instrument, and bearing both a purpose and attitude, occur in evolving and varying temporalities. That is to say, acts begin, create various responses, proceed in one direction, change, and proceed in another, and may eventually terminate at a point that was not anticipated. One possible consequence of such proceedings may be that the meaning of the scene will change, and that the nature of the agent will change as well, just as will the relevant attitude, purpose, and even the agency. Indeed, there is no way one can avoid insisting that a perspective and a method that uses drama as a fixed form must add yet another key term in order to become complete. That term is *temporality*. In fact, St. Augustine, in the course of his search for God, proposed that at any given moment a human is *remembering* and *attending* and *anticipating* (Ricoeur, 1985). These terms parallel the different moments of time–consciousness—the past, the present, and the future—and can be used to describe the process by which an organism minds the world. It has a memory that it exercises, it attends to what is happening, and it anticipates further events or developments. That anticipation, however, is fraught with uncertainty, since one may be anticipating an action while simultaneously realizing that it may not happen. That is, memory, attention, expectation, and anticipation may be exercised at any given moment and be thwarted or fulfilled in the succeeding moment. Anticipation, then, a complex and structured event in which are nested positive and negative values, becomes manifested as *peripeteia* in the various forms by which minding is accomplished. At every moment, an uncertainty of outcome is made real and each participant will experience it as a peripeteia; that is, as the possibility of an abrupt and unexpected turn of events or situations.

This temporal dimension of the "nature of the world as men experience it" was an essential part of Burke's analysis, although not featured in his terminological stencil. Using Shakespeare's *Othello* to illustrate his method, Burke wrote:

> to be complete [one] should trace the development of the plot, stressing particularly the way in which the playwright builds the "potentials" (that is, gives the audience a more or less vague or explicit "in our next" feeling at the end of each scene, and subsequently transforms such promises into fulfillments). The potentialities of one scene would thus become the actualization of the next, while these in turn would be potentials from the standpoint of the unfolding still to come. (1964:179).

Another fundamental principle of the dramatic then is that all present moments lead into a future predicated on the discursive creation of a past and a present. All minding activity of the organism can be conceived as being in one of these three moments and often in all three simultaneously. Insofar as the minding activity encompasses a past, a present, and a future, a human, in focusing on the world, seeks a connection between the past and the present, and the present and the future. (Mead, 1964:289). In dramatically constituted forms, these connections are assembled as syntagmatic chains. One element of this chain leads logically, thematically, and temporally into the next one, establishing a coherent relationship of entailment that elicits the attention, and at times the engrossment, of an audience. Consciousness of time, its development, and its movement become thematized in the plot and narrative development of the drama and in the destiny of the characters enmeshed in them, with temporal sequences thematized as *causal* relationships.[1]

Minding is an ongoing activity that proceeds by means of processing signs. Time itself is experienced, may even be created, by the manipulation of signs. Insofar as "there can be no conception of the absolutely incognizable" (Peirce, 1958:35), time, ephemeral, evanescent, and fleeting though it may be, needs signs and assemblies of signs to be cognized. Peirce, it will be recalled, wrote, "We have no power of intuition, but every cognition is determined logically by previous cognitions" (1958:41). In minding a world, a mind experiences it as a temporal process and cognizes it as a sequence of signs, each determined by a previous one. And, *if there can be no cognition that is not determined by a previous cognition, it follows that current cognitions will beget further cognitions that beget others*, and so on. Temporal emergence, cognitive continuity, and semiosis become unified into a continuous process. It is this feature of the process of minding that enables an interaction to develop its dialogistic character and a "dialogical logic"—the existence of a cognitive continuity between signs.

The minding activity has a developing and progressive character and, like the universe itself, is developing in one direction only. Its recollections of the past are not a return to a past, but a construction of events from the past in the ever present, and these recollections too move forward, pregnant with the future. Such a process nevertheless is not so much a stream of consciousness as a canal with checks and balances, with sluices and gates, which can be said to possess a processive concreteness. These features of the canal of consciousness are human constructions that give the minding process definition and content. Once such a definition and content are given, the mind and the self become located in space and time. Dramas of life help situate and locate a self in both social space and social time and are a way for a self to try to get rid of feelings of alienation and absurdity. That is, location in space and time is accomplished by casting the self in a drama of human relations, in a story with developing sequences.

Paul Ricoeur has argued that two concepts borrowed from Aristotle will complete Augustine's thesis: *muthos* (emplotment) and *mimesis*. Notes Ricoeur, "Imitating or representing is a mimetic activity inasmuch as it produces something, namely the organization of events by emplotment" (1985:34). Mimetic activity is one of the basic ingredients, the very defining feature of stage plays and is a common component of everyday life as well. Such mimesis, and the emplotment that results from its success, is achieved by giving the situated self certain features that, presented discursively and behaviorally, mesh with the features others in the situation are presenting. *Mimesis and the consequent emplotment of the product with other such mimed products, enables emotions to be directed at oneself and others in a very precise and controlled manner.* Investing one's presentations of self with characteristics that vary from one situation and moment to the next allows one to generate whatever attitudes and emotions any particular situation and moment call for. Thus a mean and nasty characterization can be replaced by one that is friendly and affectionate the moment one's child enters the situation, a change that affects the ensuing nature of the plot and interaction.

Emplotment and characterization, or muthos and mimesis, are the figures with which the temporality of experience is manifested. Emplotment itself embodies the onward structuring of temporality by creating characters and putting them in episodes or creating episodes and putting characters in them. Each episode has an incompleteness and uncertainty to be resolved when a denouement is reached that is paralleled in the minding of the reader or listener. This feature of a drama, discursively created, may be called *programmed uncertainty*, because the uncertainty introduced is a measured and calculated one with the implication that, unlike those in real life, it will be resolved soon. This is similar to what Erich Auerbach calls the "retarding element." In discussing Homer's use of suspense and anticipation, he argued that narratives as such contain this retarding element. Citing the work of Goethe and Schiller, he describes the retarding element as the "going back and forth by means of episode" (1957:3), episodes that must be constructed so that they will "not fill the present entirely, will not put the crises, whose resolution is being awaited, entirely out of the reader's mind and thereby destroy the mood of suspense; the crisis and the suspense must continue, must remain in the background" (1957:3). These mimetic and emplotment activities are inseparable from temporal structures, temporality itself being created by management of mimesis and muthos. Muthos and mimesis have, in Ricoeur's words, an "interweaving reference" (1985:32). They implicate each other, subsume each other, one becoming the ground for the other.

The essential feature of the dramatic mode of experiencing the self in a world of other selves and things is its transformation through discursive acts. Discursive acts are more than what Kenneth Burke called "symbolic actions" since they use multiple forms of transformation. It is these complex transformational processes that are used to constitute acts, scenes, agents, agencies, purposes, and attitudes to implicate them in varying temporalities and mimetically create character and plot to lead them to a conclusion. In the discourses of everyday life, as in the grand rhetorical feasts of professional orators, one can discern the presence of dramaturgical principles. Drama in discourse, in fact, manifests itself in two fundamental modes: (1) The articulating self casts itself and various others into roles and conducts itself in and through these roles. This is discernible in its discourses, as in other forms of self-presentation. (2) Articulating selves introduce various dramatic constructions into their discourses to constitute and enhance discursive relationships and dialogic moments. Conversations, then, have a rhetorical form through which self and others are deployed in many graces and conceits. Although all discursive texts will have these dramaturgical properties as their constituent features, I will select certain examples to illustrate them separately.

## The Drama of Conversations

All discursive texts addressed to another will use one or more of the principles of dramaturgy; the longer the text the more likely are they to use them all. It is impossible not to use some of these categories in any piece of discourse, though admittedly they will be deployed in varying ratios. It can be said, however, that the less they are deployed and the less efficient their distribution, the less effective the text will be. The presence of acts, scenes, agents, agencies, and attitudes gives a discourse its fundamental presence in the world, its essential quiddity. Take the following brief exchange on a telephone:

A: May I help you?
B: Well, I don't know. My brother suggested that I call you.
A: I see. Well, he must have had a reason for making the suggestion. Has there been some personal problem or difficulty that you are experiencing?
B: Yes. I just lost my wife and I feel awfully depressed.

(Labov and Fanschell, 1977:25)

A telephone call to a stranger, albeit a therapist, needs an explanation, and the caller B first proposes another agent as the cause: my brother suggested it. The therapist A helps the caller along by asking for a purpose, and elicits it: "I just lost my wife and I feel awfully depressed." The act of calling implicit in the discourse is framed in the agency of the prospective patient and his brother, and a purpose is established in the exchange. The discourse, which is textured with these features, becomes persuasively intelligible and sufficient in its own terms to sustain a discursive moment and function as an initiating fragment for a relationship.

Consider the following text:

A:  You know, I saw Sam and Carol today, walking on the street.
B:  She works for him. . .
A:  Yeah I know. But you know there is walking and there is walking. . .
B:  What do you mean? Oh come on. . .
A:  I was in this slow-moving bus—caught in traffic you know—and there they were walking on the street. The bus and they were abreast for two and a half blocks.
B:  So?
A:  They were so close and earnest in their talk and you know there was an intimacy in the walking. . .
B:  Oh Jean. . .you always read too much in things. You are a scandalmonger.
A:  I wonder whether his wife knows. . .
B:  You are not going to tell her?
A:  No?

(Field Notes)

The simple act of walking together in a road scene is described, and a special reading is made of it. The exchange is invested with a purpose that is shared by the agents, a purpose inferred from the manner of the walking, its rhythm, and intimations of its intimacy. The mere observation of a physical proximity between two people becomes the occasion for a *muthos* between them in the eyes of the beholder. The scene, in other words, bears a ratio of intimacy. It further establishes a peripeteia by the implication that she may tell the wife of the man—or again she may not. It was dismissed as scandalmongering by the recipient, but she listened anyway.

Management and control of the interactions and relationships through dramatic principles is the method by which order and concordance are introduced into one's life, and the presentations of self through discourse become compositional acts in which the disjointed events and discordant experiences of a life are talked into a coherence and a concordance. One may not succeed in verbally unifying the events and experiences of a life into a tragic poem, as Aristotle would have wanted, but certainly one seeks to put it together in a narrative coherence. In the following example, an agent is seeking to introduce some sort of order into her life through the various discursive acts she is presenting. The following text is an opening gambit in a therapeutic session (A is the patient and B the therapist):

A:  Last week, when I was supposed to come—just about 20 minutes before I was leaving to come here—my boss came over and—They have just changed over companies and this was the final thing . . . all paperwork

and everything. So C that I work with didn't come in. So he came over
and said—he handed me a big printout and says "This gotta be done." I
said "All right. No problem". And I say—and I says, "Well, when do you
need it by?" And he says, "Today," and I says, "Well, I have got 20
minutes—how's that, you know?" And he says, "I really need it today."
So I went over to this other girl and asked her if, uh, she had anything
she had to do. I says, uh, "I'll start it, can you finish it?" And she says,
"Well, I have to do this." So I went back to him and I says "Does this
really have to be done today?" And he says, "I'd really like it." I says,
"Well, you know, I leave—." I says, "There's nobody else here." I says,
"If it has to be done, I'll stay." He said, "Well, if you would." I says,
"O.K." So I felt in a way, I was doing him a little bit of a favor . . . not
much, then you know.

B:   Did he know that you, uh, that you had an appointment?
A:   Yeah. So I felt like, in a way, that I was doing him a favor.

(Gill and Hoffman, 1982)

While not an extraordinary story, its gripping quality is created by the
seemingly artless use of dramatic principles. The patient first establishes
the scene with a few deft strokes: the office at the company that has just
changed hands, the boss coming over to her, and she going over to the
other typist. The act is then described: a typing job, but a job with a
problem attached in that it is an emergency job and the office is about to
close. There are various agents in the story—a boss, an uncooperative
confederate, and the protagonist. Because the teller of the story casts
herself in the role of the protagonist, the story is depicted from her
perspective. Agencies become dominant: she seeks her confederate's
assistance, but then agrees to do the job herself. Her purpose, too,
becomes the crucial one, though intertwined with that of the boss: he
needs the document today, and she will stay overtime and do it as a
"little bit of a favor." That is, she is not being ordered to do it, and she is
not doing it because she is a supplicant and a subordinate, but as a more
or less voluntary gesture toward her employer. Moreover, even a shade
of character is presented, a character and attitude that become elements
of the muthos and mimesis of the text. A's attitudes are rather involved
and convoluted. She is ready and obliging toward her boss: "All right.
No problem," she says at being presented with a big job. But then she
discovers it is an urgent job that has to be done immediately and she has
only twenty minutes before closing time. Her attitude toward this discovery is that she is not going to work beyond her hours readily and
voluntarily, so she tries to get someone else to do the job and then asks
the boss whether it is really urgent. When he tells her yes, it is only as a
last resort that she agrees to stay late and work. Even so, she is not
obeying the orders of the boss but doing him a favor.

This discourse, an elaborate account of why A failed to keep an appointment with her therapist, achieves its narrative power and fundamental plausibility by the presentation of details that add a certain verisimilitude, as well as by the use of plotting and mimetic structures. Further, in this brief report of certain events in her office, the patient is also able to bring a number of other characters into the discursive presence of the therapist, enriching the moment of the interaction insofar as more selves are now present in it, albeit as reports and representations.

In less elaborate discursive interactions, the structures of dramatic temporality are created as serialed acts. Such orderings of discursive acts, made to constitute a peripeteic series, create a developing continuity of signification. Each and every moment of the series begets the next, until the "expectation of endings," as Frank Kemode (1979:65) puts it, is fulfilled. In such exercises, memory, attention, and expectation are served: in the very structure of the discourse the contexts are assembled so that they maintain at least a semblance of continuity from the past, elicit attention, and leave things in the discourse in such a way that the recipient will be able to maintain a continuity on his or her own. The responsive sentences in fact seek to and usually succeed in maintaining a semantic interlocking between the preceding and succeeding elements of the discourse. Consider:

A:   What time is the next train to New York?

This is a question that implies the existence of past, present, and future trains, and also reflects a memory of past trains, attends to the present by the question, and anticipates a future train. The question, itself directed toward a future, is poised for a continuity in a response, and the questioner is now caught in an expectation and tentative moment with an act yet to be completed. This simple and ordinary question has created a momentum in which the self of the questioner will become implicated in a momentum that will soon implicate the respondent as well. The semantically interlocked response the question calls for is provided with:

B:   The next train is at 10:20.

The ubiquitousness and the importance of such a relationship is also attested to by the way Abbott and Costello make the interlocking itself ambiguous and therefore a source of humor:

A:   Now on the St. Louis team, we have Who's on first, What is on second, I don't know is on third.

B: That's what I want to find out. I want you to tell me the names of the fellows on the St. Louis team.

A: I am telling you. Who's on first, What's on second, I don't know is on third.

B: You know the fellows' names?

A: Yes.

B: Who is playing first?

A: Yes.

(Anobile, 1975:08)

In transcribing this passage the clue to its proper interlocking interpretation is given by the fact that the initial statement does not have a mark of interrogation and is in fact a nominative sentence, thus making *Who* into a proper noun and the subject of the sentence, whereas in the later usage by B *who* becomes a pronoun and the sentence an interrogative one.

Consider also the following: "He is an awful idiot. . . that is putting two and two together—saying I really do not know. Saying Cathie and so I observe and flowers. An orange and shoe laces" (Abse, 1971:55). This is a transcription of a statement from one diagnosed as schizophrenic. Its syntactic and categorical structures are unclear and no intentional act can be interpreted from it—at least not a lucid and pointed one. It is obviously impossible to respond in a semantically continuous way to this utterance. In its own terms, it makes it impossible for a respondent to enter significantly into a discourse to create an interaction with the initiator. In other words, the initiator's statement lacks dramatic potential and will only lead to arrested momentum. Needless to say, this is an extreme example, but nonschizophrenics also can present us with dry and impenetrable statements, leaving us with no potential for semantic consummation. It is not so much that in such encounters one cannot take one's turn that prevents it from being considered a conversation, but that no continuous dramatically appropriate response can be made to it. The schizophrenic's statement, by forestalling the other from taking a turn, not only prevents a conversation from emerging but more importantly prevents a social organization from emerging.

Typically, then, an assertion, a declaration, a question, or even an exclamation leaves some matters *incomplete* or *implicatory* so that others can enter the discourse. Such statements indicate an imminence and an uncertainty, which call for a responsive completion that implicates an anticipation of the semantic intention of the initiator. The absence of such a response will indicate a state of interruption, a lack of effect in one's signifying acts, and a frustration of any emerging interaction. Conversations need the tempo of successive exchanges warranted by the nature of the situation and the character of the participants. A slowness to respond to a statement in the form of a question will indicate a number of significations, for example, a lack of interest in continuing the conversation or allowing the conversation to take the turn the question has already defined. In either case, the interaction at that moment confronts a contingency: (1) to proceed with the line already initiated; (2) to change it; or (3) to abandon the conversation altogether. If on the other hand, a quick and ready response had been given to the question, further questions, or assertions would have been forthcoming and the conversation would have proceeded apace. That is, the dialogue would have continued, the interaction been maintained, and the relevant selves been validated. Let us go back to a familiar conversation found in Loman (1967:1).

> Michael J.:   I bet you a nickel
> George J.:    What?
> Michael J.:   Gotta to see some money. . . . Bet you a nickel that I'm looking sharper than you

When the conversation reached this stage, its life persisted, because George said the right thing, and maintained a tight string, so to speak. Consider an alternative.

> George J.:    O.K.
> Michael J.:   What?
> George J.:    O.K. Whatever you say. . .

A certain slackness would have developed here, leaving Michael in a state of incompleteness and not knowing exactly where to go next. The same would have happened had George merely shrugged his shoulders in a gesture of indifference. What George actually said was,

> George J.:    No you wasn't

This is a responsive statement, short, and contradictory and it will no doubt contribute a necessary tautness to the conversation. By his response, George introduces drama at two levels: (1) at the level of the controlled crispness of the retort, a short and staccato construction; (2) by denial of the other's claim, introducing an agonistic into the discourse.

The next exchange introduces and develops these themes further:

> Michael J.:   No, you had your play clothes on (laughter)
> George J.:    I ain't have my play clothes on.
> Michael J.:   You had your Batman socks on too.

> George J.:   I did (Laughs) did not
> Michael J.:   You did (Laughs) so. You did so.

Michael now charges George with wearing play clothes and Batman socks, and not only laughs himself but elicits laughter from George. A playful contradiction between them is achieved in this exchange, emphasized both by the use and repetition of the word *so*. The agonistic and the tautness remain in the discourse, although George has introduced a new element into the proceedings: the teasing and the laughter. Had he merely repeated his earlier claims or had Michael merely asserted his again, the conversation would have experienced a slackness and, no doubt, deteriorated or been terminated. Indeed, Michael senses this and anticipates an ending to the conversation with:

> Michael J.:   Got something else to say?

George does in fact have something else to say. He introduces an invidious comparison and criticism. He also quickly and readily makes a new move:

> George:   Wait a minute—let me tell you something. Greg Barker look better than you. You come in here with your clothes hanging down all the way down to here (laughs)

He also emphasizes the humorous and teasing nature of the interaction by laughing as he succeeds in putting Michael on the defensive:

> George J.:   You come here with your shirt going all the way down here and your shirt sticking out.
> Michael J.:   What? [George presses home his advantage.]

Noticeably, in this second allusion to the ungainliness of Michael's clothes, George does not repeat the phrase "clothes hanging out." Rather, he introduces a stylistic variation: "Your shirt going all the way down here and your shirt sticking out."

Michael goes further on the defensive and can now only utter a monosyllabic response:

> Michael:   Who?
> George:   You.

The conversation proceeds along these lines: a give and take, a change of position on various sartorial issues, with a sustained tautness. The sartorial part of the conversation soon exhausts itself, and Michael introduces a new topic, a new beginning:

Michael J.:   I bet you I got more money than you. I got cash money in my
              pocket now.

George still does not want the conversation to slacken and terminate. He
wants, one can surmise, it to continue so he can be in the dialogue and
experience social contact and reciprocal signification. He jumps into
Michael's conversational trap:

George J.:   *You ain't* got no cash money.

This segment of the conversation proceeds with the necessary tautness,
the following exchanges once again containing ready responses and
agonistics and teasing laughter:

Michael J.:   You want to bet? (laughs)
George J.:    You ain't got nothing but fifty cents and you got to buy a
              notebook with that. (laughs)

As it proceeds, the conversation takes a number of new turns. The
money talk becomes notebook and pencil talk, rises to a crescendo at
which stage a third party intervenes, and then to girl talk and tennis ball
talk. Throughout the conversation, the sense of challenge and response,
albeit a playful one, is maintained by the *leit motif* of a bet. "I bet you a
nickel," "I bet you," "I bet you five dollars," "I bet you ten dollars."
Betting one's money against another, of course, is the quintessential as
well as the simplest dramaturgical ploy in many societies. It puts one's
self, encapsulated in one's monetary or at least exchangeable worth, into
a contest the outcome of which is in doubt. The clearest example of this
is poker. But many games of chance have the same feature of becoming
instruments by which dramas are created in otherwise mundane lives.
Such games become transformed into everyday conversational vocabularies, so that even when no money is being wagered, they function in
the same way by introducing dramatic tautness and uncertainty into the
discourse and interaction.

### The Mimesis of the Self

People can put a self into play in everyday life by using their multifaceted powers of transformation. They give it action and momentum
and, using their powers of choice and selectivity as well as linguistic
facility, define it and enable others to define it in variable terms. Indeed,
in each interaction with another, not only does one pay attention to
one's own identity and role, but also to the changing shades and colora-

tions of such identities as they develop in the discourses produced in the interactions. Such shades and colorations may be termed character, and are meant to suggest not only a developing alteration in the identity of the participants but also an enrichment of the identity. Goffman (1961b), in his examination of the distance that actors bring to the performance of certain roles, gives us a lucid example of such mimetic transformation. A surgeon in the operating room banters and jokes with the attending staff of nurses and aides and thereby creates a mood of ease and slackness in the tension that is likely to be present in a surgical situation. The surgeon, momentarily becoming a jester, adds a dimension to his self as a surgeon, and plots it with the cooperative and easeful performance of the aides, which helps to ensure a successful operation. One creates a character for the self in a situation by mimesis and it becomes temporally and dramatically integrated with those of the others:

| | |
|---|---|
| Chief Surgeon Jones: | A small Richardson please. |
| Scrub Nurse: | Don't have one. |
| Dr. Jones: | O.K., then give me an Army and Navy. |
| Scrub Nurse: | It looks like we don't have one. |
| Dr. Jones: | (lightly joking) No army or navy man here. |
| Intern: | (dryly) No one in the armed forces, but Dr. Jones here is in the Boy Scouts. |
| Scrub Nurse: | Will there be more than three [sutures]? We are running out of sutures. |
| Dr. Jones: | I don't know. |
| Intern: | We can finish up with Scotch tape. |
| Intern: | (looking for towel clamps around body) Where in the world. . .? |
| Scrub Nurse: | Underneath the towel. (Intern turns to the nurse and in slow measure makes a full cold bow to her.) |

(Goffman, 1961b:118)

In these exercises, an actor can be seen to be creating, more or less deliberately, the emotionality and intellectuality of the interactions. To quote Denzin again, "Emotions are temporally embodied situated self-feelings that arise from emotional and cognitive social acts that people direct to self or have directed toward them by others" (1984:19).

In a dating encounter between two strangers, the conversation can be used by both parties to define qualifications to the identities already projected by the revelation of information, display of views, attitudes, and feelings about things, people, and issues in the world. In such an encounter between two people who have met for the first time, one party might begin by referring to an item in the newspaper about events in South Africa. In the ensuing conversation both parties will be able to discern the political and social philosophy of the other as liberal/radical, antiracist, and so forth. This characterization could soon be followed by one party's attempt to connect certain features of quantum physics to political processes. While on the whole this could fail to convince his partner, he will have nevertheless established another facet of his character as a serious and imaginative person and an expert in the abstruse fields of physics. She, on the other hand, by having listened to him patiently, and by announcing decisively that she is not convinced by his analogy, will have indicated her character as both a patient listener and as anything but a patsy willing to go along with whatever the other is asserting.

In this case the topic of the conversation itself will have served to define a character for the respective participants. In other circumstances, other strategies serve to define character. Events that intrude into the conversation function to provide opportunities for the definition of the character of the participants. An attempt by a third party to insult the female half of an interaction has often served to allow the male half to assert himself by challenging the insulter, perhaps fighting him, thus altering the nature of the interaction. Indeed, a number of dramaturgic points are achieved by these events: the man in the interaction has shown himself to be one who is willing to commit his self to some extent to the other's interests and reputation, and he has also declared himself to be capable of courage and determination. These features will now color not only the character of the man but also the course of the interaction, just as a failure to "stand up and be counted" would. Similar payoffs can be expected in ongoing conversations where an opportunity presents itself for a participant to defend his or her beliefs, principles, religion, country, or ethnic group. Standing up for these will introduce tension into the proceedings and enhance its dramatic qualities as well as define the character of the participant in question.

In short, character is created by the discourse that one produces, through the details and description that they contain, and by using the opportunities that present themselves during the course of the interactions to create the events that display character. Developing sensitivity to the changing shades of character achieved by mastering the acts of interpreting the emerging signs and symbols becomes a feature of competent and skillful interactors.

Consider another example where the development of character, and adding color and nuance to it, is achieved by managing discourse. Humans often find themselves in conversational exchanges on various general topics. At parties and in other social gatherings, one person can take a strong position on politics or a politician, for example, forcing others to agree or disagree with him or her in varying degrees. A dramaturgically and conversationally adroit person, by taking an opposite position, can create tension and peripeteia. Emotions will be roused, adrenalin released, and perhaps some of those present will never speak to each other again, but the conversation and the encounter will have been saved from dullness. Such self-characterizations, I venture to say, normally occur in a conversational series: each party hugs a position that is different from that of the conversational other, thereby creating a logically separate identity for himself or herself. As social psychologically and epistemologically necessary as these moves are, they are also dramaturgically sound ones, since different characters are brought into the discursive interaction and what G. H. Mead called the "psychology of ennui" is avoided. "The psychology of ennui and of satiation, so far as it is wearying, is found in the irritability of certain types of response and the wearing-out of the particular stimulations which have aroused them. What is sought under these conditions are novelties in the form of stimulations, not in the whole activity" (Mead, 1938:6). Instances that represent the psychology of ennui are conversations that do not have a minimum of the agonistic in them. For example, a partner who (1) agrees with everything you say, (2) has no input of his or her own to make to the conversation, (3) does not take the conversation into the next stage on his or her own initiative, (4) does not indicate a new topic when the earlier topic is about to wear itself out can be considered an ennuic other.

Ennui is obviated in conversations at the simplest level by disagreements, demurrals, and challenges to the dominant theme of the conversation, or by an incremental and essentially different agreement. Thus, a simple statement can achieve this by making the self a protagonist able to enter into a dramatic syntacticity with another. Once can literally talk himself or herself into a drama. Consider the following:

A:    Nixon is not so bad after all. Everyone in politics is a crook up to a point.
B:    Not so bad? Not so bad? He was not like other politicians. He was tricky all the way—from his first election to the last.

(Field Notes)

This contradictory response of the other sets up a situation in which there is an immediate dramatic tension, a relevant differentiation of character between the two partners and, above all, creates an incline that will give momentum to the conversation. These features of this simple exchange ensure at least a minimum duration for the interaction and a distinct elevation of emotionality.

On the other hand, the conversation could have proceeded as follows:

A:    Nixon is not a bad fellow after all. Everyone in politics does something wrong.

B:   Of course he is not a bad fellow at all. He was merely a victim of a liberal
     conspiracy. They framed him.

There is some dramatic tension here too. By upscaling his essential
agreement with A and then adding a new element into the conversation,
B has opened a new avenue to take, a new quarry to pursue, or even a
new conflict to be faced with A denying the likelihood of a conspiracy.
Further, B and A are now differentiated from each other on relevant
issues, although there is a basic agreement on the major theme.

If B had responded to A's remarks with a mere "Yes", "Indeed", or
"If you say so," then the conversation can be said to have been in some
danger of termination or developing ennui. By such a response, B will
have allowed the conversation to become slack, failed to differentiate his
character from that of A, and undermined the emergence of the agonistic in it. By offering no input of his own to the conversation, however,
his self will have become irrelevant to the interaction. If the self of either
partner is absent in the conversation, the interaction becomes empty
and the maintenance of an ongoing relationship stymied.

The characters that emerge in the course of an interaction produce
their own story. In the above conversation about Nixon, the plot, however minimal, seems to be the contest between the two characters for
dominance. They bring arguments and data to support their claims. As
the characters are defined, the plot is thickened, and as the plot is
thickened, characters are developed. The plot develops too by the introduction of new incidents. The conversation about Nixon, for example,
can be developed by the addition of the comments about Nixon being a
victim of a liberal conspiracy. This can elicit further additions, leading to
an enrichment of the story and the development of the plot. Such
enrichment and development are achieved by cultivating a semantic
interlocking and a logical progression from one stage of the plot to
another. This will create an agonistic dimension to the discourse as well
as a sense of imminence. In ordinary conversations, the denouement is
usually not very dramatic but nevertheless there is typically an ending of
a line of the discourse and a new beginning.

The life of an articulator can function as an inexhaustible source for
anecdotes. Bare facts will not elicit the attention of the audience, however, since they need to be embellished and put into suitable dramatic
forms. Consider the following:

A:   I hear you have got yourself a good deal at Ohio State. . .
B:   Yeah, I have indeed—and I didn't even think about leaving Minnesota.
A:   What happened?
B:   One of my students called me up and told me about this ad in the
     *Chronicle*. . . He said the position seemed tailor-made for me.
A:   That's nice.

Here the dramatic element is forcefully introduced: I did not even seek the position actively, I did not even know about it, suggesting an implicit theme: it is my fate, my destiny, that made this happen, and not my intentional self, not my will, insofar as I came to this position by happenstance. Once this is established the following is presented:

A: I asked to teach only one course per semester, a hundred thousand dollars in salary and research support, you know.
B: And what happened?
A: They met all my terms.

The heroic theme is presented here: I vanquished my enemies; I bested them; they gave in to my demands. Such stories can also bring people into the dialogic moment in that they represent the success of a friend or colleague, and since there are no feelings of resentment or envy, they can lead to a shared sense of success. However, there is always an inherent danger in the strategy of creating dialogic connections. If one goes across the thin boundary line and elaborates the drama more than is warranted or embellishes the heroism, a good self-story becomes a boast and a brag and will *alienate* the audience. It will put the auditors on the defensive, and they may seek to leave not only the conversation but also the place and the person.

This process of discursive mimesis of the self is taken to its ultimate point in therapeutic encounters. A self is able to enter a dialogic relationship in which he or she is a hero, or at least the chief protagonist for a while, and can talk and talk and others will share the limelight only if they are brought into the discourse by the narrator with only a minimum of interruption. The talker can cast his or her self in any role and give it whatever character he or she wants for a ready, willing, and attentive audience. In these therapeutic interactions, one is able not only to present a self, but to create one as he or she talks along. In such dramas, the therapist himself or herself soon comes to play a supporting role with the real and fictional characters of the patient's life story, the two of them thereby becoming almost inextricably intertwined. The meaning of the session of therapy for the patient, and no doubt for the therapist, is in the continuous present of the continuing, if interrupted, sessions themselves. In them, through discursive acts and dramatic realization, the presence of a meaning is fully experienced, leading at times both to an "ecstasy" as well as a breaking of several external bonds.[2]

### The Mimesis of the Other

If the dramatic elements cannot be introduced into the ongoing conversations by making oneself a protagonist, as in the events presented so far, the participant introduces narratives in which others, real or imaginary, become the protagonists. These typically take the form of anecdotes, jokes, and riddles. Anecdotes are talk in which little dramas are created about people one knows. Acts and scenes are presented and various features depicted that create an opportunity for the play of emotions and the experience of peripeteia. Consider the following, delivered in the course of an interaction between two friends:

> A:  Did you hear what Kevin did? He has been going out with this girl—I think her name was Karol—for a couple of months . . . and she wouldn't put out for him . . . kept on saying no, not now, and he went mad. He stopped calling her and sent her a bill for all the money he had spent on her.
> B:  Not really? You are kidding.
> A:  Honest . . . Itemized and dated too.
> B:  Come on now . . . Even Kevin can't be that silly. . .

> (Field Notes)

In the text a character known to both participants is introduced, and certain events that happened to him are described. The initial segment of the anecdote contains a very normal event: Kevin is taking Karol out. This segment is followed by another, which describes an event that is slightly abnormal: she refuses intimacy, though by the current mores of the community in question she was expected to provide it. The final segment produces a climactic denouement: Kevin, considering the relationship more a contractual one than a romantic quest in which the likelihood of disappointment is an essential part, demands the return of the earnest money. The anecdote by itself introduces into the ongoing relationship a moment of interest and attention and frames an expectation: what can this anecdote lead to about the Kevin that we both know? It becomes the matter with which the interaction is sustained and momentarily fills the space between the friends and keeps their connection intact. This is done artfully by means of talk that contains a character, a series of acts, and a denouement that is unexpected and unusual. In addition, it creates a dialogic moment for the two participants by introducing an emotion, a shared whimsy, and mild contempt, regarding the silliness of Kevin's conduct. The anecdote breaks the expectations that one has about conduct in courting situations, thus breaking what George Meredith has called the "malady of sameness" (in Sypher, 1956:ix). Indeed Kevin's conduct, as described in the anecdote, constitutes the essence of comedy: a change in expected conduct that elicits both laughter and ridicule not unaccompanied by pity and compassion. Meredith wrote that a test of one's comic perception is whether or not one can "detect the ridicule of them you love, without loving them less: and more by being able to see yourself as somewhat ridiculous in dear

eyes, and accepting the correction their image of you proposes"
([1877]1956:42).

Anecdotes of the kind about Kevin are usually referred to as gossip. Often discussed in a pejorative way, it is nevertheless an essential element of the discursive life. Gossip ties at least three people together into a discursive relationship: the party who is telling, the party who is listening, and the party or parties about whom there is the telling. The latter become socially present and communally alive as a result of such discussions, while those who have no discourses about them are socially dead. Further, gossip contains actors who are known to the interactants, thereby obviating the need for characterization of any sort. The mere naming of the persons introduces the characters and their characteristics, enabling an economy in the telling of the story. The teller can proceed directly to the episode in which the relevant characters are involved and in a series of smooth moves produce a denouement. The narrative content of the gossipy anecdote, to achieve dramatic efficacy, often develops a theme in which a violation of an accepted rule or custom is the central problematic. This gives one the opportunity to exercise one's emotions and assert one's values and create a dialogic moment by displaying a sharing of the emotions and the values explicated by the anecdote. Consider the following:

A:  I went to see Arnold Brown last night . . . you know him don't you? He was shooting crap with his daddy and you know, he was cheating the old man all the time.

B:  He did? I didn't know he was like that.

(Hannerz, 1967:21)

This anecdote puts Brown in a bad light and describes the violation of certain standards. To cheat at craps is bad enough but to cheat one's own father, an old man, is to describe the violation of a relationship that is almost sacred. One takes care of one's father, one defends and protects him in his old age, and to cheat him at a game where additional rules are in operation is certainly a matter worthy of interest, attention, talk, and the evocation of emotions. Perhaps not amounting to an oedipal crime, the act is yet a violation of norms.

If anecdotes either about people in the teller's own social circles or a public figure known to the audience are not forthcoming, a fictional story that is typically part of a culture of subculture is recounted. These stories that sustain the interaction and maintain a dialogue are produced in the course of a conversation. Jokes, or what should really be called joke-stories, are well-made dramas that are recalled and recounted at the proper moment to fill the spaces between people with discursive structures that have the capacity to elicit attention and anticipation and give play to emotions.

Sigmund Freud ([1905]1960), in his masterly analysis of jokes, examined the techniques and purposes of jokes in detail, their mechanisms of pleasure, and their motives. He concluded with an examination of their relationship to dreams and the unconscious and to the comic elements in culture. One feature of the joke that he missed was its relationship to the events that took place just before the joke was introduced, and the events thereafter, and the significance of the joke for the interaction in which it is recounted. Needless to say, these are minor lapses in a major work, but discussing them seems important in an analysis of the discourses of everyday life.

In the hands of Legman (1967), one of Freud's disciples, the treatment of jokes as clues to the unconscious has been taken further. For Legman, jokes are the means of "infinite aggressions by everyone against everyone. In the culminating laugh by the listener or observer, whose position is often really that of a victim or butt, the teller of the joke betrays his hidden hostility and signals his victory by being, theoretically at least, the one person who does not laugh" (1967:9). This humorless view of jokes and the social acts in which they occur may well be true of some jokes and situations. However, one must distinguish between jokes addressed to the other in which he or she is the pilloried one, and jokes where a third party is the victim. Further, it is important to distinguish between grades of aggressiveness—from mild agonistic elements to extreme degrees of hostility. In any case, whatever unconscious elements they may subsume, jokes are preeminently dramatic features of discursive relationships.

Indeed, it is important to examine the conscious meanings of jokes as they occur in discourse, and to study their place and role in ongoing dialogic moments and relationships before one can come to the unconscious or hidden significance. The conscious or "surface" significances of jokes can be found in their dramatic form and placement in the development of the discourse. Typically they contain characters, albeit rather roughly and readily sketched ones, a tight if somewhat truncated plot, a decisive denouement, and often verbal play and display. At the moment of telling, they are able to elicit immediate attention and interest, create an emotional resonance within the social act, and define the contours of the selves participating in the joking. In fact, such stories are best described as monodramas in which a narrator verbally enacts a short play all by himself or herself, although as in the morality plays of medieval Europe, the audience may participate as well.

In the course of a conversation, one finds that he or she has to keep listening and talking to the other or that he or she would like to talk and listen to the other, and that certain strategies have to be used to achieve either aim. Further, it is mandatory to produce narratively coherent and thematically integrated words. Insofar as this is not always easy and the other may not be interested and attentive, jokes come in handy for doing the job. The telling, the attention and the listening, the smiles and the laughter, or for that matter the protests and derision that result from a bad joke keep people together and in dialogic emotionality. This can happen only if the joke is introduced at the appropriate moment in an ongoing conversation with an appropriate audience. But above all, the internal structure of the joke must be able to elicit attention and create a surprising denouement.

Consider one of Freud's jokes:

> Mr. and Mrs. X live in fairly grand style. Some people think that the husband has earned a lot and so has been able to lay by a bit . . . ; others think that the wife has lain back a bit . . . so has been able to earn a lot. ([1905]1960:33)

This is a joke that depends on a verbal parallelism between two idioms, the second of which produces a radically different meaning but still maintains thematic unity with the point of the joke. Freud notes, "A really diabolically ingenious joke! And achieved with such an economy of means!" ([1905]1960:33). In addition, the joke creates a problematic situation: How is it possible for Mr. and Mrs. X to live in such a grand manner? This moment of uncertainty is quickly resolved, but resolved ambiguously: he earned it and saved it and invested it, or she earned it by whoring. This unusual set of alternatives is made dramatic by the punning idiom. The issue, however, is still not resolved. We still do not know how the Xs earned their fortune, but it scarcely seems to matter. Rather, experiencing a momentary peripeteia and a semblance of a resolution that takes the mind in a different direction seems to suffice.

In this case another feature of the joke that enhances its emotional potential is that it concerns, as many jokes do, a sexual activity, and a deviant one at that. Such jokes are tantamount to talk about sex occurring between intimates. Such sex talk is emotionally alive and suggestive, and it brings selves together and redeems the mechanical and masked nature of many relationships and makes them into personal ones. Ordinary relationships between the sexes are regulated by a barrier of rules, of manner, decorum, and taste and protect the selves and defend the ego. But the breaking of the barriers gives feeling tones to the discourse. Such a breaking of the taboos and the emergence of feeling tones creates new bonds of intimacy or renews old ones. Further, these jokes often have a cognitive element that makes the hearers *work* at deciphering either an ambiguity or construing the structure of the joke, thus eliciting their interlocking participation in the proceedings. The surprise that comes at the end—at the unexpected "turn of events" (i.e., the line of the plot) and the novel "turn of phrase"—functions as a climax to the story and enlivens the social act. The participants are more securely interlocked semantically, more fully resonant emotionally, and each has made a contribution to the social act either in the telling of the joke or in the construing of its various elements, and in the shared savoring of its dramatic and literary riches.

Finally, the joke does contain an aggressive component. It can slander a woman, for example, with the oldest slander of patriarchal society. While this is politically reprehensible, it is also the source of the emotionality of the dialogic moment: we are together in this act of demeaning a woman, and through her, the husband. Culturally induced anxieties about straying wives, envy of the couple's wealth, verbal play, and discursive drama are all unified into a short text.

Auerbach's "retarding element" comes into play in the telling of many jokes (1957). In Homer's description of Odysseus's return home and his recognition by the servant Euriclea, he interposes a flashback to a boar hunt that occurred during Odysseus's boyhood. This retards the development of the immediate story by postponing the denouement—the discovery by Penelope that the stranger she had invited was in fact her lost husband Odysseus. From the narrative viewpoint, such a retarding of the development of the immediate line of the plot, in addition to creating suspense and anticipation, enables the author to introduce other narratives that can frame the impending story and give it shape and contour. According to Auerbach, this interruption by Homer enables him to introduce to the reader/auditor relevant information about Odysseus's grandfather Autolysis, "his house, the precise degree of kinship, his character, and no less exhaustively than touchingly, his behavior after the birth of the grandson. . . all narrated again with such complete externalization of all the elements of the story and their interconnections as to leave nothing in obscurity" (1957:2).

The erotic joke-story, like the Homeric one, employs similar means (the going back and forth of its elements) to achieve their effects as in the following one that Harvey Sacks analyzed for his rather different purposes:[3]

Ken:   You wanna hear my sister told me a story last night?
Roger: I don't want to hear it. But if you must.
  Al:  What's purple and an island? Grape Britain. That's what his sister . . .
Ken:   No. To stun me she says there was these three girls and they just got married?

Roger:   Ehhh/heh/heh.
Ken:     Ah uh.
Roger:   Wait a second.
Ken:     (Silence)
Al:      Heh.
Roger:   Drag that by me again hehh/hehh.
Ken:     There . . . there was three girls. And they were all sisters. And they
         just got married to three brothers.
Roger:   You better have a long talk with your sister.
Ken:     Wait a minute.

                                                                  (1974:338)

Ken introduces a joke and to all appearances is eager to tell it, but he
has a number of interruptions to handle as he goes along. However,
they are not so much interruptions in the conversation as they are
elements of a conversation in which the telling of the joke is merely one
element. That is, they are discursive acts by each participant in a dialogic
moment. Ken's friends, while he wants to tell the joke as part of his
discursive act, contribute their acts by means of the various interjections. In the overall structure of the telling and the effects it mobilizes,
they function as retarding elements. They delay the development and
denouement and yet introduce details that add to the import of the
story. Ken's sister, though absent from the interaction, is an important
feature of the dialogic moment. Like Odysseus's grandfather, she helps
to frame the story and makes her physical absence felt as a presence.
Her presumptive innocence, initially indicated by the childish joke
about "grape Britain," is contradicted by the main story itself, and the
interjections introduce this theme as a retarding element: She was innocent and she has now grown up. Indeed, the Sacks version of the story
begins with an allusion to the sister and ends with another. In artfully
constructed narratives, these features can be deliberately introduced by
an author and seem to occur in naturally emerging discourses. In the
completely interactional event between the three young men, the joke
itself becomes a medium in which the selves of the various participants
are manifested. This becomes vividly apparent as the telling proceeds.
Each participant listens and seeks understanding of the proceedings and
makes some contribution of his own, even if it is only a noise of assent.
Ken continues:

Ken:     Wait a minute.
Roger:   Oh, three brothers.
Al:      Heh.
Ken:     And uh . . . so . . .
Al:      The brother of these sisters?
Ken:     No they are different.

Al:      Heh.
Ken:     You know, different families.
Roger:   Is closer than before.
Ken:     So.
Al:      Eh eh.
Ken:     Quiet.
Al:      He hh hh.
Ken:     So, first of all, that night, they are . . . on their honeymoon and the
         mother-in-law says well, Why don't you all spend the night here and
         then you can go on your honeymoon in the morning. First night the
         mother walks up the first door and she hears this uuuuuuuuhh.
         Second door is HHOOOOHH. Third door there is nothing. She
         stands there for about twenty minutes waiting for something to
         happen . . . nothing.
Ken:     Next morning, she talks to the first daughter and she says, how
         come you went YEEEAAGGHH last and the daughter sez well, it
         tickled mummy, and the second girl, how come you screamed and
         she says, Oh mummy it hurt. The third girl, walks up to her and . . .
         Why didn't you say anything last night? You told me it was impolite
         to talk with my mouth full hh hyok.
Al:      Ha Ha Ha Ha Ha.
Ken:     Eh h heh hehh.
Al:      Heh heh heh.
Roger:   Delayed reaction.
Al:      Had to think about it a while.
Roger:   Hhh heh; You mean the deep hidden meaning there doesn't hit you
         right away. Hehhhh.
Al:      What he meant to say is . . .
Roger:   Kind of got psychological overtones.
Al:      (        )
Ken:     Little sister is getting older.
Roger:   Heh heh heh.

                                                                (1974:338–340)

   The punchline produces continuing discursive interactions; there is
shared laughter and appreciation at the beginning, then Roger takes his
turn at directing an irony at Al and then an analytical comment and Ken
offers a summary judgment on his sister. A quintessential dialogic
moment, with the joke functioning as medium for each actor to play his
part vis-à-vis the others, has been created. The joke occurs as an en-
hancement of the ongoing conversation and is achieved by the dramatic
structure of the joke, its temporal and narrative elements, and the
introduction of various characters. The sister telling the joke initially to
her brother Ken introduces an added touch of piquancy to the story. The
sister's sexual status and knowingness is thrust into the interaction and
is made discursively available to the brother's friends.

However, the most striking aspect of this joke's course is in the participatory nature of the encounter. What at first encounter may appear to be unwarranted interruptions by the listeners are really contributions made by them to the effectiveness of the joke. They constitute clarifications, apostrophes, and underlinings of the thematic and cultural content. In a very striking way, the entire episode recalls the dramas of past ages. The chorus of the Greek plays, which was at one time the audience of the ritual theater, certainly is similar to the group around Ken. The audience participated vociferously and vigorously in the morality plays of the Middle Ages, in the religious discourses called *harikata* and *katapirasangam* in India, and in the black churches in the American South. Such audience participation is not an intrusion but an essential element of the dialogic nature of these rituals. It brings the audience into the heart of the action, and the actors and preachers become parts of a larger cast than in the modern theater or the modern church. In the telling of the joke, the audience also refuses to be mere auditors and becomes part of the cast, with its own cues to follow and lines to deliver. The entire structure of the telling becomes a collective enterprise binding the participants into a community.

The structures and thematic content of joking encounters of this kind, commonplace in adolescent and adult male subcultures, can also be compared to the Dionysian ritual of old Greece, the dithyramb, as well as to other forms of erotic rituals and folk theater found in many parts of the world. There is entertainment as well as certain forms of ritual degradation for the participants involved in these presentations, although worship and regradation can become involved in some variations. The Dionysian ritual was wild and orgiastic, in which a chorus chanted responsively to an improvisational song or story by a leader. Eventually, the dithyramb ceased to be improvisational, becoming rather conventionalized, but the basic form and matter remained the same (Pickard-Cambridge, 1927).[4] The interactional effect of these structures is to bind the initiator and the respondent together into one unit.

Mimetic transformation of the other, and wordplay, also occur in the telling and unraveling of riddles. An almost universal practice in folk cultures, as in modernized ones, a riddle is defined by its linguistic features as well as by its dramaturgic ones. In a recent study of riddles, W. J. Pepicello and J. A. Green (1984) noted that the genre involves a *performance*, insofar as it is addressed to an audience in appropriate contexts and that it uses the structural features of language— phonology, morphology, and syntax as well as the shades and nuances of meaning. These features of riddles, however, are used in strategic interactional moments for achieving dramaturgic purposes. Thus, a riddle is offered to another who is expected to provide a suitable answer that must be fitting, witty, and in some way provocative. The form of the riddle, then, creates suspenseful anticipation, however momentarily, a brief development in temporal terms, and a denouement produced either by the respondent or the initiator. The dramatic and linguistic features of the riddle together create opportunities for presentation of stylized selves and dialogic moments, and typically occur in dialogic relationship. There may be a *play* on words at the phonological, morphological, and syntactical levels in riddles and jokes, but the real play is between the articulator and the audience. Consider the following:

Do you know why they don't give Transylvanians coffee breaks?

The riddle is a question that seeks completion in the response of the other. If this is not forthcoming, then the riddler will produce it, thereby becoming another to himself or herself as well as to his or her respondents, thereby drawing them all into a circle of laughter:

Because it takes too long to train them.

The value of riddles of this kind is their unmatched economy of means; in just two sentences wittiness is produced, a peripeteic situation and an agonistic subject are introduced, and a denouement announced.

The category of jokes called "sick jokes" uses an additional resource. By deliberately violating the common standards of awe and veneration, compassion and pity, these jokes harvest an emotional response that is an addition to the ones gathered by the structure of the joke itself. Consider the following, current during the mass media's coverage of the Ethiopian famine:

Question:   What do you call an Ethiopian walking a dog?
 Answer:   A caterer.
Question:   What do you call an Ethiopian walking two dogs?
 Answer:   An entrepreneur.

(Jules-Rosett, 1986:26)

They arrest one's attention with a question that is paradoxical or witty in its own right by combining obviously disparate elements together and then give an answer that is as startlingly offensive as it is unexpected. The paradoxical pairing and the witty combination can be more obviously seen in the following:

Question:   What do Yoko Ono and Ethiopians have in common?

Yoko Ono, a media star in her own right, was married to John Lennon, one of the members of the musical group, the Beatles. She is of

Japanese descent and has therefore nothing in common with the Ethiopians. Local cultural literacy is demanded in this riddle and the combination of Ms. Ono, a single individual, and the nation of Ethiopians
provides a truly metaphysical relationship. The dénouement connects
the two disparate elements by means of a pun:

Answer:   They both live off dead beatles.

(Jules-Rosett, 1986:1)

It is cruel to Ms. Ono, sarcastic about the Ethiopians, and displays an
extreme want of sympathy and compassion for the bereaving widow
and a famine-stricken nation. Further, it is in sharp contrast with the
abundantly displayed public sympathy for both Ms. Ono and the Ethiopians, and elicits shock by the deliberate presentation of cruelty and
thoughtlessness. Benetta Jules-Rosett notes that there are certain "eth-
noaesthetic principles" involved in these jokes. "Economy" refers to
processes of condensation, she writes, "symmetry" refers to the fact
that jokes are balanced by a division into subject and predicate and
appear in riddle form. Thus, they are not monologues or narratives
relying solely on the laughter of the audience for a response, because the
listener attempts to answer the riddle and so gets drawn actively into the
interaction.

If an interactant has no story or riddle about real or imaginary characters to recount, stories can be told about archetypical characters. This,
too, had its place in the history of the theater. In the morality plays,
various characteristics and tendencies were represented by converting
common nouns and verbs into characters in the plots and discourses of
plays. The most famous such strategy is in the play *Everyman*. In addition to Everyman, Death, Kindred, Beauty, Worldly Goods, and Good
Deeds are characters. In the modern storyteller's repertoire characters
named the Jew, the Black or the Negro, the Pole, the Jewish American
Princess, and other ethnic archetypes. Each of them summarize historically and culturally derived stereotypes and make them the animating
motive of the plots. The story typically portrays the archetypical characters in a way that enables the participants to achieve a *differentiation* of
their selves from the archetypes depicted in the plotting and the motiva-
tion, and at the same time to *share* such differentiation with each other.
Once again there is a binding and a communion analogous to the ones in
the morality plays themselves: we the God-fearing and the God-loving
against the sinners and the damned.[6]

## Play and Display of Self

Witticisms are different from jokes in that they are spontaneous verbal
and mimetic plays that make use of the material available in the moment

of the social encounter itself. Presented to the face of the others in the situation and, directly or indirectly, involving the self of the others, they are constructed and addressed to the other then and there and are therefore fundamentally creative acts. Taking advantage of the situation in which he or she finds himself or herself, a wit constructs linguistically artful and dramaturgically appropriate texts that elicit a start and a laugh simultaneously. However, they must not be wanton and profligate displays of verbal virtuosity but should rather bear a direct and intimate relationship to the discourse and drama that occurred immediately before the witticism. In so responding, an articulator displays, in Patricia Spacks's happy phrase, "a talent of ready utterance" (1986:147). These ready utterances come before and after other discursive acts and constitute interludes that add significance to the interaction.

Witty remarks, exchanges, repartees, or bon mots deliberately turn the immediate context and situation into an unexpected and still logically, semantically, and culturally coherent comment. This arrests the others in their conversational and linguistic tracks to be able to respond to it. The original comment and its response demand a creative attention to words and situations. For the wit, there is the display of a mastery over the medium, its simplicities, subtleties, and graces, its inner qualities, and its infinite flexibility and sensitivity. The making of a witticism displays the alertness of the articulator, as a full response shows the recipient's alertness (Redfern, 1984:6). In the production of witticism's and in the ready responses to them there is a double dose of what Bakhtin has termed being "actively responsive." He wrote, "The fact is that when the listener perceives and understands the meaning of . . . speech, he simultaneously takes an active responsive attitude to it. He either agrees or disagrees with it . . . augments it, applies it, prepares for its execution and so on" (1986:68).

Consider the following: A man who had recently bought a house is wandering in his backyard. A neighbor joins him. The owner points to a tree in their vicinity and observes:

A:  Isn't that a lovely ash tree?
B:  Ash tree? That is not an ash—it is a peach tree.
A:  I don't know: Noel dropped in yesterday and he told me it was an ash tree.
B:  Noel? What does he know about trees? He doesn't know an ash from a pole in the ground.[7]

Here a serious bit of information about a tree is converted into a witticism by correctly converting a common cliche into a double and appropriate pun. Its effects are complex: it creates a surprise, almost a climactic denouement by turning not one pun, but two within the same expression while keeping semantic and syntactic relations intact, and it puts another person in his place and thus creates a certain agonistic situation and provides an opportunity for the play of emotions as well. Moreover, it calls attention, in a punning way, to an implication of moronity, and effectively subsumes the subject of the discussion of an ash tree into the sense of the sentence and the structure of the witticism itself. Further, it becomes the medium with which the self of the articulator gets presented and defined as the sort of person capable of such nuances and sensitivities, and, finally, the ensuing mirth binds the two selves together in a dialogic moment.

These various effects are achieved by the dramatic nature of the text that was produced whereby an information-giving and confirmation-eliciting exchange becomes transformed into a self-presenting act with the creation of a victim and a display of verbal felicity. The startle that results from such attention to nuance and shade in discourses establishes a sensuous relationship between the words and the producer of the words. It also seeks to establish a relationship characterized by communication that is subtle and complex in intentions and demanding similar qualities of response. As Henri Bergson put it, instead of treating ideas "as mere symbols the wit sees them, he hears them and, above all, makes them converse with one another like persons. He puts them on the stage, and himself, to some extent, into the bargain" (1956:129).

In many ways wits are like gamblers. Gamblers display their ownership and mastery of money by risking it, playing with it, throwing it away, and generally being *casual* about this most, or at least the second most, widely used sign of self and instrument of exchange in society. Gambling is a wonderful medium for showing off these qualities. Organized with elements of uncertainty, it needs an audience, creates interaction between players, and nearly always leads to a change in one's fund of cash and esteem, usually a lowering of it. The witticism that emerges in the course of conversations offers a similar display, a promiscuous use of the most important medium of exchange in society: words. Witticisms make words dance and lisp, amble and indeed suggest a certain flirtationness. They are never what they seem on their mere surfaces on first encounter. Wit needs an audience and puts the self at risk, for the witticism can flop and leave the self with lowered esteem. This is the case with that most common of witty exercises, the pun; but it is also true of other forms of wit. Displaying mastery over words, an actor also displays his or her self, a certain dramatic awareness, and a deep knowledge of the culture.

However, one must not be profligate with the accumulated resources of language. Rather, one is obliged to be both parsimonious and circumspect in using them. One can pun and be witty, produce bon mots and double entendres, but there is a point at which such exercises must stop.

Otherwise, communication becomes impossible, and the announcement of intentions, the creation of an identity, and the presentation of a self, as well as the reception and validation of same from interactional others, will be stymied. Indeed, that way madness lies—literally. Profligacy in the use of syntax and promiscuity in the use of words will bring the medium of communication as well as the communicator into disrepute because they will be debasing the very coinage of the human realm. However, those who use these properties of language circumspectly, who can fit them into contexts and situations as they develop, are able to bring the drama of the unexpected turn into a tightly defined conversational occasion, enlivening both dialogic moments and dialogic relationships, the basic processes in the relentless drama of the human species, and so achieve a communion and a continuity of selves.


## Notes

1.    In recent years a number of sociologists have developed an interest in the analysis of time and temporality. David Maines, Noreen Sugrue, and Michael Katovitch in a very instructive paper (1983) have examined G. H. Mead's theory of the past. In another publication Maines related temporal issues to the study of aging (1985). Eviatar Zerubavel has done pioneering work in the study of time as well (1976, 1979, 1986). He has sought to relate the issue of temporality to the developments in recent structuralist thought. Zerubavel in the latter paper explored "how people manipulate various dimensions of temporality (e.g., duration, speed, frequency, timing) as virtual semiotic codes through which they manage to convey various social messages (e.g., about priority, importance, commitment, and respect) without having to articulate them verbally" (1986:343). See also Denzin, (1987).

2.    See Marvin Scott (1988) for an illuminating discussion of the procedures by which narratives are used to present a self. Peter Barham's (1984) study of the relationship between schizophrenia, science, and society develops these points very lucidly. Relying on the work of Alasdair MacIntrye (1981) he notes, "Narrative thus provides the appropriate form for understanding the actions of others or, as the case may be, for not understanding such actions." I may add, however, that not only does one understand the actions of others by putting them in a narrative context, but one constructs narratives in order to make one's life comprehensible to both self and other.

3.    Harvey Sacks's studies of talk in everyday life has introduced, indeed discovered, a whole field for research by students of human societies. His interest was mainly in the formal aspects of talk. In his analysis of the telling of a joke he focused on the "course of the telling" and showed that "it has a single most decisive feature: the joke is built in the form of a story." The decisiveness of that feature involves the fact that, "there being means for sequentially organizing the telling of a story in conversation . . . [t]his telling is composed, as for stories, of three serially ordered and adjacently placed types of sequences which we call the *preface*, the *telling* and the *response* sequences" (1974:337; italics added). The original transcription of the joke was made with a certain phonetic

fidelity; in the version presented here these markers have been removed and the jokes printed in standardized forms.

4. In this connection, see the classic study of the origins of Greek religion and theatrical ritual by Jane Harrison [1912] (1948). The structure of the medieval play has been discussed in Chambers (1903). See also Young (1933). A description and analysis of the Indian *harikata* and Radha-Krishna *bhajanas* can be found in Milton Singer (1972). A discussion of the dithyramb and its role in the emergence of Greek tragedy and comedy can be found in the early and erudite treatise by A. W. Pickhard-Cambridge (1927) and in Gilbert Murray's *The Origin of Greek Theater* (1933). Lyman and Scott have also developed this argument and examined the connections between *theoria, theater,* and *theory* (1975:1–3, 101–114).

5. See Alan Dundes (1987) for a collection and commentary on such jokes.

6. Rose Coser (1960) has reported a study of the "serious import of humor." She argued that humor is used for various organizational purposes. Gary Allan Fine has argued that humor is used for the social construction of meaning. Humor plays "an important role in shaping identities and in structuring situational definitions" (1984a:83). Michael Flaherty (1984) has done an ethonographic study of humor and concludes humor is used as part of the "reality work" of social interaction. Robert Stebbins (1979) has also studied the occurrence of jokes, pranks, and witticisms during the course of a play rehearsal and concluded that they produced "relief" from the tensions of the social encounter. Such joking also served to allow the actors to present their own selves and define the boundaries between themselves and the characters they were becoming in the play. Important as these contributions are in understanding the cultural significance of jokes, my focus has been on the accomplishment of jokes as semiotic and dramatic acts.

7. Reported by James McCartney as having occurred in his newly acquired backyard.

# References

Abrahams, Roger. 1974. "Black Talking on the Streets." In *Explorations in the Ethnography of Speaking*, edited by R. Bauman and J. Scherzer. Cambridge: Cambridge University Press.

Abse, Wilfred. 1971. *Speech and Reason*. Charlottesville: University of Virginia Press.

Anobile, Richard. 1975. *A Fine Mess: Verbal and Visual Gems from the Films of Abbott and Costello*. New York: W. W. Norton.

Allport, Gordon. 1968. *The Person in Psychology*. Boston: Beacon.

Aristotle. 1961. *Topica*. Cambridge, MA: Harvard University Press.

Auerbach, Eric. 1957. *Mimesis*. New York: Doubleday.

Austin, J.L. (1961)1970. "A Plea for Excuses". *In Philosophical Papers;* edited by J.O. Urmson and G.J. Warnock.

_____. 1975. *How to Do Things with Words*. Cambridge, MA: Harvard University Press.

Averill, James. 1980. *Anger and Aggression: An Essay on Emotion*. New York: Springer-Verlag.

Bakhtin, M.M. 1981. *The Dialogic Imagination*. Austin: University of Texas Press.

_____. 1986. *Speech Genres and Other Later Essays*. Austin: University of Texas Press.

Barham, Peter. 1984. *Schizophrenia and Human Value*. London: Duckworth.

Barthes, Roland. 1974. *S/Z*. New York: Hill and Wang.

_____. 1975. *The Pleasure of the Text*. New York: Hill and Wang.

Bateson, Gregory. 1972. *Steps to an Ecology of Mind*. New York: Ballantine Books.

Behan, Brendan. 1958. *Borstal Boy*. London: Hutchinson.

Bennett, Adrian. 1981. "Interruptions and the Interpretation of Conversations" *Discourse Processes* 4:171–188.

Benson, Kenneth. 1977. "Organizations: A Dialetical View." *Administrative Science Quarterly*, 22(1):1–21.

Bercovitch, Sacvan. 1975. *The Puritan Origins of the American Self*. New Haven, CT: Yale University Press.

Bergson, Henri. 1956. "Laughter". In *Comedy*, edited by W. Sypher. New York: Doubleday.

Bever, T.G., J.R. Lackner, and R. Kirk. 1974. "The Underlying Structures of Sentences Are the Primary Units of Immediate Speech Processing". In *Noam Chomsky: Critical Essays*, edited by G. Harman. New York: Doubleday.

Birdwhistell, Ray. *Kinesics and Context*. Philadelphia: University of Pennsylvania Press.

Blumer, Herbert. 1955. "Collective Behavior". In *Outline of Sociology*, edited by A.M. Lee. New York: Barnes and Noble.

_____. 1969. "The Sociological Implications of the Thought of G.H. Mead". In *Symbolic Interactionism: Perspective and Method*, Englewood Cliffs, NJ: Prentice Hall.

Boothe, Wayne. 1974. *The Rhetoric of Irony*. Chicago: University of Chicago Press.

Brazil, D.C. 1975. *Discourse Intonation*. English Language Research, University of Birmingham.

Brazil, D.C. 1985. *The Communicative Value of Intonation*. English Language Research Monographs. University of Birmingham.

Brown, R. and Gilman, A. 1972. "The Pronouns of Power and Solidarity." In *Language and Social Context*, edited by P. Giglioli. Baltimore: Penguin Books.

Buber, Martin. 1970. *I and Thou*. New York: Scribner.

Buber, Martin. 1972. *Between Man and Man*. New York: Macmillan.

Buczynaska-Garewitz, H. 1983. "Sign and Dialogue." *The American Journal of Semiotics* 2(1–2):27–44.

Burke, Kenneth. 1962. *A Grammar of Motives and a Rhetoric of Motives*. Cleveland: World Publishing.

———. 1964. *Perspectives by Incongruity*. Bloomington: Indiana University Press.

———. 1966. "Definition of Man." In *Language as Symbolic Action*. Berkeley: University of California Press.

———. 1968. "Dramatism." *The International Encyclopedia of the Social Sciences*. New York: Macmillan.

Burke, Peter. 1987. *The Historical Anthropology of Early Modern Italy: Essays on Perception and Communication*. Cambridge: Cambridge University Press.

Carrithers, Michael, S. Collins, and S. Lukes, eds. 1985. *The Category of the Person*. New York: Cambridge University Press.

Cassirer, Ernest. 1967. *An Essay on Man*. New Haven, CT: Yale University Press.

Chambers, E.K. 1903. *The Medieval Stage*. Oxford: Clarendon Press.

Chatman, Seymour, 1978. *Story and Discourse*. Ithaca, NY: Cornell University Press.

Chomsky, Noam. 1969. *Syntactic Structures*. The Hague: Mouton.

———. 1972. *Language and Mind*. New York: Harcourt, Brace.

———. 1983. *Dialogues in the Psychology of Language and Thought*, edited by R.W. Riber. New York: Plenum.

———. 1986. *Knowledge and Language: Its Nature, Origin and Use*. New York: Praeger.

Corry, John. 1977. *The Golden Clan: The Murrays, McDonnells and the Irish Aristocracy*. New York: Houghton Miffin.

Coser, Rose. 1960. "Laughter Among Colleagues," *Psychiatry* 23:81–95.

Coulthard, Malcolm. 1985. *An Introduction to Discourse Analysis*. London: Longman's.

Covelli, Lucille, and S.O. Murray. 1981. "Accomplishing Topic Change". *Anthropological Linguistics* 22(Dec.):382–89.

Cruttenden, Alan. 1986. *Intonation*. Cambridge: Cambridge University Press.

Culler, Jonathan. 1982. *On Deconstruction*. Ithaca: Cornell University Press.

Cuddihy, John Murray. 1978. *No Offense*. New York: Seabury.

Dawood, N. J. 1973. (translator) *Tales from a Thousand and One Nights*. Baltimore: Penguin.

Denzin, Norman. 1984. "The Temporality of Everday Moods." in *Social Referencing, Infancy and Social Psychological Theory*, edited by S. Feinman. New York: Plenum.

———. 1985. *Understanding Emotions*. San Francisco: Josey-Bass.

———. 1987. "Under the Influence of Time: Reading of the Interactional Text". *Sociological Quarterly* 28(3) 327–341.

Derrida, Jacques. 1976. *Of Grammatology*. Baltimore, MD: Johns Hopkins University Press.

Derrida, Jacques. 1981. *Positions*. Chicago: University of Chicago Press.

Doyle, Bertram. 1971. *The Etiquette of Race Relations in the South*. New York: Schocken.

Dundes, Alan. 1987. *Cracking Jokes: Studies of Sick Humor Cycles and Stereotypes*. Berkeley, CA: Tenspeed Press.

Elias, Norbert. 1978. *The Civilizing Process*. New York: Urizen.

Empson, William. 1964. *Seven Types of Ambiguity*. New York: Meridian Books.

Empson, William. 1969. *The Structure of Complex Words*. London: Chatto and Windus.

Fine, Gary Alan. 1984a. "Humorous Interaction and the Social Construction of Meaning." Pp. 83–101 in *Studies in Symbolic Interaction*, Vol. 5, edited N. Denzin. Greenwich, CT: JAI Press.

———. 1984b. "Negotiated Orders and Organizational Cultures." *Annual Review of Sociology* 10:239–62.

Fitzgerald, John. 1966. *Peirce's Theory of Signs as a Foundation of Pragmatism*. The Hague: Mouton.

Flaherty, Michael. 1984. "A Formal Approach to the Study of Amusement in Social Interaction." Pp. 71–82 in *Studies in Symbolic Interaction*, edited by N. Denzin. Greenwich, CT: JAI Press.

Fodor, J., and Garrett, M. 1967. "Some Syntactic Determinants of Sentential Complexity." *Perception and Psychophysics* 2:289–96.

Fodor, J., Garrett, M., and Bever, T. 1968. Some Syntactic Determinants of Complexity." *Perception and Psychophysics* 3:453–61.

Fowler, Roger, ed. 1975. *Style and Structure in Literature*. Oxford: Basil Blackwell.

Frank, Arthur W., III. 1979. "Reality Construction in Interaction." *Annual Review of Sociology* 5:167–191.

Freud, Sigmund. (1905) 1960. *Jokes and their Relation to the Unconscious*, edited and translated by J. Strachey. New York: Norton.

Geertz, Hildred. 1959. "The Vocabulary of Emotion: A Study of Javanese Socialization Process." *Psychiatry* 22:225–237.

Geertz, Clifford. 1979. "From the Native's Point of View: On the Nature of Anthological Understanding." In *Interpretive Social Science*, edited by P. Rabinow and W.M. Sullivan. Berkeley: University of California Press.

Genette, Gerard. 1980. *Narrative Discourse*. Ithaca, NY: Cornell University Press.

Georges, Robert. 1969. "Towards an Understanding of Story-Telling Events." *Journal of American Folklore* 82:313–28.

Giddens, Anthony. 1979. *Central Problems in Social Theory: Action, Structure and Contradiction in Social Analysis*. Berkeley: University of California Press.

Giddens, Anthony. 1982. *Profiles and Critique in Social Theory*. Berkeley: University of California Press.

Giddens, Anothy. 1984. *The Construction of Society*. Berkeley: University of California Press.

Gill, Merton and I. Hoffman. 1982. *Analysis of Transference*, volume II, *Studies of Nine Audio Recorded Psychoanalytic Sessions*. New York: International University Press.

Gilsenan, Michael. 1976. "Lying, Honor and Contradiction". In *Transaction and Meaning*, edited by B. Kapferer. Philadelphia: Institute for the Study of Social Issues.

Goffman, Erving. 1959. *The Presentation of Self in Everyday Life*. New York: Doubleday.

———. 1961a. *Asylums*. New York: Doubleday.

———. 1961b. *Encounters*. Indianapolis: Bobbs-Merrill.

———. 1963. *Behavior-in Public Places*. New York: Free Press.

Goffman, Erving. 1967. *Interaction Ritual*. New York: Doubleday.

Goode, Eric. 1985. "Deviance". In *Essays in Interpretive Sociology*. edited by H. Farberman and R.S. Perinbanayagam. Greenwich, CT: JAI.

Gross, Edward, and G.P. Stone. 1970. "Embarrassment and the Analysis of Role Requirements". In *Social Psychology through Symbolic-Interaction*, edited by G.P. Stone and H.A. Farberman. Boston: Ginn-Blaisdell.

Handke, Peter. 1973. *Kaspar*. New York: Farrar, Straus and Giroux.

Hannerz, Ulf. 1967. "Gossip, Network, and Values in a Negro Urban Slum." Washington, D.C.: Center for Applied Linguistics.

———. 1969. *Soulside*. New York: Columbia University Press.

Hansell, Mark, and Cheryl S. Ajirotutu. 1982. "Interpretations in Interethnic Settings." In *Language and Social Identity*, edited by John Gumperz. Cambridge: Cambridge University Press.

Harman, Gilbert, ed. 1974. *On Noam Chomsky: Critical Essays*. New York: Doubleday.

Havens, Leston. 1986. *Making Contact*. Cambridge: Harvard University Press.

Harrison, Jane. 1912. *Themis: A Study of the Social Origins of Greek Religion*. Cambridge: Cambridge University Press.

Hebdige, Dick. 1979. *Subculture: The Meaning of Style*. London: Methuen.

Helm, David. 1985. "Exclusionary Practices." (Unpublished paper) Boston: Boston University.

Henry, Jules. 1936. "The Linguistic Expression of Emotion." *American Anthropologist* 38:250–56.

———. 1973. *Pathways to Madness*. New York: Vintage Books.

Hewitt, John, and R. Stokes. 1975. "Disclaimers". *American Sociological Review* 40:1–11.

Hirschkop, Ken. 1985a. "Bakhtin, Discourse and Democracy." *New Left Review* 160:93–113.

Hochschild, Arlie. 1977. Comment on Thomas Scheff's "Distancing of Emotion in Ritual." Current Anthropology 18:494.

———. 1979. "Emotion Work, Feeling Rules and Social Structure." *American Journal of Sociology* 85(3):551–75.

Huizinga, Johan. 1964. *Homo Ludens*. Boston: Beacon.

Jakobson, Roman. 1962. *Selected Writings*, volume I, *Phonological Studies*. Gravenhage: Mouton.

Jakobson, Roman. 1971. *Selected Writings*, volume II, *Word and Language*. The Hague. Mouton.

Jakobson, Roman. 1978. *Sound and Meaning*. Translated by John Mepham. Cambridge, MA: MIT I Press.

Jakobson, Roman, and M. Halle. 1956. *The Fundamentals of Language*. The Hague: Mouton.

Jameson, Frederic. 1982. "The Symbolic Inference or Kenneth Burke and Ideological Analysis." In *Representing Kenneth Burke*, edited by H. White and M. Brose. Baltimore, MD: Johns Hopkins University Press.

Kemper, Theodore, D. 1987. "How Many Emotions Are There? Wedding the Social and Autonomic Components." *American Journal of Sociology* 93(2):263–89.

Kermode, Frank. 1979. *The Genesis of Secrecy*. Cambridge: Harvard University Press.

Kevelson, Roberta. 1982. "Peirce's Dialogism, Continuous Predicate and Legal Reasoning". *Translations of the C.S. Peirce Society* 18(2):159–76.

Kierkegaard, Søren. 1965. *The Concept of Irony*. Bloomington: Indiana University Press.

Kierkegaard, Søren. 1986. "The Rotation of Crops". In *Either/Or*. New York: Harper and Row.

Labov, William. 1972. "Rules for Ritual Insults". In *Studies in Social Interaction*, edited by D. Sudnow. New York: Free Press.

Labov, William, and Fanschell, D. 1977. *Therapeutic Discourse: Psychotherapy as Conversation*. New York: Academic Press.

Laing, R.D., and R. Esterson. 1970. *Sanity, Madness and the Family*. Baltimore, MD: Penguin Books.

Langer, Suzanne. 1953. *Feeling and Form*. New York: Scribner.

Langer, Suzanne. 1967. *Mind: An Essay on Human Feeling*, volume I. Baltimore, MD: Johns Hopkins University Press.

Langer, Suzanne. (1942) 1970. *Philosophy in a New Key*. Cambridge, MA: Harvard University Press.

Langer, Suzanne. 1972. *Mind: An Essay on Human Feeling*, volume II. Baltimore, MD: Johns Hopkins University Press.

Leach, Edmund. 1974. *Claude Levi-Strauss*. New York: Penguin Books.

Leach, Edmund. 1976. *Culture and Communication*. Cambridge: Cambridge University Press.

Legman, Gershon. 1967. *The Rationale of the Dirty Joke*. Volume 1 New York: Grove.

Levi-Strauss, Claude. 1967. *Structural Anthropology*. New York: Doubleday.

Levi-Strauss, Claude. 1979. Myth and Meaning. New York: Schocken Books.

Lewis, Hywel. 1982. *The Elusive Self*. Philadelphia: Westminister.

Liszka, Jakob. 1981. "Peirce and Jakobson: Toward a Structuralist Reconstruction of Peirce". *Transactions of the C.S. Peirce Society* 18(1):41–61.

Little, Lester. 1970. "Formules Monastiques de Malediction aux ixe et xe siecles." *Revue Marbillon* LVIII.

Loman, Bengt. 1967. *Conversations in a Negro American Dialect*. Washington, D.C.: Center for Applied Linguistics.

Lyman, Stanford, and M.B. Scott. 1970. *A Sociology of the Absurd*. New York: Appleton Century.

Lyman, Stanford, and M.B. Scott. 1975. *A Drama of Social Reality*. New York: Oxford University Press.

Lyons, Williams. 1980. *Emotion*. Cambridge: Cambridge University Press.

Lyotard, Jean-Francoise. 1988. *The Postmodern Condition*. Minneapolis: University of Minnesota Press.

MacIntyre, Alasdair. 1981. *After Virtue.*, IN: University of Notre Dame Press. London: Duckworth.

Maines, David. 1982. "In Search of Meostructure: Studies in the Negotiated Order." *Urban Life* 11:267–79.

Maines, David. 1985. "On Time, Timing and the Life Course." *Interdisciplinary Topics in Gerontology* 17:182–93.

Maines, David, N. Sugrue, and M. Katovitch. 1983. "The Sociological Import of G.H. Mead's Theory of the Past." *American Sociological Review* 48(2):161–73.

Malcolm, Norman. 1966. "Knowledge of the Other Minds". In *Philosophical Investigation: A Collection of Critical Essays*, edited by G. Pitcher. New York: Doubleday.

Marr, David. 1982. *Vision*. New York: W. H. Freeman.

Mascaro, Juan. ed. 1973. The Dhammapada. Penguin Books.

Mauss, Marcel. (1985) (1988). A Category of the Human Mind: The Notion of Person, the Notion of Self". In *The Category of the Person*, edited by Michael Carrithers, S. Collins, and S. Lukes. New York: Cambridge University Press.

McCarthy, E. Doyle. 1988. "Emotions are Social Things." In *The Sociology of Emotions*, edited by D. Franks and E.D. McCarthy. Greenwich, CT: JAI.

Mead, G.H. 1934. *Mind, Self and Society*. Chicago: University of Chicago Press.

————. 1938. *The Philosophy of the Act*. Chicago: University of Chicago Press.

————. 1964. *Selected Writings*, edited by A.J. Reck. New York: Bobbs Merrill.

Meredith, George. 1956. "An Essay on Comedy". In *Comedy*, edited by W. Sypher. New York: Doubleday.

Mills, C. Wright. 1940. "Situated Actions and Vocabularies of Motive", *American Sociological Review* 5(Oct.):904–13.

Morris, Wesley. 1979. *Friday's Footprint*. Columbus: OH. Ohio University Press.

Morson, Gary Saul. 1985. "Dialogue, Monologue and the Social: A Reply to Ken Hirschkop". *Critical Inquiry* 11:678–85.

Murray, Gilbert. 1933. *The Origins of the Greek Theater*. Oxford: Clarendon.

Murray, Stephen, 1985. "Toward a Model of Members' Methods for Recognizing Interruptions." *Language and Society* 14:31–40.

Murray, Stephen, and L. Covelli. 1982. *Women and Men Speaking at the Same Time*. Berkeley, CA: Kroeber Anthropological Society.

————. 1987. "Power and Solidarity in 'Interruption': A Critique of the Santa Barbara School's Conception." *Symbolic Interaction* 10(1):101–10.

Myrdall, Gunnar. 1962. *An American Dilemma*. New York: Harper and Row.

Ortega y Gassett, José. 1956. The Dehumanization of Art and Other Essays. New York: Anchor.

Peirce, Charles Sanders. (1931–1958). *Selected Papers*, 1–6, edited by C. Hartshorne and P. Weiss. Cambridge, MA: Harvard University Press.

————. 1955. *Philosophical Writings*, edited by J. Buchler. New York: Dover.

————. 1958. *Selected Writings*, edited by P. Weiner. New York: Dover.

———. 1958. *Selected Writings,* volumes 7 and 8, edited by A.W. Burks. Cambridge, MA: Harvard University Press.

———. 1977. *Semiotics and Significs. The Correspondence of Charles S. Peirce and Victoria Lady Welby,* edited by C.S. Hardwick. Bloomington: Indiana University Press.

Pepicello, W.J., and J.A. Green. 1984. *The Language of Riddles: New Perspectives.* Columbus: Ohio State University Press.

Perinbanayagam, R.S. 1985. *Signifying Acts.* Carbondale: University of Southern Illinois Press.

———. 1986. "The Meaning of Uncertainty and the uncertainty of Meaning." *Symbolic Interaction* 9(1)105–126.

———. 1990. "How to Do Self with Things". In *Beyond Goffman,* edited by S. Riggins. Berlin: Mouton-de Gruyter.

Pettit, Phillip. 1975. *The Concept of Structuralism.* Berkeley: University of California Press.

Pfeutze, Paul. 1954. *Self, Society and Existence.* New York: Harper and Row.

Pickhard-Cambridge, A.W. 1927. *Dithyramb, Tragedy and Comedy.* Oxford: Clarendon.

Radcliffe-Brown, A.R. 1961. *Structures and Function in Primitive Society.* Cambridge and New York: Free Press.

Radin, Paul. 1956. *The Trickster: A Study in American Indian Mythology.* New York: Philosophical Library.

Ransdell, Joseph. 1980. "Semiotics and Linguistics." In *The Signifying Animal,* edited by I. Raush and G.F. Carr. Bloomington: Indiana University Press.

Read, Herbert. 1967. *Art and Alienation.* New York: Horizon.

Redfern, Walter. 1984. *Puns.* Oxford: Blackwell.

Ricouer, Paul. 1985. *Time and Narrative.* Chicago: University of Chicago Press.

Rochberg-Halton, Eugene. 1982. "Situation, Structure and the Context of Meaning." *Sociological Quarterly* 23(Autumn):455–76.

———. 1986. *Meaning and Modernity.* Chicago: University of Chicago Press.

Root, Michael. 1975. "Language Rules and Complex Behavior." In *Language, Mind and Knowledge,* edited by K. Gunderson, Minneapolis: University of Minnesota Press.

Rosenthal, Sandra. 1986. *Speculative Pragmatism.* Amherst: University of Massachusetts Press.

Sacks, Harvey. 1974. "An Analysis of the Course of a Joke's Telling in Conversation." In *Explorations in Ethnography of Speaking,* edited by R. Bauman and J.S. Sherzer. New York: Cambridge University Press.

Sacks, Oliver, 1987. *The Man Who Mistook His Wife for a Hat and Other Clinical Tales.* New York: Harper and Row.

Sacks, Oliver, and R. Wasserman. 1987b. "The Case of the Colorblind Painter." *New York Review of Books* 19:25–34.

Sacks, Harvey, E. Schegloff, and G. Jefferson. 1974. "A Simplest Systematics for the Organization of Turn-Taking for Conversations." *Language* 50:696–735.

Saussure, F., de. 1959. *Course in General Linguistics.* New York: McGraw-Hill.

Scheff, Thomas. 1977. "The Distancing of Emotion in Ritual." *Current Anthropology,* 18:485–505.

Scheff, Thomas. 1979. *Catharsis in Healing, Ritual and Drama*. Berkeley: University of California Press.

Schegloff, Emmanuel. 1968. "Sequencing in Conversational Openings." *American Anthropologist* 70(6):1075–95.

––––––. 1972. "Notes on a Conversational Practice: Formulating Place." In *Language in Social Context*, edited by P.P. Gigliolo. Baltimore: Penguin.

––––––. 1973. "Recycled Turn Beginnings." (Unpublished) cited in A. Bennett (1973).

Schmalenbach, Herman. 1977. *Society and Experience*. Chicago: University of Chicago Press.

Scholes, Robert. 1982. *Semiotics and Interpretation*. New Haven, CT: Yale University Press.

Scott, Marvin. 1988. "Sociology Encounters Psychoanalysis". In *Sociology of Emotions*, edited by D.D. Franks and E.D. McCarthy. Greenwich, CT: JAI.

Scott, M.B., and S. Lyman. 1968. "Accounts". *American Sociological Review* 33(Feb.) 46–62.

Seckman, Mark, and C. Couch. 1989. "Jocularity, Sarcasm and Social Relationships." *Journal of Contemporary Ethnography* 18(3):327–44.

Siegel, Lee. 1987. *Laughing Matters: Comic Tradition in India*. Chicago: University of Chicago Press.

Shott, Susan. 1977. "Emotions and Social Life: A Symbolic Interactionist Analysis." *American Journal of Sociology* 84(6): 1317–34.

Shotter, John, and K. Gergen, eds. 1989. *Texts of Identity*. Newbury Park, CA: Sage.

Simmel, George. 1950. "Coquetry." In *The Sociology of George Simmel*, edited by K. Wolff. New York: Free Press.

Singer, Milton. 1972. "The Radhakrishna Bhajanas of Madras City". In *When a Great Tradition Modernizes*, New York: Praeger.

Singer, Milton. 1982. "Personal and Social Identity in Dialogue". In *Psychosocial Theories of the Self*, edited by B. Lee. New York: Plenum.

Singer, Milton. 1984. "Signs of the Self". In *Man's Glassy Essence*. Bloomington: Indiana University Press.

Smith, Neil, and Deidre Wilson. 1979. *Modern Linguistics*. New York: Penguin.

Spacks, Patricia Meyer. 1986. *Gossip*. Chicago: University of Chicago Press.

Spitzer, R.L., and Williams, J.W. 1984. *The Initial Interview: Evaluation Strategies for DSM III*. New York: BMA Audio Cassettes.

Stebbins, Robert. 1979. "Comic Relief in Everyday Life: Dramaturgic Observations of a Function of Humor". *Symbolic Interaction* 2(1):95–104.

Stone, Gregory. 1970. [1962] "Appearance and the Self", In *Social Psychology through Symbolic Interaction*, edited by G.P. Stone and H. Farberman. Waltham, MA: Ginn-Blaisdell.

Strauss, Anselm. 1978. *Negotiations*. San Francisco: Josey-Bass.

Sypher, Wylie. 1956. "Introduction". In *Comedy*, edited by W. Sypher. New York: Doubleday.

Tambiah, S.J. 1985. "Animals Are Good to Think and Good to Prohibit". In *Culture, Thought and Action*. New York: Cambridge University Press.

Todorov, Tzvetan. 1977. *The Prose of Poetics*. Ithaca, NY: Cornell University Press.

Turner, Ralph. 1962. "Role-Taking: Process versus Conformity". In *Human Behavior and Social Processes,* edited by A. Rose. Boston: Houghton Mifflin.

United Nations. 1989. "Operation Life Line Sudan." (Situation Report 1, Africa Bureau) 11 April 1989.

Wardhaugh, Ronald. 1985. *How Conversation Works.* Oxford: Basil Blackwell.

Weber, Max. 1958. *Essays in Sociology,* edited by H.H. Gerth and C.W. Mills. New York: Oxford University Press.

Welsford, Enid. (1935) 1966. *The Fool: His Social and Literary History.* Gloucester, MA: Petu Smith.

Wheeler, John. 1984. "Bits, Quanta, Meaning." Unpublished paper, Center for Theoretical Physics, University of Texas, Austin.

Whigham, Frank. 1984. *Ambition and Privilege.* Berkeley: University of California Press.

Willeford, William. 1969. *The Fool and His Scepter.* Evanston, IL: Northwestern University Press.

Wittgenstein, Ludwig. 1958. *Philosophical Investigations.* New York: MacMillan.

Woodward, A., and Bernstein, R. eds. 1974. *Presidential Transcripts.* New York: Avon.

Young, Karl. 1933. *The Drama of the Medieval Church.* Oxford: Clarendon.

Zerubavel, Eviatar. 1976. "Timetables and Schedulings: On the Social Organization of Time". *Sociological Inquiry* 7:87–94.

Zerubavel, Eviatar. 1979. *Patterns of Time in Hospital Life.* Chicago: University of Chicago Press.

Zerubavel, Eviatar. 1987. "The Language of Time: Towards a Semiotics of Temporality." *Sociological Quarterly* 28(3):343–350

Zimmerman, Don, and C. West. 1975. "Sex Role, Interruptions and Silence in Conversations". In *Language and Sex,* edited by B. Thorne and N. Kenly. Rowley, MA: Newbury House.

# Index